Contents

Personal Effectiveness

Alexander Murdock and Carol Scutt

_in association with
of Management_

17

WITHDRAWN

_the Institute
of Management_

FOUNDATION

To Denise and John

Butterworth-Heinemann Ltd
Linacre House, Jordan Hill, Oxford OX2 8DP

A member of the Reed Elsevier group

OXFORD   LONDON   BOSTON
MUNICH   NEW DELHI   SINGAPORE   SYDNEY
TOKYO   TORONTO   WELLINGTON

First published 1993

British Library Cataloguing in Publication Data
Murdock, Alexander
 Personal Effectiveness
  I. Title   II. Scutt, Carol
  658

ISBN 0 7506 0665 7

Printed and bound in Great Britain by Clays, St Ives plc

Series adviser's preface

This book is one of a series designed for people wanting to develop their capabilities as managers. You might think that there isn't anything very new in that. In one way you would be right. The fact that very many people want to learn to become better managers is not new, and for many years a wide range of approaches to such learning and development has been available. These have included courses leading to formal qualifications, organizationally-based management development programmes and a whole variety of self-study materials. A copious literature, extending from academic textbooks to sometimes idiosyncratic prescriptions from successful managers and consultants, has existed to aid — or perhaps confuse — the potential seeker after managerial truth and enlightenment.

So what is new about this series? In fact, a great deal — marking in some ways a revolution in our thinking both about the art of managing and also the process of developing managers.

Where did it all begin? Like most revolutions, although there may be a single, identifiable act that precipitated the uprising, the roots of discontent are many and long-established. The debate about the performance of British managers, the way managers are educated and trained, and the extent to which shortcomings in both these areas have contributed to our economic decline, has been running for several decades.

Until recently, this debate had been marked by periods of frenetic activity — stimulated by some report or enquiry and perhaps ending in some new initiatives or policy changes — followed by relatively long periods of comparative calm. But the underlying causes for concern persisted. Basically, the majority of managers in the UK appeared to have little or no training for their role, certainly far less than their counterparts in our major competitor nations. And there was concern about the nature, style and appropriateness of the management education and training that was available.

The catalyst for this latest revolution came in late 1986 and early 1987, when three major reports reopened the whole issue. The 1987 reports were *The Making of British Managers* by John Constable and Roger McCormick, carried out for the British Institute of Management and the CBI, and *The Making of Managers* by Charles Handy, carried out for the (then) Manpower Services Commission, National Economic Development Office and British Institute of Management. The 1986 report, which often receives less recognition than it deserves as a key contribution to the recent changes, was *Management Training: context and process* by Iain Mangham and Mick Silver, carried out for the Economic and Social Research Council and the Department of Trade and Industry.

It is not the place to review in detail what the reports said. Indeed, they and their consequences are discussed in several places in this series of books. But essentially they confirmed that:

- British managers were undertrained by comparison with their counterparts internationally.
- The majority of employers invested far too little in training and developing their managers.
- Many employers found it difficult to specify with any degree of detail just what it was that they required successful managers to be able to do.

The Constable/McCormick and Handy reports advanced various recommendations for addressing these problems, involving an expansion of management education and development, a reformed structure of qualifications and a commitment from employers to a code of practice for management development. While this analysis was not new, and had echoes of much that had been said in earlier debates, this time a few leading individuals determined that the response should be both radical and permanent. The response was coordinated by the newly-established Council for Management Education and Development (now the National Forum for Management Education and Development (NFMED)) under the energetic and visionary leadership of Bob (now Sir Bob) Reid of Shell UK (now chairman of the British Railways Board).

Under the umbrella of NFMED a series of employer-led working parties tackled the problem of defining what it was that managers should be able to do, and how this differed for people at different levels in their organizations; how this satisfactory ability to perform might be verified; and how an appropriate structure of management qualifications could be put in place. This work drew upon the methods used to specify vocational standards in industry and commerce, and led to the development and introduction of competence-based management standards and qualifications. In this context, competence is defined as the ability to perform the activities within an occupation or function to the standards expected in employment.

It is this competence-based approach that is new in our thinking about the manager's capabilities. It is also what is new about this series of books, in that they are designed to support both this new structure of management standards, and of development activities based on it. The series was originally commissioned to support the Institute of Management's Certificate and Diploma qualifications, which were one of the first to be based on the new standards. However, these books are equally appropriate to any university, college or indeed company course leading to a certificate in management or diploma in management studies.

The standards were specified through an extensive process of consultation with a large number of managers in organizations of many different types and sizes. They are therefore employment based and employer-supported. And they fill the gap that Mangham and Silver identified – now we do have a language to describe what it is employers want their managers to be able to do – at least in part.

If you are engaged in any form of management development leading to a certificate or diploma qualification conforming to the national management standards, then you are probably already familiar with most of the key ideas on which the standards are based. To achieve their key purpose, which is defined as achieving the organization's objectives and continuously improving its performance, managers need to perform four key roles: managing operations, managing finance, managing people and managing information. Each of these key roles has a sub-structure of units and elements, each with associated performance and assessment criteria.

The reason for the qualification 'in part' is that organizations are different, and jobs within them are different. Thus the generic management standards probably do not cover all the management competences that you may need to possess in your job. There are almost certainly additional things, specific to your own situation in your own organization, that you need to be able to do. The standards are necessary, but almost certainly not sufficient. Only you, in discussion with your boss, will be able to decide what other capabilities you need to possess. But the standards are a place to start, a basis on which to build. Once you have demonstrated your proficiency against the standards, it will stand you in good stead as you progress through your organization, or change jobs.

So how do the new standards change the process by which you develop yourself as a manager? They change the process of development, or of gaining a management qualification, quite a lot. It is no longer a question of acquiring information and facts, perhaps by being 'taught' in some classroom environment, and then being tested to see what you can recall. It involves demonstrating, in a quite specific way, that you can do certain things to a particular standard of performance. And because of this, it puts a much greater onus on you to manage your own development, to decide how you can demonstrate any particular competence, what evidence you need to present, and how you can collect it. Of course, there will always be people to advise and guide you in this, if you need help.

But there is another dimension, and it is to this that this series of books is addressed. While the standards stress ability to perform, they do not ignore the traditional knowledge base that has been associated with 'management studies'. Rather, they set this in a different context. The standards are supported by 'underpinning knowledge and understanding' which has three components:

- Purpose and context, which is knowledge and understanding of the manager's objectives, and of the relevant organizational and environmental influences, opportunities and values.
- Principles and methods, which is knowledge and understanding of the theories, models, principles, methods and techniques that provide the basis of competent managerial performance.
- Data, which is knowledge and understanding of specific facts likely to be important to meeting the standards.

Possession of the relevant knowledge and understanding underpinning the standards is needed to support competent managerial performance as specified in the standards. It also has an important role in supporting the transferability of management capabilities. It helps to ensure that you have done more than learned 'the way we do things around here' in your own organization. It indicates a recognition of the wider things which underpin competence, and that you will be able to change jobs or organizations and still be able to perform effectively.

These books cover the knowledge and understanding underpinning the management standards, most specifically in the category of principles and methods. But their coverage is not limited to the minimum required by the standards, and extends in both depth and breadth in many areas. The authors have tried to approach these underlying principles and methods in a practical way. They use many short cases and examples which we hope will demonstrate how, in practice, the principles and methods, and knowledge of purpose and context plus data, support the ability to perform as required by the management standards. In particular we hope that this type of presentation will enable you to identify and learn from similar examples in your own managerial work.

You will already have noticed that one consequence of this new focus on the standards is that the traditional 'functional' packages of knowledge and theory do not appear. The standard textbook titles such as 'quantitative methods', 'production management', 'organizational behaviour' etc. disappear. Instead, principles and methods have been collected together in clusters that more closely match the key roles within the standards. You will also find a small degree of overlap in some of the volumes, because some principles and methods support several of the individual units within the standards. We hope you will find this useful reinforcement.

Having described the positive aspects of standards-based management development, it would be wrong to finish without a few cautionary remarks. The developments described above may seem simple, logical and uncontroversial. It did not always seem that way in the years of work which led up to the introduction of the standards. To revert to the revolution analogy, the process has been marked by ideological conflict and battles over sovereignty and territory. It has sometimes been unclear which side various parties are on − and indeed how many sides there are! The revolution, if well advanced, is not at an end. Guerrilla warfare continues in parts of the territory.

Perhaps the best way of describing this is to say that, while competence-based standards are widely recognized as at least a major part of the answer to improving managerial performance, they are not the whole answer. There is still some debate about the way competences are defined, and whether those in the standards are the most appropriate on which to base assessment of managerial performance. There are other models of management competences than those in the standards.

There is also a danger in separating management performance into a set of discrete components. The whole is, and needs to be, more than the sum of the parts. Just like bowling an off-break in cricket, practising a golf swing or forehand drive in tennis, you have to combine all the separate movements into a smooth, flowing action. How you combine the competences, and build on them, will mark your own individual style as a manager.

We should also be careful not to see the standards as set in stone. They determine what today's managers need to be able to do. As the arena in which managers operate changes, then so will the standards. The lesson for all of us as managers is that we need to go on learning and developing, acquiring new skills or refining existing ones. Obtaining your certificate or diploma is like passing a mile post, not crossing the finishing line.

All the changes and developments of recent years have brought management qualifications, and the processes by which they are gained, much closer to your job as a manager. We hope these books support this process by providing bridges between your own experience and the underlying principles and methods which will help you to demonstrate your competence. Already, there is a lot of evidence that managers enjoy the challenge of demonstrating competence, and find immediate benefits in their jobs from the programmes based on these new-style qualifications. We hope you do too. Good luck in your career development.

Paul Jervis

Acknowledgements

The authors specifically acknowledge the following sources: The Institute of Management for permission to reproduce diagrams from their Certificate in Management package; Melrose Films (1991), 'Certificate in Management' package; The Open University (1990), Open Business School Certificate in Management for their eight barriers to effective communication; Peter Honey and Alan Mumford (1990), *The Manual of Learning Opportunities*, Honey; Charles Handy (1985), *Understanding Organizations*, Penguin Books, for ideas and concepts used in Chapter 8; W. G. Hardy (1990), *Effective Business Writing*, Institute of Management, for an extended version of his 'purpose for writing'; John Adair for the use of ideas and concepts in managerial decision making; Steve Cooke and Nigel Slack (1991), *Making Effective Managerial Decisions*, Prentice Hall, for permission to reproduce Figure 5.3; Gary L. Cooper, Rachel D. Cooper and Lynn H. Eaker (1988), *Living with Stress*, Penguin Books, for permission to reproduce Figures 7.2 and 7.3; The London Borough of Enfield, Boots plc and the Woolwich Building Society and their managers for assisting the authors in the provision of case material to illustrate personal effectiveness. Other sources are acknowledged in the body of the text or in the bibliography.

1 Introduction

Introduction to the book

This chapter aims at introducing the manager to the idea of managerial competence:

- the personal effectiveness skills involved in the gaining of competence;
- it describes how people learn and what it is that enables personal change;
- it identifies the central role of communication in all aspects of personal effectiveness;
- it shows the relationship to the Management Charter Initiative's (MCI) units of managerial and personal competence at Certificate in Management level.

Background to the MCI units of competence

As the result of various research carried out by such leading authorities in the field of managerial competence as Charles B. Handy, The National Forum for Management Education and Development was established to identify the competences required by British management and to obtain employer commitment to the development of their managers. The National Forum is the industry lead body recognized by the Training Agency for the development of competence-based standards in the area of management.

Recruitment of employers, academic institutions and private agencies has been achieved through approaches by and public relations exercises launched through the Confederation of British Industry (CBI), Institute of Management (IM) and other National Forum members and founder members of the MCI.

Detailed guidelines for implementing the MCI Code of Practice were published in February 1989 and were reviewed at the October 1989 National Conference after which the first major achievements of the MCI were published.

The principal activity was the development of a three-tier structure of qualifications at Certificate, Diploma and Masters levels corresponding to junior, middle and senior management roles. Certificate level guidelines were publicly launched in October 1989 and pilot courses were run during the year 1989/90. Certificate level courses were launched in the autumn of 1990.

The Diploma level guidelines were launched with pilot courses running during the academic year 1990/91 and programmes were fully launched in 1991/2. Masters level courses are to be launched in 1992/3.

Once they were piloted, refinements were made and the following Units and Elements of Competence at Certificate level are those which are being addressed and improved by providers of courses and advisers of programme participants (see Table 1.1). This book addresses aspects of elements of managerial competence under Units 1, 5, 6, 7, 8 and 9.

Table 1.1

Units	Elements
1 Maintain and improve service and product operations	1.1 Maintain operations to meet quality 1.2 Create and maintain the necessary conditions for productive work
2 Contribute to the implementation of change in services, products and systems	2.1 Contribute to the evaluation of proposed changes to services, products and systems 2.2 Implement and evaluate changes to services, products and systems
3 Recommend, monitor and control the use of resources	3.1 Make recommendations for expenditure 3.2 Monitor and control the use of resources
4 Contribute to the recruitment and selection of personnel	4.1 Define future personnel requirements 4.2 Contribute to the assessment and selection of candidates against team and organizational requirements
5 Develop teams, individuals and self to enhance performance	5.1 Develop and improve teams through planning and activities 5.2 Identify, review and improve development activities for individuals 5.3 Develop oneself within the job role
6 Plan, allocate and evaluate work carried out by teams, individuals and self	6.1 Set up and update work objectives for teams and individuals 6.2 Plan activities and determine work methods to achieve objectives 6.3 Allocate work and evaluate teams, individuals and self against objectives 6.4 Provide feedback to teams and individuals on their performance

Table 1.1 (continued)

Units	Elements
7 Create, maintain and enhance effective working relationships	7.1 Establish and maintain the trust and support of one's subordinates
	7.2 Establish and maintain the trust and support of one's immediate manager
	7.3 Establish and maintain relationships with colleagues
	7.4 Identify and minimize interpersonal conflict
	7.5 Implement disciplinary and grievance procedures
	7.6 Counsel staff
8 Seek, evaluate and organize information for action	8.1 Obtain and evaluate information to aid decision-making
	8.2 Record and store information
9 Exchange information to solve problems and make decisions	9.1 Lead meetings and group discussions to solve problems and make decisions
	9.2 Contribute to discussions to solve problems and make decisions
	9.3 Advise and inform others

Personal competence

In order to achieve the competences outlined above, managers need to develop the personal competences shown in Table 1.2. Each chapter identifies the areas of personal competence involved in gaining overall competence. Chapter 1 focuses on the dimensions of personal competence 3 – Managing oneself to optimize results.

The other chapters in the book

Chapters 2 and 3 analyse, in turn, the art of interpersonal communication, including active listening and assertiveness; their effects on motivation and delegation; factors facilitating and impeding it; written and impersonal communication within and between organizations (the hard data prevalent in organizations); how and when to use them and the advantages and disadvantages of each.

Chapters 4, 5 and 6 analyse the role of communication in resolving problems, making decisions and setting and prioritizing objectives. Various skills and techniques are developed and examined for their effectiveness in communicating information, agreeing actions; methods of review and evaluation are also discussed. Chapter 7 concentrates on managers working under stress and the problems of 'distress'.

Table 1.2 Personal competence

Clusters of personal competence	Dimensions of personal competence
1 Planning to optimize the achievement of results	1.1 Showing concern for excellence 1.2 Setting and prioritizing objectives 1.3 Monitoring and responding to actual against planned activities
2 Managing others to optimize results	2.1 Showing sensitivity to the needs of others 2.2 Relating to others 2.3 Obtaining the commitment of others 2.4 Presenting oneself positively to others
3 Managing oneself to optimize results	3.1 Showing self-confidence and personal drive 3.2 Managing personal emotions and stress 3.3 Managing personal learning and development
4 Using intellect to optimize results	4.1 Collecting and organizing information 4.2 Identifying and applying concepts 4.3 Taking decisions

Chapters 8 and 9 examine effective working relationships inside and outside organizations respectively; the development of relationships; establishing customer needs; the use of negotiation; handling disagreements and conflicts/objections; the use of PEST and SWOT analyses and so on.

In conclusion, Chapter 10 summarizes the key issues, examines further the importance of self-knowledge and the knowledge of others and develops an approach for the construction of the various action plans for change outlined at the end of each chapter.

What is personal effectiveness?

Personal effectiveness is herein defined as a distinct set of competences, which are a group of skills embedded within all work related activities. Personal effectiveness relates to the MCI Standards of Managerial and Personal Competence as defined above.

Each unit of competence has a specific set of performance criteria required by participants when providing evidence as proof of their achievements.

The importance of self-knowledge

To understand one's own strengths, and maximize them; to know one's own weaknesses and learn how to overcome them through self-development, not only improves a manager's own opportunities and prospects but also provides him/her with the ability to facilitate the identification of the strengths and weaknesses of others. It also provides the opportunity to agree how to address others' self-development needs.

Objective setting for personal effectiveness development

Within the organizational context, it is important for people to recognize that individuals have their own objectives as well as the organization in which they work. Objectives (in this case those for personal effectiveness development) must be set, involving an analysis of what they might be, and have action plans in order to achieve them; it is then necessary to evaluate (how, when, why, where, what) the objectives were achieved (and to analyse reasons when they have not) in order to develop them and the action plans further.

It is also necessary to balance the objectives of the organization with individuals' personal objectives. In order to do all these things, effectively and efficiently, managers need to develop their own and others' personal effectiveness skills. Objective setting improves the performance of managers in their jobs and equivalent benefits outside work will flow from a personal objective setting exercise.

Objective setting should be SMART:

- Specific,
- Measurable,
- Agreed,
- Realistic,
- Time-related.

Objective setting takes place at every level of society and in every organization and, since organizations serve a function for stake-holders and this function is defined in its objectives, they often clarify not only what it is necessary or desirable to achieve but also the route in which success may be achieved. Objectives are therefore key to organizational and individual change and development.

Objective analysis

It can sometimes be difficult to define what our objectives should be, particularly when discussing those attached to becoming more 'personally effective'. These can be vague and elusive although very important. It is helpful, therefore, to concentrate on the outcomes desired from our behaviour, rather than the processes involved in the behaviour in order to clarify our objectives. Therefore, to ascertain the objectives for the less tangible outcomes, we would translate them into the desired 'outcomes' as demonstrated by the examples below.

Intangible statement	Tangible 'outcome' demonstrated by behaviour
<ul><li>developing self-confidence</li><li>be more creative</li><li>understands role conflict</li><li>appreciates the need to inform others</li></ul>	<ul><li>has self-confidence</li><li>is creative</li><li>identifies and deals with conflicting priorities, etc.</li><li>communicates appropriately, within and between departments, etc.</li></ul>

How people learn and what enables personal change

In a sense everything that happens, nice or nasty, planned or unplanned, is a learning opportunity. Unfortunately, opportunities do not come neatly packaged and labelled as such. Opportunities tend to reside in the eye of the beholder, more a matter of perception and recognition than of incontrovertible fact. This means that learning opportunities, in common with any other sort of opportunity, are easily missed. A major task, therefore, for trainers and development specialists [and managers generally] is to get people to recognise and make use of opportunities for learning. The ultimate goal is the complete integration of all kinds of activities and learning (Honey and Mumford (1990))

Honey and Mumford use the model shown in Figure 1.1 to show how learning takes place and subsequent change is effected:

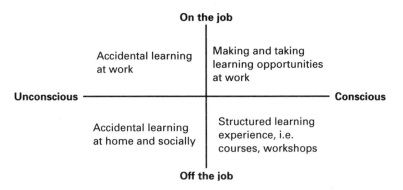

Figure 1.1 *Learning opportunities*

Most people believe learning from experience to be an accidental, unconscious process. They consider such experiences to be a matter of 'serendipity' if they happen consciously to realize they have learned something from them.

Learning through competence identification and objective setting can crystallize the meaning of experiential learning and facilitate clear action planning and performance criteria identification.

The advantages of being a learning opportunist

Honey and Mumford go on to say that learning opportunism (i.e. identifying and utilizing learning opportunities) has many potential benefits including:

- adding an interesting, extra 'learning' dimension to all you do;
- making learning from experience a more conscious and deliberate process;
- making one more purposeful; determined to extract learning even from unremarkable, routine events;
- helping one to learn from successes not just from mistakes;
- making it more likely that one will transfer learning from one specific situation to a broad range of other situations;
- meaning one can articulate what one has learned and communicate it to others;
- provides a recipe both for one's continuous improvement and helping others to improve;
- helps one to keep ahead of, and attuned to, change.

The learning opportunist, say Honey and Mumford, who reaps all these learning benefits finds that, in addition, their overall performance is enhanced (see Table 1.3).

Once people's minds are focused on the idea that every experience, generating reflection and self-appraisal, becomes an opportunity for development not previously conceived as possible, all experiences take on a new value and are seen as beneficial.

It is important to overcome any feelings of self-recrimination, embarrassment or shame over mistakes. The only time there is a need to judge ourselves, is when we have wasted the opportunity to learn from such mistakes and then continue to make them!

This process is common to all aspects of life; if we do not learn and develop as a result of experiences, the same mistakes and unfortunate experiences will continue to confront us, and our progress will be arrested; when successes are accepted without understanding their meaning, then the actions taken to create those successes, being accidental, are unlikely to be repeated.

Table 1.3   Work-related experiences likely to provide learning opportunities

---

- Situations – within the organization
    - Meetings
    - Tasks – familiar
          – unfamiliar
    - Task forces
    - Customer visits
    - Visits to plant/office
- Situations – outside the organization
    - Voluntary organizations
    - Domestic life
    - Industry committees
- Processes
    - Coaching
    - Counselling
    - Listening
    - Modelling
    - Problem-solving
    - Observing
    - Questioning
    - Reading
    - Negotiating
    - Selling
- People
    - Bosses
    - Mentors
    - Network contacts

- Managing changes
- Social occasions
- Foreign travel
- Acquisitions/mergers
- Closing something down

- Professional meetings
- Sports clubs

- Mentoring
- Public speaking
- Reviewing/auditing
- Clarifying responsibilities
- Walking the floor
- Visioning
- Strategic planning
- Diagnosing problems
- Decision-making

- Peers
- Consultants
- Subordinates

Source: Honey and Mumford (1990).

Learning styles

From their Learning Styles exercises, Honey and Mumford (1990) identified four preferences in individuals' learning approaches: the 'Activist' who prefers to get on with the job and will try anything once; the 'Reflector' who spends a lot of time thinking about what has been done and what is to be done; the 'Pragmatist' who is happy as long as things make practical sense; and the 'Theorist' who likes to analyse situations and behaviour and make philo-sophical sense of situations, without necessarily needing to prove them empirically (see Figure 1.2).

Different learning style preferences lead most people to distort the iterative process of the Learning Cycle by placing a greater emphasis on some stages than on others. Thus Reflector/Theorists tend to linger at Stages 2 and 3, preferring to postpone getting into planning and action, whereas Pragmatist/Activists tend to leap-frog Stages 2 and 3 in their haste to do

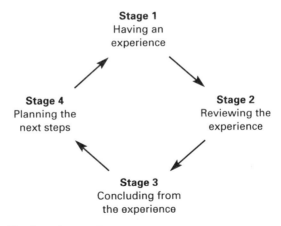

Figure 1.2 *The learning cycle*

something! There are, however, other tendencies which become apparent when one examines how people learn from experience (Honey and Mumford (1990))

As the result of Alan Mumford's survey of 144 directors, Honey and Mumford have identified four different approaches to learning with hindsight and with foresight:

- *The intuitive approach* − involving learning from experience, but not through a conscious process; it is claimed that learning is an inevitable consequence of having experiences.
- *The incidental approach* − involving learning by chance from activities that jolt an individual into conducting a 'post mortem'; usually when something out of the ordinary has happened or when something has not gone according to plan.
- *The retrospective approach* − involving learning from experience by looking back over what happened and reaching conclusions about it; especially provoked by mishaps or mistakes − these people are also inclined to draw lessons from routine events and success.
- *The prospective approach* − involving all the retrospective elements plus planning to learn before an experience; where future events are treated as opportunities to learn.

The central role of communication in these activities

What is workplace communication?

The provision and passing of information and instructions which enable a company or any other employing organization to function efficiently and effectively and employees to be properly informed about developments.

It covers information of all kinds which can be provided; the channels along which it passes; and the means of passing it. (ACAS)

Why good workplace communications are important?

- It is a two-way process between people at all levels, within all functions and disciplines, it takes place upwards, downwards and sideways:
- it ensures efficiency and success;
- managers have a responsibility to communicate;
- it creates trust, especially if employees are involved in developing systems and procedures;
- it facilitates job satisfaction;
- it is vital in employee relations/industrial relations consultation, information exchange, negotiation etc;
- it reduces misunderstandings;
- it involves people — staff want to know:
  - what is happening and why,
  - the way their jobs can contribute to organizational prosperity and effectiveness,
  - the future prospects of the organization;
- there are legal obligations in organizations with union recognition;
- employees are able to contribute.

Who is responsible for communications?

- It involves everyone, but management is primarily responsible which should ensure:
  - a positive lead from the 'top',
  - that policy is put into practice,
  - that practice is properly maintained,
  - that policy and practice are regularly reviewed,
  - that adequate facilities and opportunities exist,
  - that adequate feedback is obtained,
  - the chain of communication is clearly understood by those involved and to keep the chain as short as possible;
- The larger the organization, the more likely specialist functions, e.g. personnel, as well as line managers, will take an active interest in employee communications — possibly involving direct responsibility.
- The principal links would be line managers/supervisors/team leaders depending upon the structure of organization.

What should be communicated?

- Information about conditions of employment:
  - written statements;

- especially: − disciplinary procedures,
                    − grievance procedures,
                    − itemized pay statements,
                    − arrangements of employee representation;

- Information about the job:
  - job descriptions,
  - operating and technical instructions,
  - health and safety information,
  - general information about workplace,
  - background information about organization,
  - information about work objectives and performance;
- Information about the organization:
  - mission, objectives, policies etc.,
  - past and present performance and progress,
  - future plans and prospects, e.g.:
    - financial performance,
    - state of the market,
    - investment,
    - sales,
    - profit and loss,
    - assets and liabilities.

Much of this information may be available to trade unions − see *ACAS Code of Practice No. 2 − Disclosure of Information to Trade Unions for Collective Bargaining Purposes*.

There are also statutory rights for employees to be informed and consulted under Section 99 of the Employee Protection Act, 1975, and the Transfer of Undertakings (Protection of Employment) Regulations 1981.

The process of workplace communications

- Effective workplace communications must be:
  - clear, concise and easily understood,
  - presented objectively,
  - presented in a manageable form to avoid rejection,
  - regular and systematic,
  - as relevant, local and timely as possible,
  - open to questions being asked and answered;
- Methods of communication:
  - face-to-face:
    - group meetings,
    - cascade networks,
    - large-scale meetings,
    - inter-departmental meetings,
    - conferences and seminars,
    - audio-visual aids,

　　　　　　　　　− team briefings;
　　　　　　　− the written message:
　　　　　　　　　− employee handbooks,
　　　　　　　　　− employee reports,
　　　　　　　　　− house journals and newsletters,
　　　　　　　　　− bulletins,
　　　　　　　　　− notices,
　　　　　　　　　− individual letters to employees.

Maintaining effective communications

　　　　− Monitor,
　　　　− review,
　　　　− communicators know their roles,
　　　　− appropriate information available,
　　　　− information reaches all who need or want it,
　　　　− information not unnecessarily restricted,
　　　　− communication bringing desired benefits,
　　　　− practice matches policy;
　　which will depend upon:
　　　　− appropriate training,
　　　　− the extent of employee co-operation,
　　　　− the quality of management decision-making,
　　　　− the level of involvement by senior managers,
　　　　− absenteeism and labour turnover,
　　　　− the employee relations climate.

Communication is one of the key skills for the competent manager. A commonly agreed definition of management is 'achieving results through people'. In order to do this we need to practise the whole range of management competences and fulfil a variety of roles. These are all predicated on our ability to communicate with our colleagues at work (and sometimes with ourselves).

If we examine the management sequence illustrated in Figure 1.3, it becomes clear that communicating is involved at every stage of

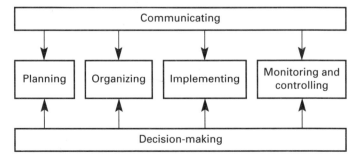

Figure 1.3 *The management context*

the process. It is therefore a critical component of almost every management skill. In this sense it can also be defined as a dimension of personal effectiveness.

The skills of communication

The means of communication (which includes the medium) can be various (see Figure 1.4). For most purposes they include:

- spoken (but may also include non-verbal aspects);
- written;
- representational;
- communication with self (thinking);
- team briefing.

The first four means of communication are discussed elsewhere in this book. We would like to look more closely now at thinking and team briefing.

Thinking

Thinking, or communicating with oneself, is something we naturally do more unconsciously than consciously. It is such an automatic process that unless we have become aware and educate ourself accordingly, much of our thinking can be wasted. It is the purest form of 'communicating' and does not necessarily involve language. If we are thinking in a structured way, we undoubtedly use our mother-language in order to proceed logically in our thinking. When unstructured thoughts come to us, they can be in the form of pictures, symbols even quite complicated conundrums at times. We frequently ignore or dismiss them as irrelevant to our present need.

There are times when our random, unstructured thinking is of extreme value; hence the gaining credibility of brainstorming exercises. It is not so easy to 'brainstorm' as some people may believe. We are all concerned, in one way or another, about our individual abilities to do what is right, our credibility in the eyes of others, fear of looking stupid and so on.

We should learn to trust our own thinking more and share random thoughts with others in the workplace. It is a wonderful way of gaining trust and support, because this is a way of refining and developing ideas and issues; allowing the contribution of others to

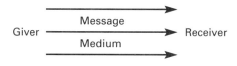

Figure 1.4 *The components of communication*

influence our values, beliefs and behaviour. Our own self-guilt often prevents our development of good thinking and communicating with ourselves.

Team briefing

While, at first sight, discussion about team briefing may more appropriately belong to another chapter, it seemed natural to bring it in at this stage having just discussed communicating with ourselves. The main point being that we all interpret information according to our own understanding based upon our beliefs, values and experiences. It is necessary to point out the dangers involved in any kind of cascading exercise which requires interpretation and reinterpretation of information as it is being conveyed.

Because so much of our thinking is unconscious, we are often genuinely unaware of the influence we personally have on the information we transmit. Study the following team briefing procedure which is a general approach made by many organizations.

What it is

Team briefing is a system of regular meetings to pass on management information to all employees. To enable this to happen quickly and effectively, a drill is established with dates, times and places for named groups to meet with their 'team briefers'; these briefers are the team leaders for that group of people. There is usually a team briefing co-ordinator to help set up and maintain the system.

What it does

Team briefing is a normal part of the manager's or supervisor's job as a communicator. It does not replace other forms of existing management communication; it complements them. The objective is to make sure that people know what is happening and why, through explanation, question and answer. It is not a group grievance session, an opportunity to discipline everyone, or group therapy!

How it works

Once established, team briefing will normally take place on a regular basis as a routine, much like regular accounting procedures. It involves everybody attending meetings on the set occasions, with briefers leading their teams. The system is likely to operate as follows:

- Throughout the period between briefings, the briefers collect 'snippets' of information and facts on team progress. A day or two before the 'briefing', they will write out their own 'team brief'. The information will be about progress, people, policy and points for action.

- The briefers' managers will check the local input that is planned to be put across and comment as necessary.
- The company board or executive meeting is held and a given time is allocated to items for briefing.
- A number of items relevant to everyone (when they exist) will be written down and copied to all briefers.
- Directors from the board meeting will meet with their teams. They will brief and explain the items on the briefing form, answering any questions. Any questions that cannot be answered at the meeting will be answered as soon after the meeting as possible. The team will take their own notes of the relevance of each item and the answers to questions.
- These briefers then add information they have just been given to their own briefs, making sure that this is all relevant. They will then brief their own teams in the same way as they were briefed. The same process continues throughout the organization.
- At the final level of briefing, notes will not be distributed, as these are only aids to the briefer.
- As far as possible, the majority of the employees will be briefed at the same time. Also the number of levels that information comes down through, should be kept to a minimum. All meetings should be kept to a minimum duration.
- After the meetings, briefers need to obtain answers to unanswered questions and feed back the reply. They also need to keep a note of absentees and brief them as soon as they return.
- After the system has been established, it will need to be monitored. Managers will sit in occasionally on their briefers meetings to keep them in touch. Members of management should 'walk the job' and chat to people informally about the brief.

There are many occasions during a procedure of this kind, regardless of how well it is implemented, that individuals can influence what is communicated by their own value systems.

This has been included in this chapter to allow managers to 'think' about how they might guard against their own influencing behaviours becoming too powerful.

Action planning

1   Determine whether each of the MCI managerial competences and personal competences are relevant to your present job.

2   If they are not relevant now, how might they become relevant in the future?

3   Are there any competence areas not encapsulated by the MCI which you believe should be included?

---

4   Make notes regarding your own learning preferences and the opportunities you have taken in the past. How might you improve them/develop them in the future.

---

5   Discuss your communication skills with your subordinates, colleagues, boss, friends, etc. How effective are you now? How might you improve them in the future?

---

2 Interpersonal communication

The overall competence focus of this chapter is to:

- create, maintain and enhance effective working relationships;
- exchange information to solve problems and make decisions.

which will be developed by the ability to:

- establish and maintain the trust and support of one's subordinates;
- establish and maintain the trust and support of one's immediate manager;
- establish and maintain relationships with colleagues
- develop oneself within the job role;
- contribute to discussions to solve problems and make decisions;
- advise and inform others.

involving the following dimensions of personal competence:

- showing sensitivity to the needs of others;
- relating to others;
- obtaining the commitment of others;
- presenting oneself positively to others;
- managing personal learning and development;
- collecting and organization information;
- identifying and applying concepts.

Objectives of this chapter

- to recognize the many forms of verbal and non-verbal communication and their importance;
- to be able to listen actively to another person;
- to recognize the importance of purpose, self-management and challenge for other people;
- to identify appropriate reasons for delegating a task;
- to match the skills involved in the task to the delegatee.

Introduction

The nature of interpersonal communication

Definition: The exchange of information, verbally and through bodily expression, between two or more people in order to influence the occurrence of action, ideas or thoughts; at work, in leisure or community pursuits, or in individuals' domestic lives.

We communicate with each other, whether we wish to or not, in order to: inform; instruct; motivate; persuade; encourage; negotiate; understand the views and ideas of others; listen because we like to and want to learn; and to seek, receive and give counselling, information, advice, decisions and so on. Types of information we wish to communicate to and receive from others can be categorized as:

- knowledge,
- data,
- attitude,
- intention,
- emotion.

Interpersonal communication can hover between being easy, good, happy and positive, and being difficult, not so good, unhappy and negative. Communication, and thereby relationships themselves, often break down as the result of not 'talking' to each other.

All this might seem obvious; that we all instinctively know this. Unfortunately, despite such common knowledge, we can see everywhere all the time, how misunderstandings can occur and resentments build by people not communicating properly with each other. If this can happen between two people in private, causing apparently irrational and immature behaviour leading to negative results, it takes little imagination to understand how people become irrational towards each other in organizations, within nations and between nations; war being the worst of all possible outcomes.

Verbal and non-verbal components to communication

We need to recognize the many forms of verbal and non-verbal communication and to 'actively' listen to others. What we say, what we do, and even our refusal to talk, all communicate messages to those with whom we interact. Yet, however well we think we communicate, there are gaps.

These gaps are nearly always unintentional and they point to the difference between the intended message, and the message received. Even with verbal communication, the words we use do not contain the whole of the message. Various commentators agree that a message is made up of 7 per cent words, 38 per cent voice tonality and 55 per cent body language!

Consider the memo, or brief note which you might leave for a colleague or subordinate because you are not going to be in the workplace for a while. If you know each other well enough, it is possible that brevity will not be a problem. If, on the other hand, you are comparatively new to your work surroundings and you are working on building relationships between the team, you leave a memo for a colleague who has recently returned to work from a prolonged leave and, as yet, the necessary trust and support has not developed between you. In your memo you simply state 'Following our meeting on Wednesday, you will be expected to assume the listed responsibilities in the coming year'.

To add to the problems highlighted by the illustration, imagine the responsibilities listed to be understood differently at the original meeting by the two people concerned. What kind of effects, then, do you suppose this kind of memo might have on your colleague and the building of relationships? It is unlikely to promote goodwill and team spirit; not even the boss is likely to put things that curtly, and yet you were addressing a colleague on this occasion.

Rudeness was unlikely to be the intention behind your communication, possibly believing all that was necessary was to confirm the discussions you had at the meeting, but antagonism is the likely result of a communication which has not been thought through properly. A good test is to read your own words as though you were the other person before sending out a memo of this kind. If you know the person well, he or she can visualize your body language and hear the intonation in your voice; it is likely that the message will read as more than the sum of the words alone, and therefore be acceptable to your colleague. However, you would be best advised not to take it for granted!

Although we are approaching communication analytically, we would stress that people's impressions are complex agglomerations of 'more than the sum of the parts' and cannot all be based on systematic analysis. They are often based more on emotion, prejudice, guesswork, and so on.

Gender and cultural differences in communications

Little research has yet been carried out on these differences, but managers are becoming more aware of the varying communication styles and individual needs exhibited by people from different racial, educational and cultural backgrounds. What may be considered by one group to be acceptable and the 'right' approach to make, could well be considered rude and unacceptable by another.

As managers, we all have a responsibility to get to know and understand those with whom we work. Even differences in people's 'perceived' class status and regional background will affect their own and others' behaviour. If we spend more time getting to know about people in the beginning, the less time will be wasted later on as misunderstandings become greater and more serious through ignorance of the subtle differences. It is these very differences which bring together the many and varied skills and abilities we need to perform effectively at work.

We should also study the differences between how men and women communicate: woman to woman; man to man; woman to man; man to woman. There are significant differences between the way men and women interrelate and communicate with and between each other which are further affected by the differences between the racial, cultural, educational backgrounds and so on, as well as people's expectations, their prejudices and stereotypical images.

All this might appear to be a very complex and daunting task for the newly appointed manager, but it can be a fascinating challenge which will help alleviate the longer-term frictions and conflicts which will occur if the need to understand the differences is ignored or postponed.

First impressions

We also judge people based on very little evidence. It is quite well known in the selling business, for instance, that first impressions are extremely important. Various commentators have suggested that we make our minds up when we are interviewing in the first 10 seconds, 2 minutes, or 5 minutes. Is it possible to elicit (or project) enough information in that time to give someone a rounded picture of ourselves?

On what information are such judgements made? Are they likely to be correct? Whatever the answers to these questions, researchers into the subject suggest, quite rightly, that we should maximize our opportunities by positively trying to create a good first impression.

What facilitates interpersonal communication?

Active listening

We all deliberately start by taking information in, rather than giving information out. In order to be personally effective we need to know other people's interests, needs and so on. We therefore need to demonstrate to our colleagues that we are interested in what they are saying.

It is therefore necessary for us to create an environment in which others can be honest and give information freely. To do this it is important that we confirm to them that we are supportive and not standing in judgement of them, by showing recognition that we have heard and understood their message by providing encouragement and feedback, rather than probing, interpreting and evaluating what has been said.

To listen actively to another person we should:

- establish rapport;
- make eye contact;

- match body language − by mirroring actions, posture, gestures;
- ask questions − to confirm, seek information and recognition;
- not interrupt or change the subject − active listening means letting the other person 'set the agenda';
- keep the focus on them, by using words such as 'you' and 'your' rather than 'me' and 'mine';
- use names.

Body language and other non-verbal communication

Body language is usually what springs to mind when we talk about non-verbal interpersonal communication clues (not to be confused with impersonal communication and the written word). Body language will be discussed here in the ordinarily accepted definition of the phrase, plus one or two other points for consideration which might not spring to mind so readily.

Characteristics

These include facial expressions; gaze and eye contact; bodily posture; gestures and use of hands in adding to, or contradicting, the spoken word; proximity (some cultures expect to be in closer proximity when in discussion than others); touch! and it also involves personal appearance (we are what we wear) are we really telling people something about ourselves by the clothes we choose to wear?

Body language is important and it constitutes an integral part of the information which people consciously or unconsciously use to assess others. The interview is a situation in which this 'activity' is particularly focused.

Important behaviours one might expect to see in others, and indeed portray oneself, would include:

- Appearance − appropriate to the context of the interview (one would not normally expect to wear jeans to a selection interview, or a formal review meeting or by contrast, to turn up wearing a pin-striped suit for an informal counselling session at a job centre).
- Eye contact − To avoid eye contact implies dishonesty, even though this is not always true (e.g. shyness, feelings of threat, etc.), therefore ensure eyes are levelled at the other person's eyes without staring or gazing for too long (this can seem like threatening behaviour) − above all *smile*.
- Body stance − The body, including the position of the feet should be pointed towards the other person to encourage mutual interest and respect. To turn away implies disinterest, impatience or lack of time. Leaning towards the other person in a relaxed non-fidgeting way shows friendliness.
- Sit comfortably − The legs should either be side by side or loosely

crossed to express comfort and a relaxed attitude. Unnecessary hand movements are best avoided. (Other than gestures which add to the positive meaning you are expressing, hand movements can be a distraction and even put across different messages to your words and facial expressions!)

- Show interest and enthusiasm – This will encourage the other person to relax, even to enjoy the session/interview by the warmth generated under these conditions.
- Listen and respond to what is said – Too often 'interviewers' are guilty of thinking far too much about the next questions they want to ask; they actually forget to listen to the answers to the current questions! Not only will the 'interviewees' stop making efforts when it is realized that they are not being listened to, the interviewers also look rather foolish if they then ask questions which have already been answered!
- Nod head to show understanding – Hold upright, straight and level. (To hold the head forward and high indicates aggression, to hold it forward and rigid denotes anxiety.)
- Hold hands open and outstretched – Hold them away from the face and offer a firm handshake. (Pointed fingers and raised hands indicate aggression; clenched fists and folded arms denote defensiveness.)
- Voice, clear and steady – Shows confidence and soft, pleasant tones indicates friendliness.

Verbal communication

Characteristics

Verbal communication, both face to face (including meetings) and on the telephone, involves: conversations; listening skills; and talking. All of which are supported by body language – even while talking on the telephone, one can 'hear' when someone is smiling, or frowning by their tone of voice!

It is very important for managers to develop their conversational skills and to present ideas and opinions verbally. Demands upon verbal articulation will increase as areas of responsibility widen both informally in general conversations and formally in planned and prepared presentations.

Speech is also used by people to communicate emotions and their innermost feelings. It is possible to communicate all of these needs by using a variety of elements of speech which can be controlled and used to good effect. Such elements would include:

- voice tone;
- speech emphasis;
- speech content;
- use of figurative language;

- humour in speech;
- speed of speech;
- pronunciation used;
- pitch of voice;
- inferred speech.

Advantages

Immediate verbal communication of efforts, good and bad, will provide positive outcomes. People will feel recognized if good work has been acknowledged and, provided people have been told in private about poor performance, will feel less foolish and will have the opportunity to correct their behaviour before it has become known generally.

A manager at a London residential care home, says that poor performance should not be avoided as 'it will not go away'. It is necessary to discuss such problems immediately with those concerned and if they are not dealt with promptly, people may deny that they were performing badly because they had not been told before. She says it is important to 'manage the little things before they become big issues. The major disasters are not always the worst to handle. Accept that you, as the manager, are not always right; know your own weaknesses and work on them'.

She also believes in discouraging negativity in others by: maintaining a sense of humour; creating an atmosphere of warmth, caring, mutual respect, regard for others' feelings and, above all, respect for all races, creeds, religions, gender, sexuality and disability.

Disadvantages

Those with 'hidden agendas' may deny that they were ever told about their performance. They may have 'remembered pain' from the past; for instance, other managers may have used such dialogues as levers to cover up their own weaknesses and inadequacies in the face of adversity. Until trust has developed in the light of current experiences, a lot of time and effort will be required to develop people beyond such behaviour.

In the meantime, it may be necessary to keep some documented evidence, signed and dated, to ensure the discussion is not ignored or denied.

Creating the environment

Some would say that a climate of independence within workgroups such that people do not feel threatened by the existence of other groups is important in facilitating interpersonal communication. That it is vital to make all information available within and between groups to facilitate good working relationships by being aware of what others are doing.

If people are aware that they need to know what is happening in other areas of the organization for their own understanding and development (they will know where to send enquiries if they do — and that enquiries about their own work will be passed on to them in return), they will look out for and enjoy being able to pass on and receive information.

Typically, if this kind of interaction is not encouraged, people will still talk to each other, but it is more inclined towards cliquish behaviour; with a tendency to gossip, start rumours and hold grumbling sessions about 'the management', other individuals and other groups.

Flexibility of staff to work in various capacities within and between departments might also be said to help the flow of information; people become less 'attached' to the more limited roles to which they may be assigned and are more inclined to develop a corporate approach in their growing awareness of the importance in giving and receiving information.

Doreen Ward, from Ian McLeod House also says it is imperative to keep people informed (in her case Enfield Social Services Department as a whole), discuss changes, give feedback, identify training needs properly and not just send people on courses because it will do them good. Courses must be relevant to the development areas identified and resources should not be used inappropriately.

What impedes interpersonal communication?

According to the Open University (1990), in their 'Effective Manager' course material, there are more than eight barriers to effective communication:

- Uncertainty of message: when we are simply not sure what to say, or how to say it.
- Faulty presentation: this might occur by choosing the wrong medium. For example a memo when a face-to-face discussion would be more appropriate. Recently one of the authors experienced an unpleasant situation where a colleague had left 'instructions' for the boss following his own inappropriate behaviour, in the form of a quick note. Clearly this required 'negotiating' with, rather than telling the boss what he should do in the future. He was naturally offended and he over-reacted as a result of his authority being challenged in this way. This was not the intention of the message communicated and only a face-to-face discussion would have avoided this.
- Limited capacity of target: or where the receivers of the message are not trained to interpret the information, e.g. financial statements,

and they feel threatened by being presented material with which they are not equipped to deal. Information thus provided is likely to be rejected or only selectively absorbed by the receivers.

- Unstated assumptions: where sender and receiver are unaware that they each have different assumptions about aspects of the message.
- Incompatible viewpoints: failure to communicate because the sender and receiver of messages view circumstances from a completely different perspective. For example, managers may view the introduction of a new computer system as providing opportunities for improving performance and saving people from the boredom of routine tasks, while employees and union representatives may see the introduction of information technology as a means of reducing staff levels.
- Deception: where the sender deliberately withholds certain aspects of information because she/he believes it to be in his/her best interests to do so.
- Interference: noisy telephone lines; the phone ringing while we are trying to write a complex letter; an emergency occurring in the office while we are trying to negotiate with a client, etc.
- Lack of channels: where people who possess information with which others might usefully benefit, and vice versa, but who are unaware of the needs of each other because there are no formal channels allowing such exchanges of information.
- Cumulative distorted communication − 'Chinese whispers': The longer the chain of people receiving and passing the information, the more distorted the message will be by the time it reaches the last in the chain.

David Hind (1989) also provides insights to various problems associated with 'inferred' language and 'speech distractions'. As an example of this problem, the writer would like to discuss the style of an ex-boss who had tremendous difficulties in making people understand what he was trying to communicate. He was a very skilled negotiator, a wheeler-dealer of some note. Under some circumstances, communication of this kind may be useful, but by and large most people do not respond very well to it. Messages are never direct; requests/instructions are often inferred rather than explicit; the words used are intended to make the receiver 'read between the lines' and statements are often the complete opposite to the communicator's intended message. Recipients can often be made to feel inadequate if it later emerges that they have not fully understood the messages being communicated.

We need to be clear about the meaning we wish to convey. We all suffer, at some time or another, from the feeling that we know what we want to say, but somehow it just does not come out the way we intend. We cannot always be prepared for this, but if we can, then so much the better.

Often people feel excluded from other departments or work units which, in turn, makes them jealously guard their own work and resent the idea of inter-communication when it does occur; they have learned not to trust people when they see them discussing something. They understandably feel 'left out', that some people are favoured over others. If information is shared easily between people, this situation does not have time to fester and produce negative attitudes.

If individuals and groups are encouraged to consider each other as 'customers' just like any other customers, they will have no reason or inclination to build resentments. They will begin to understand that everyone, including themselves, needs positive and friendly interaction in order to do their jobs to the best of their ability. (See also Chapter 9, 'Communicating effectively outside the organization'.)

Individuals can make themselves indispensable by withholding information for their own purposes and not allowing others within the group, let alone beyond it, know what they are aware of or where information might be obtained. They misguidedly believe that this kind of behaviour will be good for their personal development and career opportunities. Making other people, including their bosses, come to them for information (which even then is likely to be sparingly given), makes them feel self-important and they think that it gains them recognition. They consider that if they are seen as the people who 'know what's what', they are more likely than their peers to gain promotion when opportunities occur. (See also Chapter 8, 'Creating and fostering effective workplace relationships'.)

Such people often do not understand the detrimental effects this kind of behaviour may have on the organization as a whole. For example when these people are away sick or on holiday, it will be difficult, if not impossible, for anyone else to cover their jobs in their absence. It is usually on these occasions that their bosses, far from believing in the indispensability of their absent subordinates, are more likely to become frustratingly aware of their lack of co-operation and corporate identity.

Conflicting views can present problems. Often we spend so much time thinking about what we want to express ourselves, we do not listen to what other people are trying to say. It is a hard, but very important lesson if we can listen to others while remembering the main points of our own arguments; sometimes these become modified when listening to other viewpoints.

How motivation and delegation affect communication and vice versa

Motivation

It is essential to recognize the importance of purpose, self-management and challenge for other people. Motivation might not readily spring to mind as involving communication skills. However, if viewed as a means of communicating shared interests and needs, it can be seen that in order to do this we also need to, once again, communicate individual and organizational needs, expressed objectives, targets and plans; it is only when there is a coincidence between these organizational and individual issues that motivation can be achieved.

From the various researches carried out; from Maslow's (1943) hierarchy of needs, through Hertzberg's (1959) hygiene and motivational needs (two factor theory) and onto Vroom's (1964) expectancy theory (after Porter and Lawler) and then to Alderfer's (1972) ERG theory (existence, relatedness and growth), it is clear that people are motivated in various ways and by various means including; financial gain, status, recognition, achievement, responsibility as well as freedom and interest, etc. We can also make certain general points about the characteristics positively associated with people who are highly motivated. These would include:

- Purpose   People who are highly motivated tend to be results or goal-oriented. This would involve a large amount of commitment which then increases work performance.
- Self-management   People seek to have a level of control over their own lives. Highly motivated people seem to desire, and to have a large measure of self-determination over their lives. This includes the ability to make their own decisions; possessing a certain level of autonomy.
- Challenge   Highly motivated people have a desire to improve and test themselves against the highest possible standards.

It can be added that people are also seen as social animals who voluntarily integrate their own goals with those of groups/organizations with which they work (or leave if they cannot).

It is interesting to note that externally imposed incentives and controls, favoured by the 'rule them with fear' school, are inefficient, as well as undesirable. This is why organizational development theory now favours the moves in management style from:

- individual to shared responsibility;
- autocratic to collaborative approaches;
- power relationships to empowerment of others.

In order to look at the question of how we can better motivate other people, we need to bear in mind not only these general points but also the extremely important principle of being able to identify the needs and goals of those we seek to motivate. In order to do this, we need to become good listeners. This is where our active listening skills begin to pay off.

To facilitate the translation of these ideas into action, Figure 2.1 is helpful:

Figure 2.1 *A perception model of motivation*

What has been discovered from what the wealth of motivation theory tells us is that if we increase effort by facilitating the motivation of others, we raise performance. From the individuals' standpoint of course, if they perceive that the outcomes are worthy of their effort, they will be willing to make the effort in order to perform and achieve the désired outcomes. The performance has to be focused however and must satisfy both organizational and personal needs. How do we do this?

- tie effort to performance;
- link performance to desired outcomes;
- look at the value of work, i.e. we must assess how much this goal is valued by the person we are trying to motivate.

The needs of individuals may be developmental; starting with small gains or focused rewards progressing to the higher needs (to use Maslow's terminology) of recognition and self-actualization (fulfilment); or move backwards and forwards along a continuum of needs depending upon occasions and circumstances. Managers need to keep up to date with their subordinates' changing needs and circumstances. Personal situations also affect individuals' motivation and their needs of the time.

Where individuals carry out limited duties, regardless of how intellectually demanding of them they may be, if they operate in isolation and with little support, people are likely to become tired and bored and feel unvalued. Such individuals can become more insular over time and keep all forms of communication with others to the barest minimum.

A manager of a London-based unitized residential care home, upon her arrival early in 1992 discovered that each unit (units are divided into categories of clients: dependent; independent; elderly mentally infirm; plus a mixture of the first three categories) had its own philosophy and culture. She was surprised to find that there were 'no cross border relationships, that staff did not share equipment, information or ideas; they just wanted to keep to themselves'.

'They were not "owning" the whole from a corporate perspective and that problems arising were passed onto those directly involved and no one else was motivated to help others when it was needed.' Each unit staff group were aware that 'their space was "their space" and colluded together on this basis'. Her aim was to change the environment to an 'open, warm welcoming one, where teamworking flourished which would then lift morale and create mutual support'.

She says that 'it is important for everyone to know what they are at the home for, and that they are getting paid to do it. Once the message is put across, that is when motivation improves, maybe staff just do things to please me, but they are now performing very well. It could be that some of the staff were unable to do what they thought was right when I first came here, because customer complaints are now diminishing. Information is provided to encourage staff because everyone needs to know everything here, even though some information is considered to be silly or unnecessary by some people'. The manager adds that while she is the manager everyone will be kept informed, which has proved right time and again for her.

Personal effectiveness skills required in order to help motivate others:

- be an active listener;
- applaud, compliment and reward;
- give considered answers;
- consult and take account of what people say;
- seek out their needs;
- give responsibility and the necessary authority;
- offer challenge.

Delegation

It is necessary to identify appropriate reasons for delegating tasks and to match the skills involved in performing tasks with those assuming responsibility.

If managing is about 'achieving results through people', then all managers should delegate. We know that managers in successful companies delegate tasks and responsibilities right down the line; yet delegation is often dealt with badly, if at all!

Some people may see delegation more as a job task that a personal skill, yet there is a personal effectiveness dimension to delegating. Many of the problems associated with poor delegation are either failure to communicate, or inability to do it properly. The following attitudes are all too typical of some managers:

- 'I would rather do it myself'.
- 'They'll only do it all wrong'.
- 'I'll have to watch them like a hawk'.
- 'I tried delegating once; it was more trouble than it was worth!'
- 'I don't want them to do my job for me!'

There are three reasons for delegating:

- to free time for yourself;
- as a training or development exercise;
- for motivational purposes.

Delegated tasks usually fail for one of the following reasons:

- wrong reason for delegating;
- wrong task(s) delegated;
- task(s) delegated to the wrong person;
- factor 'X'.

Delegation works in a management context that is increasingly emphasizing the notions of empowerment and shared responsibility. So sharing and delegating both tasks and responsibility, with the necessary authority, is becoming the norm. However, the three reasons are very different and when a task is delegated, one should be clear about the motives for doing so.

Freeing time for yourself

For a manager, this is a perfectly legitimate reason to delegate. However, it is worth asking yourself if you always delegate only menial tasks, tricky assignments and whether you keep certain tasks for yourself as 'hobbies'.

Training and development exercises

This is an excellent way to develop skills and confidence in your staff. However, if it is a training exercise, the skills to be learned and practised should be clearly spelled out.

Motivation

The importance of self-management and challenge in this context has already been discussed.

Delegating the wrong task and/or to the wrong person

Many more delegation exercises would be more successful if the tasks were matched more carefully to the person. The following six rules should be followed for successful delegation:

- Clarity: the purpose should be spelled out.
- Matching delegatee to task: the skills required should be carefully considered. The level of the task should be challenging, but appropriate.
- Discussion: the task, from the purpose through to the fulfilment, should be talked through.
- Resources: sufficient resources, particularly time, should be made available.
- Monitoring: the rewards should be discussed and progress should be regularly checked.
- Review: achievement should be checked against objectives.

Factor 'X' — the unpredictable element

There is little control possible over factor 'X'. This means that even where we have been careful to identify our purpose in delegating tasks and responsibility, and even where we have followed the six rules, things can still go wrong. However, a crucial issue is to determine what should be done to be realistic and accept that sometimes things do go wrong — the element of risk!

It is important to allow failure; progress can only be made if we accept occasional failures. It should be a part of the review process to try to identify why things may have gone wrong and to learn the lessons without blaming anyone.

Another manager at a residential care home talks of recognizing people's abilities, communicating praise, and reward and agree areas of delegation with staff in order to motivate them. She had made considerable efforts to make the skills of one young assistant manager known to the department more widely. He was transferred into the Civic Centre to continue the implementation and development of a budget system across the department (an extension of his achievements at this home).

The management team here are also being encouraged to identify their own strengths and weaknesses and not to feel threatened by other members' skills. 'They must acknowledge the ideas of others', claims the manager, 'and to always reward good work, to always be ready to listen and learn, share knowledge and experience and to delegate — to support others — but to let them get on with it'. She also believes they should always encourage others' contributions and let them sometimes think some ideas are their own, even where the managers may already have had such ideas themselves. This, she says, will also facilitate staff motivation!

Assertiveness and how to develop it

What is assertiveness?

Assertiveness is about speaking one's mind openly and objectively, without undue emotion or 'emotional blackmail'. It is the art of clear and direct communication. Being assertive enables you to: express personal feelings to others; be direct and ask for what you want; say 'No' clearly and firmly without causing offence when you do not want to follow a certain course of action. It allows you to take responsibility when necessary; say what you mean clearly and confidently and stand up for your rights (David Hind, 1989).

The most important distinction which must be made is between assertiveness and aggression. It is much easier for some people to be aggressive, but it is very ineffective. Those for whom aggression is the norm are unable to demonstrate their assertiveness for some reason; it may be that their experience has led them into this behaviour as the result of others not listening to them. It may simply be that they are insufficiently confident in their own abilities or the strength of their arguments and, believing others will not accept their 'reasons' under any circumstances, they have to force their opinions and beliefs onto others.

Aggressors tend to rally support from surrounding colleagues and subordinates; they achieve this either through others' fear of their power or as the result of their perceived past successes.

Aggressors' behaviour towards those with opposing views who are not themselves sufficiently assertive, will either breed aggression in return, or be avoided by those whom they wish to influence 'or bully'. Either way, nothing will be achieved and the problems will continue.

Assertiveness is about standing up for our beliefs and interests and at the same time taking into account the beliefs and interests of others. Displaying aggression is about taking an extreme stand in communicating our beliefs and interests. Assertiveness is about knowing your own mind and confidently and politely communicating it to others as necessary, in order to achieve individual and organizational objectives.

Making and refusing a request

If we transmit to those concerned the full facts relating to our reasons for making or refusing a request, in most cases people will genuinely understand and do their best to assist us when trying to achieve our objectives. No excuses, of course, but in detailing exactly what our situation is, most people would respond positively, and assertively in return. Agreements are mostly reached when both parties are behaving reasonably and considerately.

As is implied in this statement, the tone of our voice and the inference behind the words we use, are important factors in transmitting our views and opinions assertively. Politeness is essential, extreme politeness is not assertiveness and would be seen as 'creeping' which is unlikely to promote the desired response in others.

Coping with refusal

There are bound to be occasions when you are denied your request. If this is genuine you need to accept the reasons positively and compromise accordingly, occasionally requiring a completely different answer to the problem. Sometimes a refusal may be made by someone who does not have the authority to refuse that request. Again, there is no need to wield your own authority; a negotiated agreement can be reached and should be attempted before moving to an alternative solution.

Standing up for your rights

Nervous or timid people sometimes have difficulty in saying 'No', even when it is justified. Such people will often take on more and more work and then everyone is surprised when jobs are not completed or not finished to the right standard. Managers must remember this when dealing with subordinates if they appear to never say 'No' regardless of how busy they are. It is the managers' responsibility to be aware of the level of work being carried out by all their subordinates and colleagues and communication of these factors must be regularly transmitted. The organizational objectives, as well as the control of individual stress levels, depend upon the managers' skills to achieve this.

Managers can help others to say 'No' appropriately by keeping in touch with how they think they are doing; whether they are overworked or not; by finding out the level of work they may be receiving from other managers and so on. When people are asked frequently about their level of involvement, they find it easier to express how they really feel because they are more relaxed and learn that the boss is a reasonable human being.

Showing appreciation

Showing appreciation for work done by others is key to the development of good working relationships as well as building assertive behaviour. Some managers appear to think it 'soft' and non-assertive to thank others for what they have done. This is simply not so; the approach will build self-confidence, trust and mutual support between team members.

Making apologies

Similarly apologizing when you are wrong will gain credibility and support from others. False apologies and empty promises will have the reverse effect, but to admit mistakes takes courage initially, which will be rewarded by positive responses from your staff and colleagues.

Passive behaviour

People exhibiting passive or compliant behaviour usually have come from a background where other people's expectations are that they should behave in this way. Women from many cultures, for example, have been brought up to be obedient to their fathers, brothers and eventually, their husbands also. It is not too difficult to understand how that then becomes translated into 'appropriate' and accepted behaviour at work, especially when the boss is a man. The working environment itself often expects particular patterns of behaviour from people of varying backgrounds and particularly between the sexes. Many organizations still hold traditional views about the roles of men and women in society.

Where men will largely be encouraged to be competitive, assertive, performance oriented and demanding, similar behaviour in women is often criticized as being jealous, aggressive, overdemanding and selfish. While many occupations are experiencing changed perspectives in the accepted behaviour of men and women, even the most enlightened organizations have their examples of work roles occupied by women exhibiting the passive, compliant behaviours still frequently expected of them, e.g. typists, cleaners, junior clerks, factory operators and assemblers, etc. The jobs themselves often attract women, and sometimes older men, interested in part-time or flexible work requiring little commitment beyond the hours actually worked.

Most of the job roles in question are of low status, poorly paid and often the first to be lost in times of recession. It is very difficult for people to exhibit assertive characteristics when their very livelihood is constantly under threat.

Manipulation

Manipulation more closely identifies with aggression than either passivity or assertiveness. It is another technique people use to 'get their own way' often used by those who are in no position to 'aggressively' pursue their interests and who are unable to demonstrate assertive behaviour. They want their own way but do not want it to be obvious to others and therefore adopt a manipulative approach to making people do and say what they want.

Those who perceive their position to be weaker than those they wish to influence sometimes use manipulative approaches; downtrodden housewives (not all housewives), victims of familial pressure and demands; secretaries who cannot stand up to their bosses; bosses who believe this is the best way to get people to do things (especially where they have learned aggression does not work) and so on. It is sometimes used as emotional blackmail.

Usually those being manipulated will, sooner or later, realize what is happening and will resent it bitterly. Aggression is sometimes easier to handle because it is more obvious; a skilled manipulator can sometimes get away with their approach for much longer periods. Women with aggressive husbands or bosses can sometimes manipulate them very successfully and they proudly discuss their behaviour with their peers and colleagues. Unfortunately for them, the women are never recognized for their achievements; it is the men who gain the kudos or go down in the history books!

Those concerned with 'getting their own way' all the time are still being the 'child' in a 'parent–child' relationship. It is immature behaviour demonstrating that they have not yet learned that other people's involvement in developing their originally identified wishes or beliefs can, in fact, bring about more positive outcomes for all concerned. They retain the obstinate belief that the self-satisfaction, or gratification of getting their own way in the first place, regardless of the consequences, is really what life is all about. Assertiveness does not necessarily mean giving up what you believe to be right, sometimes people agree to requests without modification or attaching conditions, so why behave aggressively or manipulatively when it is never appropriate?

Body language and assertiveness

As an only daughter of well meaning but old fashioned parents, the author as a child was not allowed to 'answer back' when being given instructions, or to ask questions about 'why, how, who, where and when' in justification of the facts expounded; the response always being 'because we say so'. However, it was always observed by the parents that the child never needed to say what she thought, her eyes said it all!

Posture and gesticulation are equally revealing 'languages', communicating individuals' real views and attitudes towards other people and situations, regardless of the words they use, and you ignore or dismiss them at your peril!

Body language is highly communicative then, in all sorts of situations and for many reasons. It may be used in compensation for being unable or unwilling to articulate verbally, it might be used deliberately to confuse messages, or it can support the words used by reflecting the spoken reality.

For more detailed analyses of the importance of body language, see Allan Pease (1988).

Assertiveness and criticism

To either give or receive criticism involves assertiveness and many people have difficulties in this area.

In receiving criticism, it can be helpful to seek advice from your critics. In discussing the advice, objectively and positively, it is possible that the initial criticism will become less daunting for both parties and a better approach to future behaviour may be developed between you.

Similarly, in giving criticism, it could prove fruitful for you to start by questioning third parties about whether they believe their behaviour was appropriate and, if they do not ask first or believe they did act appropriately, offer advice for developing a better approach in the future. Whatever discussions ensue, those receiving criticism should be in no doubt that you are giving it, but at the same time, must be assured that you are prepared to help them improve whatever you are not happy about.

Challenging the status quo

Ms Marchant at Arnos Grove says that 'now the care assistants know what is expected of them, they are beginning to "challenge" each other on best practice. They have the ability to gain the knowledge, she says, and become assertive with each other and the managers, which is created out of management support and encouragement'.

Action planning

1 Discuss your effectiveness as a 'person to person' communicator with your boss, your colleagues, subordinates, friends and relations.

2 Prompt their responses by asking about your behaviour under the various headings in this chapter and try to record them objectively (do not disagree with them, just think about what they have to say).

3 Were there any surprises? Were there areas of agreement between the various responses? If so, record your reactions and thoughts concerning them. What about the varying responses? Whom do you believe to be the most accurate in their observations of your behaviour and why? Be honest with yourself, this is all about self development, not punishment for ineffective behaviour.

4

What are your development needs? How do you intend to address them?

3 The art of formal communication

The overall competence focus of this chapter is to:

- seek, evaluate and organize information for action;
- exchange information to solve problems and make decisions.

which will be developed by the ability to:

- obtain and evaluate information to aid decision making;
- record and store information;
- lead meetings (and presentations) to solve problems and make decisions;
- advise and inform others.

involving the following dimensions of personal competence:

- showing sensitivity to the needs of others;
- relating to others;
- obtaining the commitment of others;
- presenting oneself positively to others;
- showing self-confidence and personal drive;
- managing personal emotions and stress;
- managing personal learning and development;
- collecting and organizing information;
- identifying and applying concepts.

Objectives of this chapter

- to deal effectively with information by controlling, assimilating and organizing it;
- to develop skills and confidence in writing;
- to develop skills and confidence in presenting verbally and visually in formal settings;
- to become familiar with and to practise techniques of graphic communication to organize information and to communicate ideas.

Introduction

At work we are constantly bombarded with information of many types and from a large variety of sources. Constantly ringing telephones distract our attention and internal memoranda, business letters, reports, agendas and minutes of meetings land upon our desks daily. We are also expected to read and know the contents of notices, newspapers, journals, books and publications of all kinds, PR literature, company accounts and annual reports, posters, pamphlets, leaflets, itineraries, job descriptions, etc. We also have to maintain our diaries so that everyone knows who is doing what, and when.

It is vitally important to be able to distinguish, from this mass of information, between the important things and the background 'noise', and to be able to sort and make sense of it.

In sorting, prioritizing and representing this information, we are communicating with ourselves, and the efficiency with which we do it affects how well we do our jobs. A key skill is to make the best use of our time and effort (see Chapter 6, 'Planning goal setting and time management').

It is often too easy to be controlled by the inflow of information, rather than controlling it. We then become reactive and lose efficiency. Sometimes we should believe in the importance of 'Don't just do something – sit there!' But in sitting there, we should be thinking about what we should be doing, instead of just getting on with it – a key to good management but an 'activity' often foreign to the way we have been brought up.

Types of impersonal communication

The written word, including writing reports and letters, effective reading and taking notes; meetings; public presentations; exhibitions and conferences; electronic communication: computerized information – internal, external (locally, nationally, internationally); electronic mail, facsimile, etc. are all examples of the impersonal communication with which managers must deal effectively and efficiently.

Use of business English

Written communication

Good writing involves not one skill, but many. Writing skill is a continuum that ranges from adequate to highly competent and flexible. Even then, the demands of writing bulletins for TV news, writing plays and writing educational materials, all make different demands on us, and no one person is likely to be an equal expert in all formats.

Each medium requires different skills, and for most of us there is also a requirement to have a technical or conceptual knowledge basis about which to write. Of course, everyone has that knowledge, and all of us can write, so the purpose here is to provide information and techniques to help you to write better. For nearly all of us, better means simpler and clearer.

The first principle in the use of business English is to 'Keep it Short and Simple' (the KISS approach). It is very tempting for managers and professionals to use jargon common to their organizations or professions. As well as not being clever, it is also offensive and rude where others are not likely to be familiar with it. The same thing applies if managers talk 'down' to their correspondees; assuming them to be unable to comprehend the nature of the ideas they are trying to transmit.

A balance must then be maintained between an acceptable, non-turgid—non-academic style of writing, free of any jargon, and a language which is common within and between English speaking organizations. Indeed the style of this book is intended to be easily readable, unambiguous and understandable!

It is important to decide the purpose, target audience and format. This will provide the requirements for the content. Clear thinking is also required in both written and oral presentation. If you understand the issues and the rules for presenting them, you will be able to argue logically and to identify any problems in the arguments of others.

The purpose could be to:

- change behaviour or beliefs;
- answer a question;
- present facts;
- present results of an audit or similar activity;
- describe situations, events, or ideas;
- provide information;
- record past events;
- recommend;
- influence decision-making;
- bring about action;
- persuade.

Source: (adapted from Hardy (1990)).

Structure

Once the purpose of writing is defined, we then need to organize the important ideas into some sort of structure. We are lucky today; indeed as I am writing this section of the book and tap out the ideas onto my computer keyboard, with the word processing package I am using I can move whole sections around; break up sentences and reorder them; delete unwanted parts and add to ideas as I come back to them afresh, without wasting paper or time or running the risk of forgetting ideas as they come to me. I can suddenly move between chapters as ideas flow from one source into another area more suited to another chapter, and return again to add further thoughts. For me this is ideal; it is not however always possible to use a computer.

When it is not possible to use information technology to develop ideas for writing, it can be a good idea to mind-map ideas first (see Figure 3.1) rather like you might do when sitting an examination and you think through in advance how you might tackle the answer, linking your ideas with arrows. You will find, especially if you are a lateral thinker like me, that your completed map will be far from linear with main ideas and associated ideas circling and spiralling all over the page. However, it is possible, once you have completed this process, to order the ideas logically, making sections and sub-sections which also help to develop the ideas further.

Another way of developing from the sub-headings would be to list ideas in bullet point format for each section. Both these approaches are called 'top-down'. With reports, a good technique is to then 'top and tail' each section. That is, for each section, write a first sentence encapsulating the purpose or key point; then write a summary containing the conclusion, or key point. It then remains only to fill in the text contained in the mind map or bulleted list.

Whichever process you use, commencing all written communication by thinking about headings and sub-headings is a perfect means for developing your ideas and allowing them to flow easily; sometimes you will add to them as you proceed; sometimes you will change or remove some of your original headings, but all will make writing easier to commence, develop and complete whatever your purpose.

Good journalistic technique says that you should put the most important point first, and then any supporting information below it. Using this technique, you should be able to 'cut off' the text at any point without missing the most important issue.

Logical reasoning

The logical form into which most arguments can be translated is known as a syllogism and consists of:

- A major premise: the statement of a general law or principle or fact.
- A minor premise: connecting a particular case with the general law, principle or fact.
- A conclusion: a new fact validly inferred from the two premises.

Developing the theme

Serial arguments

These are commonly used in reports and technical papers where the conclusion of one argument becomes the premise of the next. E.g. if we develop managers to delegate effectively to their workgroups, individuals will become more competent in their jobs, be more satisfied with their performance, which will, in turn, allow their managers to develop new skills and spend more time thinking creatively, which will also, in turn, provide the basis for the learning organization to evolve and develop into new areas of strategic thinking, and so on.

Lateral thinking

When we think laterally, we develop new and innovative solutions to problems by approaching them from entirely different directions. It is vital to write clearly and explain the rationale behind new ideas when writing. Where logical thinking is about linear, progressive, deductive approaches to problem-solving, lateral thinking is about the use of unorthodox or apparently illogical methods of approaching the problem and is likely to need a certain amount of defending (especially where individuals' backgrounds are technical or scientific i.e. logical!).

Writing style

The major objective here is to get over the key points in a way that is clear and effective. As already mentioned, this usually means simpler and clearer. Many people forget this, but the most difficult ideas can often be put over in a simple way, using straight-forward language.

Correctness of language

Dictionaries record the accepted usage of most educated people of the day, so that when we talk of correctness, in this context, we mean the speech or writing of formally educated people. However, it is necessary to use the rules as a guide rather than a rigid formula because English in all its forms is fluid and constantly changing. Without rules for language, however, there would be endless con-fusion of meaning.

Obstacles to thinking clearly

Identification of any obstacles to your own clear thinking can help you avoid them:

Language

This can be an obstacle. Names used for things are rarely ambiguous, however more abstract terms can mean different things to different people, e.g. 'right' and 'wrong', 'good' and 'bad'.

Preconceived ideas

Attitudes and opinions can be major obstacles to clear thinking. These are based upon our background, education and experience and become our convictions. They are often just prejudices which prevent us from thinking clearly on certain subjects. They are strongly held beliefs which usually collapse if put to the test of logical reasoning. Prejudices should not be confused with criteria for judgement.

Self-interest

Suspect your own opinions and those of others when it is obvious that the need to change them poses a threat to your own or others' security or happiness. This is not easy to do for yourself, however, objective scrutiny of your own motives is very helpful for self-development as would be your facilitation of that of others.

Generalizations

Be careful of sweeping statements in arguments which might hide the important issues. They are sometimes also based on prejudices. It is helpful to make general statements more precise by inserting words like 'most', 'sometimes', 'always', etc.

Attract and maintain the interest of the reader

Write to 'express to' not 'impress' your reader. Inexperienced writers often try to impress others and while they might talk with their own voice, they will try to be someone else when they write. The resultant use of unfamiliar words and meandering sentences will be foggy writing which irritates rather than communicates.

One of the advantages of the top-down approach discussed above (apart from helping us to structure the information and the logical flow), is that it focuses attention on the main points and at the same time it also helps to attract and maintain the interest of the reader. Some useful guidelines:

Words

As well as avoiding jargon as already mentioned, avoid the use of complicated words and phrases where simple ones will do.

Sentences

The shorter your sentences, the better. It is not always possible, but if you aim for ten to twenty words a sentence, that makes your work very readable. 'Punchy' statements are also more likely to be remembered.

Paragraphs

Three to five sentences per paragraph also break the words up into manageable chunks and are best if they contain details of one idea or issue at a time. Words which are spread out between paragraphs with plenty of blank paper showing between them and between sections, encourage continued reading. Cramped paragraphs and lengthy sections are likely to bore readers and divert their attention to wondering how much longer they need to concentrate, rather than on how interesting and absorbing the information is.

Active verbs

These give a stronger and clearer sense of meaning. Why say 'it is undergoing problems of a functional nature', when you really mean 'it doesn't work'?

Name it

Another common mistake is to go all round the houses to say something that is quite direct. Ask yourself the question — if someone said to you 'but what does that mean?', how would you tell them? If you rehearse a simple verbal explanation, it may help you to write it. In other words, many people would be much better writers if they wrote like they spoke!

Create mental pictures

So many words are abstract and represent concepts rather than things. It is much harder to say just what you mean. In shifting from thinking to communicating, place yourself in the position of the reader. If that person is an outsider or a newcomer, try to remember how little you knew before you learned the special knowledge you now have.

Assumptions

Many people start with the 'but if's' first, before the main point. This only obscures what they have to say. If you stick to the Point, Evidence, Conclusion style, you will avoid this.

Idea overload

It is common for people to try to say two things in one sentence. This usually results in neither having the required impact. If you want to make two points, write two sentences. A slight variation on this theme is the 'sentence within a sentence'.

Common mistakes
Search through some of your writing and check for the following:

- 'This' and 'It' — Is it obvious what?
- 'You' and 'We' — Is it obvious who?

Right first time
Many people agonize over their written work precisely because it is not right first time. You need to realize that nobody gets it right first time It is much better to write it and revise it.

Perfection in grammar, style, spelling
People do get overconcerned about grammar, but if it sounds right, it is likely to be right. As a final check — read it aloud. Real howlers should stand out when you say it aloud. There is not a great deal you can do about spelling — except that you should be honest if you are not always accurate. In that case, use a spell-checker on your word processor, or get someone to check it for you. Even when you would normally spell something correctly, it is easy not see your own mistakes, but for someone else it is likely to 'stick out like a sore thumb'.

Punctuation
Do not punctuate to observe some rule, do it because the sentence you are writing demands punctuation if it is to be understood. Punctuation enables the reader to read quickly and without ambiguity. Common sense and logic are the best guides to punctuation.

Fitness for purpose
Match your style to the application. A company annual report has to be formal, but most other documents do not. You can also use creative layout or other visual ideas.

Above all, there is the need to know who your reader is. When writing to other managers, or send them copies of letters you have sent to others, it is vital to be aware of the relevance of the information to them (and the language they use); it should either be pertinent to their jobs, their professions or to their wider interests.

The large amounts of information received by managers means that anything which is not directly relevant will either be 'binned' or, at best, 'filed' unread. This is not only a waste of time and resources, but also impacts upon the wider environment and the unnecessary waste of paper, world-wide.

The presentation and interpretation of data

Most written communication is presented in report form for management purposes. Simple methods should be used to display the data in a way which captures the essential aspects.

In presenting any data it is important to use a neutral approach in your use of language, avoiding emotive words or statements, such as may be used by the popular press for instance. Avoid language as a smokescreen to hide features of your study, for example; obscure quotations, long and complicated sentences and excessive footnotes which can be distracting and even completely off-putting for the reader.

Honesty is vitally important. Look for the strengths and weaknesses in the work of others you use (and discuss it) and also reveal in your report the strengths and weaknesses of your own work.

Types of report format

There are various types of report format. The public sector generally, and local government particularly, are inclined to be lengthy and complicated approaches to report writing. It is our intention here, however, to discuss concise and effective approaches to presenting findings in report format.

Reports are structured documents and are commonly organized in sections:

- Title and author.
- Intended readership.
- A table of contents with actual headings and sub-headings to allow readers to determine the nature of the report.
- Terms of reference: the authorization and purpose of the report.
- Every good report will provide management with a summary of the main points of other sections, conclusions and any recommendations in order to tempt readers to delve into the detail within the report.
- Background and history: generally speaking, it is necessary to devote a small section to the background of the report and the relevant history. This will usually identify the problem(s) or issue(s) identified as requiring attention. It will also be useful if specific objectives for the investigation, or required outcomes are identified here.
- Method of investigation: specific research will require the author to discuss alternatives and identify the preferred methods with full justification. A general management report will require the investigator to identify which approaches have been used. Both types of

report will need to include any constraints envisaged and how these may be overcome.

- General and specific findings of the investigation itself: this section will detail the circumstances and issues arising out of the investigation. This will be a factual account, reporting the findings in as subjective a manner as possible. If interviews have been carried out, these should be reported based upon the actual answers given to questions.

When seeking information from others, particularly when researching attitudes and opinions, certain guarantees should be made, these might include:

- all information obtained will be treated as strictly confidential (i.e. names of respondents will not be used when discussing their responses if they do not wish them to be so);
- if interviews are carried out, the persons concerned will have the opportunity to see and verify the recorded statements;
- those participating will be entitled to a copy of the final report if they wish;
- if the research is to be used by an academic institution for examination purposes, the question of subsequent publication will require the permission of participants.

- Criteria for analysis, highlighting strengths, weaknesses, opportunities and threats.
- Analysis.
- Discussion.
- Conclusions drawn from the investigation. These will be based upon the actual analysis of the data collected with no new material included.
- Recommendations to senior management based upon your enquiry or investigation. This is the 'action centre' of the report and should meet the defined purpose of the report.
- Appendices: these are pieces of supplementary data not essential to the main findings, or updates of information which will eliminate the need for re-writing. They may include glossaries of technical terms and a list of abbreviations.
- Acknowledgements: thanks to people who helped prepare the reports.
- Bibliography: sources of references used in the research.
- References: unpublished material not generally available, e.g. company papers.

Reviewing the report

Having written the report, leave it for a day or two before revising and editing it. This allows time to think about what has been written and how. New thoughts may emerge, their inclusion will improve the report. Type or print out the first draft when it will be easier to:

- read the material objectively;
- assess the contents;
- decide if it looks good;
- review the language, logic and sequence of presentation;
- determine whether the main body supports the recommendations;
- decide whether it is convincing;
- know if you are proud of it.

Graphic communication

Graphic communication is the use of visual techniques to aid communication. There are many ways in which the techniques of graphic communication can enhance your ability to communicate clearly and effectively.

Among the many different types of graphic communication techniques are:

- Lettering and typography,
- Illustration and design,
- Graphic enhancement – signs and icons,
- Maps and diagrams (see Figure 3.1).

Both lettering/typography and illustration/design are really specialist functions best left to professional designers. However, they are usefully discussed in the context of word processing and DTP (Desk-top publishing).

We live in a fairly rich visual culture, and in a technological and fast-changing world we are used to dealing with huge amounts of information. We learned a long time ago that much information can be assimilated quickly, and that graphic design and logos can help to carry simple messages with great impact. Many companies also appreciate the importance of visibility, and pay hefty consultants' fees to have their corporate logos designed.

Of course, such devices can be used at a more modest level by all of us. We can incorporate icons or logograms into our documents and presentations to enhance the visual impact and the message.

Flow diagrams

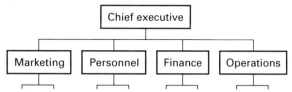

Structure diagrams

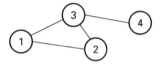

Project diagrams
(a) PERT diagrams

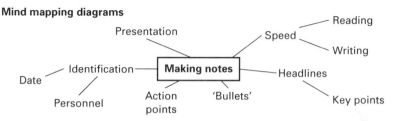

(b) Gantt charts

Mind mapping diagrams

Figure 3.1 *Diagrams used in visual presentations*

Information technology

The use of desk-top PC computers has opened up many more options for the graphic illustration of information. The main applications are:

Word processor
This offers the ability to manipulate numerical information — like financial information or stock/production levels — on a grid. The most sophisticated ones offer the ability to illustrate the information in diagrams such as pie charts or bar charts.

Desk-top publishing (DTP)
This adds to word processors the ability to design pages, complete with illustrations. There have been many claims that the advent of DTP will turn us all into designers. Of course, this is not true. It may well not be an efficient use of your time to spend hours slaving over a hot computer to produce a perfect document. However, for the computer literate, documents and OHPs can be produced with much higher quality if you can acquire the basic skills.

Statistical presentation

These forms of presentation are used almost exclusively for illustrating numerical data. They include pie charts, various types of bar chart and line graphs (see Figure 3.2).

Visual/aural presentations

Making information visually attractive is particularly important when making presentations to colleagues or potential customers. As well as attention to the visual, this is an opportunity to use available technology to its full potential. When planning such a presentation, there are several elements to bear in mind:

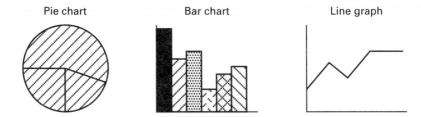

Figure 3.2 *Statistical presentation*

Purpose

We need to identify what the presentation is intended to do — it is necessary to ask two things here, what is the purpose for you and what is the purpose for your audience? There may be differences. This provides the focus, the structure and the style for the presentation.

Expectations

Both your own and the audience's expectations need to be considered.

Objectives

These too might differ between you and your audience.

Target audience

We speak to colleagues in a different way than we do to potential customers. The nature of the audience will influence the level of formality. The size of the audience will influence the style.

You — the speaker

You must ask yourself three further questions:

- Am I the right person to make this particular presentation to the audience?
- What makes me a suitable person to do this?
- Why will I be considered credible?

Resources

This will be decided to some extent by the nature of the target audience, by the available resources, and by the nature of the venue. For a small, informal group, it may be appropriate to hand out copies of discussion documents, but it is possible, in most cases, to use an overhead projector or a flipchart. It can be very useful to hand out hard copies of the OHP slides for reference and for taking notes.

Slides, video and audio mediums are also available increasingly at many venues for major presentations. Many chief executives of major companies will expect to use a teleprompter for a major speech these days.

Timing

As a general rule, the shorter the better. Few people can concentrate for longer than about 20 minutes on a single speaker. However sometimes it is necessary to speak for longer. In this case, try to enliven your presentation by breaking it up, by adding an extra element, or by seeking the involvement of the audience. This interactive element always helps to interest the audience. It can be done by simply asking questions at regular intervals.

Physical surroundings

Consider the most appropriate place to present, the size of the audience and the seating arrangements in relation to whether everyone will be able to see, hear and take notes if they wish.

Once these basic planning factors have been analysed, you can then move on to the detailed construction of the presentation itself. In doing this you should pay attention to the following:

Structure

It should be broken down and organized into a coherent and logical structure. Obviously this is dependent on the application itself, but it should include:

- purpose;
- overview;
- background/introduction;
- the body of information (including claims and evidence, if appropriate);
- summary.

Layout

It is often tempting to put too much information onto an OHP. It is better to limit text to a minimum. You should use headings and 'bullet point' lists are also very effective. It is useful to remember that people seem to be able to remember points more easily if they come in threes. When using an OHP it is very tempting to read the words on the slide. This is a mistake, and a lost opportunity − they can all read for themselves. You should use your commentary to amplify, emphasize or to digress.

Visual

Remember to use diagrams, charts, tables, icons, etc. where possible.

Commentary/style

You first have to make a choice of method of presentation before deciding how to remember the substance of it. You can read from a script; speak from prepared notes or speak without notes. The choice will depend on your skill and confidence.

Interacting with an audience

The rapport you create with your audience is a most important ingredient in ensuring that the message of any presentation gets across. This will depend upon your looking and smiling at individuals (not the same ones all the time); maintaining good eye contact; and asking questions where appropriate. It is also necessary to be relaxed; well prepared; well rehearsed; appropriately dressed; confident; enthusiastic; audible; and clear.

It can be effective if you make good use of humour. You must control the pace of your delivery, and you should never apologize for your presence or denigrate yourself. You should not distract the audience by your mannerisms or go on for too long.

Creating a visual presentation is an ideal opportunity to use the facilities of the computer to help you create visual material of a high standard. Some people feel more at home using traditional aids such as the white board, overhead projector, films/video films, slide projector and handouts.

However, too much visual material can cloud a point rather than illuminate it; the audience will concentrate more on the equipment itself and the techniques rather than on what you are saying. It is therefore vital to ensure that the use of any visual aids support, illustrate and reinforce points and they should be short, concise, simple and easy to see and hear.

Use of statistical analysis

General measures

Averages

Mode (the most frequently occurring incidences); median (dividing the data, once ranked, into two equal halves; the arithmetic mean (the sum of all the observations divided by the number of the observations) — this is the most commonly calculated measure of central tendency.

Measures of dispersion

For example, the spread of employees' length of service within a department may be more valuable than the average length of service of all employees. This will check the appropriateness of your chosen measuring device. (The mean deviation or the standard deviation.)

Percentiles

These show the percentage of a distribution falling above or below a given value and are therefore an extension of the mode. They are useful for making general comparisons between data but difficult to handle mathematically.

Relationships

These are measured on ratio or interval scales and frequencies plotted on scatter diagrams.

Populations and samples

In order to make predictions about a population as a whole, samples of behaviour are plotted on a graph which will give a normal distribution curve (beware of bias and error which will 'skew' the results). Use computers or programmable calculators for this.

The process of observation and communication

Different people observe things differently (does anyone have the whole 'picture'?). Also, beware of ambiguity, contradictions and inconsistencies in the process of communication. All observations and their interpretation of written material will be influenced by your own background knowledge, training and objectives of the investigation.

It is very easy to omit important material. One cannot use it all, therefore it is necessary to be highly selective and ruthless. You will need to use your judgement to balance the need for completeness in reporting or presenting with brevity to meet your purposes. Beware your hidden assumptions which are not openly explained and which underlie the approach you use.

Stages involved in critical evaluation

- clarity of purpose for reading and evaluating;
- skim-reading of material;
- reviewing your general orientation;
- marshalling your external knowledge relevant to the purpose;
- evaluating the report/presentation.

Effective reading

We all have to read – to keep informed, to keep up to date, and so on. But most of us could make our reading work much more efficiently for us.

Reduce your reading time

This can be done by judicious scanning. Before even beginning to read, you should look at the contents to identify sections of importance (and of no importance). Then you should look at the subtitles only, again to identify sections of particular interest. Thus, before you begin reading you should know what you are looking for, and where in the document you are most likely to find it.

When you do read, you should scan — do not expect to read every word. Most documents will contain only a few key ideas that you will wish to retain. The major task is to identify those.

Record what is important

When you have identified those few key ideas, you need to be able to remember them or to mark them for future reference. One way to do this to use a highlighter pen as you go along. Another is to write a very brief summary and attach it to the front page of the document. Action points should be marked in a different colour, or a different style.

Taking notes

Have you ever looked at the notes you have made of a meeting and wondered what on earth you have written? We often tend to take notes as a means of keeping ourselves occupied rather than with an eye for future use. We have all been guilty of reducing the effectiveness of our notes because we fail to record the most basic, and often the most important information. Notes should always be dated, and should include the names of those present, if they relate to a meeting.

A good habit to get into is to begin notes with a statement of their purpose — why you are recording this information, and what it is to be used for. Other points to take account of are:

- Selectivity: notes should not be too long, and should contain only summary information which can be of potential use later on.
- Organization: the rules of any good writing apply. Information should be grouped, and organized into headings.
- Presentation: again, diagrams can be useful ways of illustrating information or dynamic processes. Bullet point lists, again, help to summarize and show information in digestible form.
- Neatness: reasonable writing, neatly presented, and without doodles helps the visual clarity of notes.
- Action points: these are among the most important items of information to record — whether they apply to you or others, yet they are often left out. Some visual device for recording action

points can be helpful. Examples might include bracketing, use of coloured pens, or use of a special right-hand column.

Remember, we make notes in many circumstances and for many reasons. These techniques will help to improve the effectiveness of your note-taking.

Diaries

Diarying can be another important form of impersonal communication, especially where they are used by more than one person. Lorna Marchant from Enfield Social Services, the manager of the Arnos Grove residential care home, says that very little information was available when she first joined about the comings and goings of clients. It is necessary to know exactly how many residents are on site; who is out, where they are and the expected time of return, etc. The practice had been for word of mouth information exchange only, this being considered sufficient, with very little written down for others to access.

There was also no pre-arranged registering of new residents; they would just arrive with no arrangements being made for their property, clothes or family/social contacts. Staff now use the diarying procedure to good effect and everyone knows what is happening, to whom and so on.

Meetings

Purpose

Meetings (the interactive processes of meetings are discussed elsewhere in this book) are a very useful way to make things happen; to agree priorities, discuss and solve problems, identify new methods of working, agree and allocate responsibilities, follow up progress and so on.

However, these purposes can be, and often are, abused. Some people simply insist upon meetings because they have always had them. Others use them as a method of checking individual performance assuming that group pressures will make people perform better. Others may use meetings as a method of group discipline.

We have all been to meetings that have been a waste of time for all concerned. Why does it seem so easy for so many meetings to turn out like this? Malcolm Peel (1988) in his book, *How to Make Meetings Work*, has identified six deadly sins:

- unnecessary attendance;
- lack of preparation;

- bad tactics;
- ineffective communication;
- personality problems;
- procedural problems.

A meeting should have a clear purpose, and it should be known and agreed by all concerned. This not only helps to integrate and focus the activities of the meeting but it also serves as a way to measure its effectiveness.

Lorna Marchant from the Enfield Social Services care home at Arnos Grove has established full staff meetings which occur every 2 months. Initially she has had control of the agenda but intends gradually to allow the staff to influence it. There are also shift meetings which the assistant managers attend every day (instead of their own separate meetings) so that everyone knows what has happened and what needs to happen. These, Lorna says, will also facilitate team-building where care plans are looked at and daily exchanges of information take place.

Planning

A meeting should be properly planned and organized. Planning involves personnel, information and resources. The first and most obvious point is that a meeting cannot take place if any key contributors are not present. As well as being forewarned of meetings, participants should receive relevant information in good time before the meeting. If the purpose of the meeting is to discuss a report, no useful contributions can be made if the report is received cold for the first time at the meeting. Good organization will ensure that transport, rooms and other necessary facilities are available.

The conduct of the meeting will depend to some extent on the level of formality, and the nature of the meeting. A working meeting — for instance to produce a draft document, or to solve a technical problem — may take some considerable time. Usually, however, the shorter the meeting the better, as long as the objective is achieved.

Elements of an efficient and productive meeting:

- purpose or objective known and shared by all;
- agenda set and followed;
- timetable set and agreed;
- notes/minutes recorded;
- input and involvement by all;
- outcomes discussed and decided;
- action points summarized at end.

There are three essential categories of membership at any meeting:

Chairperson

She/he is responsible for calling the meeting in the first place as well as its purpose and the content of the agenda. She/he must also, at the meeting itself, co-ordinate the issues, control participation and ensure optimum contributions from the relevant membership as well as handle any conflicts. Above all, the chairperson must not dominate the meeting him/herself; must seek clarification of any technical or other complex concepts; and should make his/her own personal notes of the proceedings.

Secretary

She/he is responsible for all arrangements before, during and after the meeting. This will include the provision of all the necessary documentation, other specific information required for the meeting, equipment, materials, any refreshments needed, and she/he may also be required to take minutes unless another member is present for the purpose.

Other members

They should ensure adequate preparation for their contributions at the meeting. These will include the relevant expert or experts required for the facts; someone who is able to identify compromise solutions; someone who is good at throwing up ideas (even if they are not all useful!); someone who can commit resources; and at least one person who is prepared to admit they do not understand, because most people are afraid to show their ignorance.

Construction of agenda

There are specific stages with coherent progression which must be addressed throughout the course of the meeting and the minutes will normally be recorded in order of discussion.

1 apologies for absence;
2 minutes of previous meeting;
3 matters arising from previous minutes;
4 list of new items in order of urgency or importance;
5 any other business;
6 date and time of next meeting.

Recording of meetings

These should simply record the facts and any decisions taken and follow-up action required under each item. It is not necessary to record verbatim comments from each member other than where they refer directly to further action or further decisions required.

It is important to ensure that an accurate account of those attending the meeting be listed at the top of the minutes with relevant roles allocated alongside the names.

Item 1 should name those who should have attended the meeting but who have apologized, for urgent or important reasons, and who have been excused by the Chair.

All members should have had sufficient time before the meeting to read the minutes of previous meetings and make any necessary notes in order to raise queries. Item 2 then requires that the minutes are agreed by all members and then signed by the Chairperson and Secretary.

Ideally, an 'Action Column' should be ruled up on the right-hand side of the minutes to identify the initials of those who have agreed at the meeting to follow up as necessary. Do not commit responsibilities to those absent from the meeting unless they have previously agreed to be involved! This is a common mistake which can result in demotivation, inaction and compromised objectives.

Item 3 will deal with the matters arising from those minutes, which may be taken in a different order depending upon any newly agreed priorities identified at the meeting.

This will then be followed by item 4 which addresses all new issues to be dealt with by the meeting, in order of priority.

Item 5 covers any other business which may not be listed on the agenda and which has been identified by members as new, although perhaps not urgent, items for discussion.

The meeting members will then agree the time, date and place of any further meeting.

Techniques for effective communication at meetings

Kiss

Keep it short and simple as discussed earlier in this chapter. You must try to be clear and concise so that what you say is understood by everyone at the meeting.

Know your own subject

Be familiar with all the written material made available before the meeting, and therefore be confident that you will be able to deliver your information and answer likely questions without fear of being unprepared.

Avoid interrupting others midstream

Let them make their points and, no matter how difficult it may be because you disagree, or are frightened you might forget what you want to say — **listen** to what is being said. Make your own notes of course so that you can come back to your points, but by listening to others without interruption, it is possible to influence the discussion if the need continues. You will gain support and credibility as a good listener with the ability to acknowledge and apply what others think to your own thought development, without upsetting or embarrassing anyone. If you do not listen, not only the speaker but also others in the group are less likely to want to listen to you when it is your turn to speak.

Humour is also helpful

This will relax everyone and help produce a conducive environment, especially where there are difficult problems to resolve or complex issues to debate. However, make sure it is relevant and that you do not become the scapegoat and ridiculed as the result of being known as a joker and never taken seriously.

Only speak when necessary

You should also be sure to speak when you have something constructive to add to a discussion and not just for the sake of being heard. A common mistake is for people to contribute to their own function or specialism and remain quiet during the discussion of issues outside their immediate control.

This not only makes them appear disinterested in the problems of others but also seem to be ignorant of them as well. Therefore listen keenly to what is being said in all topics and allow your ideas to form accordingly. It can reveal to others where they have been less than efficient in transmitting information.

Be ready to compromise

It is important to do this where you are able and not just 'stick to your guns' as a matter of principle. Uncompromising attitudes, unless the implications are too great for those you are representing — when you should explain them very clearly to the rest of the meeting — will achieve nothing. It could also damage your reputation as a good manager if you do not have the ability to view situations from a wide perspective.

Identify areas of agreement

If you are negotiating, identify those areas with which there is agreement and spell them out before making strong points over which you are seeking acceptance, but are less easy for the other members to agree with.

Acknowledge the strengths and achievements of others at the meeting

This should include those who are not present. This also has positive effects on others' views of your abilities and perceptions.

One of the managers interviewed for this book, found staff meetings very traumatic when she first arrived in post because of one individual within the group. No one wanted to discuss things because the person concerned was always on the defensive, making it impossible for others to air their views and opinions. The manager then concentrated on small group meetings to much greater effect; others found it easier to contribute and develop their self-confidence. When she finally ran a full staff meeting, the manager had been able to remove the individual's defensiveness who then had little to say beyond relevant issues making a more constructive and positive meeting in all. The manager's main tip for effective meetings: 'Always plan and prepare thoroughly, or you will look stupid. Take it from one who knows!'

As a final comment on the art of communicating impersonally, the manager would add, 'Remain focused on the end-product or outcome. Take time to read everything; policies, procedures, everything relevant. Past course materials make excellent reminders, especially if bad habits are creeping in. Keep up to date with things, it is no good having manuals of procedures and then allow the dust to settle on them. They have a purpose, so use them. Really understand the essence of their existence not just to act by the book, but to internalize their purpose and be party to their development'.

Action planning

1 Do you have problems sifting through and reading all the material that lands upon your desk? Try out some of the simple rules discussed in this chapter and keep a log of the information you have gathered, recorded and stored.

2 Discuss with your boss the effectiveness of any reports you have submitted recently and make notes of any areas of development required. (Remember to assess your language – including use of jargon; any aids you have used to support your arguments – visual and otherwise; note-taking and other secondary information used in your reports.)

3 Discuss with those with whom you regularly 'meet' your effectiveness at meetings and group discussions. Detail your strengths and areas for development.

4 Communication and resolving problems

The overall competency focus of Chapters 4 and 5 is to:

1 seek, evaluate and organize information for action; and
2 exchange information to solve problems and makc decisions.

which will be developed by the ability to:

- obtain and evaluate information to aid decision-making;
- record and store information;
- lead meetings and group discussions to solve problems and make decisions;
- contribute to discussions to solve problems and make decisions;
- advise and inform others.

involving the following dimensions of personal competence:

- monitoring and responding to actual against planned activities;
- obtaining the commitment of others;
- showing self-confidence and personal drive;
- managing personal learning and development;
- collecting and organizing information;
- identifying and applying concepts;
- taking decisions.

Introduction and objectives

This chapter and Chapter 5 will introduce you to problem-solving and decision-making. You may have considerable experience in solving problems and making decisions. Managers are expected to do this. However the problem-solving and decision-making methods used may be ineffectual or otherwise inappropriate.

Management writers argue about the relationship between problem-solving and decision-making. Some claim that problem-solving is part of decision-making. Others feel the reverse and argue that decision-making is part of problem-solving. There are those who feel that problem-solving and decision-making should be seen as similar terms to describe the same process.

Here the view adopted is to see them both as part of a process.

The focus of this chapter is on the concept of a problem which has to be identified, understood and solved. The focus of Chapter 5 is upon the manager making decisions about what to do, who to involve and how to communicate effectively for action.

By the end of Chapters 4 and 5 you should:

- understand the nature of problem-solving and decision-making and their importance in management;
- understand the difference between 'closed' and 'open-ended' problems;
- have a good grasp of how to approach problem-solving;
- understand what creative thinking is and what helps and hinders it;
- be able to tackle a problem in a systematic fashion;
- be familiar with a range of techniques for:
  - identifying and describing a problem,
  - generating options in response to a problem,
  - selecting a solution from various options (Chapter 5);
- be aware of when and how to involve others in problem-solving.

An overview of problem-solving

Consider a day in the life of Sandy Jones, a manager, in terms of a succession of problems encountered. As you read the problems confronting Sandy consider what your reaction might be.

1 Sandy learns from the news that the train services are delayed which will create a problem in getting to work for an 8.30 meeting.
2 On arriving at work Sandy has to cover for the absence of a senior colleague who has been taken ill.
3 Sandy receives a letter from an aggrieved customer complaining about poor service.
4 Sandy's boss discovers that all the managers wish to take holidays in August and asks Sandy to come up with some ideas in response to this.
5 The telephone bills run up by Sandy's section are twice as high as the same time last year. The finance manager calls Sandy about it.

Before reading any further take a sheet of paper and write down your reactions. If you have a colleague or friend to hand share the problems with them, then compare your reactions with theirs.

Some of Sandy's problems might require an immediate solution. Others might be satisfactorily resolved with investigation. Some may not have any obvious solution. Some, on reflection and investigation, may not be problems at all!

It is not the nature of the solutions themselves that you propose which is of interest, as much as whether you actually propose any at all!

Sandy's reaction to the first problem almost certainly would be based upon personal knowledge and experience. Perhaps Sandy has an alternative to using the train. A telephone message could be passed to the person chairing the meeting. Possibly the meeting may be postponed. After all other people attending the meeting may also be affected by the travel delays.

The second problem would require Sandy to establish what the colleague had scheduled for the day; Sandy would need to find this out from the colleague or those familiar with his/her schedule. Perhaps some of the responsibility could be delegated. If the colleague had a tight schedule then Sandy may well have to rearrange priorities and postpone meetings. Sandy may be quite familiar with the colleague's work and work contacts. Alternatively the colleague's work may be very unfamiliar to Sandy.

The letter of complaint could require urgent investigation. Much would depend upon the context and the expectations of the organization. If the organization was well used to receiving complaints it may be almost a routine response. On the other hand the company may be concerned about any complaint because of the quality standards or nature of the product. In such an organization complaints may have the highest priority and be handled at quite a senior level.

The situation of holiday leave is one where there is likely to be different priorities in operation. The managers' interests may differ from that of the organization.

The use of the telephone may not in fact represent a problem. However, in order to establish this Sandy would need to provide information to explain why the bill had gone up. Possibly Sandy's organization does a lot of telephone selling and the usage is a sign of an active salesforce. Alternatively it could represent a lack of control over resources − or even deliberate abuse of resources by staff making many personal calls.

How did you respond to Sandy's problems? Did you see them in terms of your own particular experience, work setting or work habits. If so then your response could probably have led you to propose 'solutions'. This would not be an uncommon reaction in managers' who are 'hands-on' and proactive. It could be said to be more characteristic of an active or pragmatist learning style.

On the other hand if your reaction was to ask questions to elicit more information then you were possibly reacting in a way less dependent upon your work setting, experience or habits. The reluctance to 'rush to judgement' associated with the desire to acquire more (and more) information can be associated with a more reflective or theoretical learning style.

You may have realized that some of the problems Sandy confronts are more amenable to group discussion than others. Similarly some have tight time constraints. The first one, for example, requires that Sandy react quite quickly or accept the consequences of 'non-action'.

Apologizing after the meeting for failing to attend is less appropriate than communicating reasons for non-attendance in advance.

Some of the problems may not be problems at all. The higher telephone usage may be an inevitable result of staff doing their work effectively. The absent colleague may have had no commitments scheduled for that day.

Some of the problems may not have any obvious solution. There may not be any possibility of building a consensus to accept a solution because those involved have incompatible and opposing priorities. The intention of all managers to take leave at the same time may fall into this category.

Some of the problems could be extremely serious. If the company made very high value products where failure was seen as having large cost implications then a complaint might be very serious. An aircraft manufacturer, for example, would take extremely seriously a complaint that vital parts of the airplane were failing.

How to categorize problems

There is a wide range of ways to categorize problems. Here are several such ways which you may find helpful in thinking about problems you encounter in your work and home life.

Tudor Rickards (1990) uses the following set of categories:

'One right answer problems'

We are all familiar with these. What is 15 per cent of 100 invites the answer '15'. You would justifiably argue with someone proposing a different solution. There is often a considerable element of creativity involved in finding the answer to such problems. The living of crossword puzzle compilers relies on this.

Insight problems

Here the answer comes from a new perspective. This involves an element of creative thinking. We have all been there at some time. People who have locked themselves out of their car or house have probably tried to think creatively about how to get in without the key.

The account of Archimedes arriving at an insight in his bath is an example. He was trying to work out how much gold was in a crown. He knew the weight of the crown but was unable to work out the volume. It was necessary to have both the weight and volume of the crown in order to know whether it was pure gold. As he sat down in his bath he realized the water level rose and he could use the displaced water to measure the volume of an object.

Wicked problems

The success of the solution requires that it be tried out. Is the reason the light won't work a defective bulb, a blown fuse or the lack of a power supply? One way to find out is to test for each possible cause in turn. It may well be a combination rather than one single cause. More commonly it occurs in organizations when a solution has to be tried out in order to see if it will solve the problem. Restructuring and reorganization are examples of this.

The introduction of water metering on the Isle of Wight is an attempt to try out a possible solution to the various problems of water supply and rationing. The concept of paying for the amount of water you use is seen as something which has to be tried out in practice. The views of experts or the results of consumer surveys would not be regarded as sufficient to support the massive cost implications of changing over a substantial part of the country. There is also the consumer reaction to be considered.

Vicious problems

A problem may seem to have a straightforward answer but the human element adds a complication. The presence of outmoded and costly work practices in both the newspaper industry and in the car industry challenged managers for many years. The solutions might have seemed obvious but the industrial relations complications were enormous. There is scope for what Tudor Rickards calls 'lose–lose' behaviours in which all those affected by the problems end up worse off.

The UK coal dispute in the 1980s offers an example where there was from the management perspective a clear need to rationalize the coal industry and make it more competitive. However, the perspective of many of the miners was of a threat to whole communities and a way of life. In hindsight we may well look back and wonder how it got to the stage of such entrenched positions. Surely there must be a more positive way of settling disputes and bringing about necessary change without so much suffering and ill-feeling?

Fuzzy problems

Here the problem is difficult to solve because straightforward logic cannot easily be applied. An example is the attempt to computerize mail services by using computers to 'read' addresses on envelopes. It works reasonably well with typed envelopes but handwritten addresses pose a major challenge. The machine can process the envelopes far more quickly than the human operator can. Yet the human operator is able to categorize the handwritten addresses.

The way the Post Office resolved this problem was to install a video camera facility which took a picture of each address the machine could not read. The letters were fed through the machine in batches and the human operator fed in the correct code for the letters whose addresses were highlighted on a video screen. The computer remembered the order of the letters in the batch. So the batch of letters could be passed through the machine a second time for the handwritten addresses to be machine coded using the information keyed in by the human operator. While the human operator was keying in the correct information the machine could be processing other batches of letters.

It is worth noting that a problem can occupy more than one category. A fuzzy problem may also be a wicked one for example.

Problems can also be seen as existing along dimensions rather than in separate categories. Here are some examples of such dimensions:

Straightforward —————— Complex

A straightforward problem usually can be identified because there is sufficient knowledge as to what would constitute a solution and the problem has clear boundaries. The recent concerns about the risks of electrically operated car windows to small children would be an example. The manufacturers are well aware of how to reduce the risk. Some cars already have the necessary safeguards installed. Government legislation to require all manufacturers to do it would constitute a solution.

A complex problem often has no obvious solution and may be unbounded. An example would be the congestion of road traffic in the London area. It is argued building more roads just leads to more cars followed by more congestion. Improving public transport on the other hand is seen as requiring enormous investment and people may even then prefer to use cars. Furthermore the problem is complicated by the wide range of reasons for travel and the need to move goods and freight. The way the problem is defined can create the complexity. Transport is related to how and where people work. It is hard to put a precise boundary around 'transport' without looking at patterns of change in work generally.

Not technical —————— Highly technical

A non-technical problem is one which is readily understood and solvable by a 'lay person' (i.e. someone who has no particular technical or professional training). We handle such problems all the time in our everyday lives — where to go shopping; when to take a holiday; who to invite to your office leaving party.

Technical problems, on the other hand, require a level of technical or professional training or experience in order to arrive at a solution. When your dentist inspects a cavity in a tooth she or he makes a judgement about whether a filling is suitable or whether a more radical solution is indicated. Similarly the experienced plumber might know from listening to that worrying groan in your central heating whether your boiler requires a service. When you pay for technical advice you are often paying a premium for the training or experience which enables the person to diagnose the problem.

Hence the oft-quoted account of the service engineer who fixes a domestic appliance by tapping it with a hammer. The customer queries the bill of £30 so the engineer divides the bill into two parts: '£1 for tapping the appliance with a hammer; £29 for the 10 years knowledge and experience which enabled me to know how hard to tap and where to tap'.

Emotionally charged —————Not emotionally charged

Some problems have a high emotional content. They arouse strong feelings in those involved and sometimes in those not directly involved. Charities involved in famine relief are well aware of the powerful images created by pictures of starving children. The issues associated with adoption of Romanian babies were both complex and highly emotional. Managers often use a shorthand phrase to describe 'emotionally charged' problems. They call them 'people problems'. What is important is to be aware of the limitations of strict logic in the resolution of such problems.

There are some problems which have little emotional content. They sometimes involve little personal involvement. The selection of your lunchtime sandwich might be an example. Others may require enormous effort and commitment to resolve. The conduct of scientific research in non-emotive areas would be an example.

Sometimes it can be helpful to use two dimensions to create a box or graph in which to locate problems. This may show, for example, that of a range of technical problems some are highly emotionally charged and thus need to be handled differently.

Figure 4.1 represents examples of how four typical office problems could fit into the categories. The use of simple devices such as this to define and present problems can be of great value to the manager in trying to understand the nature of a problem. They also can serve

Technical	Repair of office equipment	Introduction of new technology
Not technical	Agreement on lunch rota	Staff reorganization
	Not emotionally charged	Emotionally charged

Figure 4.1 *Using boxes to categorize problems*

as a useful communication tool in consulting with staff about work-place problems. The box diagram (see Figure 4.1), could be used to show staff that uncertainty and unease over reorganization is in a different category from the lunch rota or getting equipment repaired. All problems can become emotionally charged if badly handled. Thus the agreement over the lunch rota could become an emotional one because of the way it was handled.

Creative thinking

Creative thinking is the relating of things or ideas which were previously unrelated.

People often feel that a problem has a 'single correct answer'. This viewpoint leads to a narrowing down of options. Narrowing down does not promote creativity.

John Rawlinson (1981) distinguishes between analytical and creative thought.

- analytical thought:
  - relies on logic;
  - aims to come up with only a few answers (or only one answer);
  - is convergent in that it aims to narrow down the range of possibilities;
  - is vertical (see below);
  - uses various techniques to close down the range of options (see below).

You will see this exemplified in the problem-solving approach of Kepner and Tregoe (1981) later in this chapter.

- creative thought;
  - uses imagination;
  - seeks many possible answers or ideas;
  - is divergent in that it aims to open up the range of possibilities;
  - is lateral (see below);
  - uses various techniques to open up the range of options.

One of these techniques is brainstorming described later in this chapter.

In practice a combination of both analytical and creative thought is usually required.

What is associated with creativity?

Henry Mintzberg and others have noted that an understanding of how the brain functions is important to understanding why people seem able to cope with some mental activities but not others. In particular Mintzberg wonders why it is that top managers often seem impervious to the sophisticated techniques of planning which they have available to them.

The brain is divided into two distinct hemispheres. Oversimplified you can think of it as an orange split into two halves. Each hemisphere controls movement on the opposite side of the body. Certain functions such as speech are primarily controlled on one side. Stroke victims can suffer major speech impairment as a result of a stroke affecting the left hemisphere of the brain.

Recent research suggests that there is also specialization between the two halves of the brain in respect of thought processes. The left side of the brain thinks in a logical fashion. Hence the fact that speech, a logical ordering of sound, is a left-brain activity. The right side of the brain, however, tends to think more in visual images. Here the way information is handled is more in terms of relationships and the broad picture rather than in terms of a logical sequence.

Therefore certain types of intellectual activity, such as understanding the logic of a mathematical proof, are left-brain focused. Other activities such as the creation of a painting or design of an advertising logo are primarily right brain.

Formal planning activities in management using scientific or logical techniques are left-brain oriented. When you follow the bakery problem using the Kempner and Tregoe technique later in this chapter you will be using the left side of your brain. However, practising managers often operate intuitively. This usually comes from experience. They recognize that problems are rarely amenable to strict logic and that we live in an imperfect world. Hence the need to use the right brain in managerial activity.

Mintzberg (1973) illustrates the 'right brain tendencies' of managers from the following findings of his research.

- Managers tend to favour verbal over written communication. This is because it enables a whole picture to be formed. The tone of voice and type of expression adds to the image.
- Much of the analysis managers undertake is not of hard numerical data but rather of fuzzy and more opinionated information. The organization grapevine is a source which managers are prone to use as much, if not more, than anyone else.
- Managers often find it hard to pass information down to people. Yet in order to delegate work this has to be done. A possible explanation is that managers rely on the right side of the brain but the source of the information is logical and held on the left side.
- Managers work in short bursts of activity encompassing considerable variety. Longer paced orderly and logically planned activities tend to be the exception.
- There are a number of managerial roles Mintzberg identifies. He regards as the most important 'leader', 'liaison', and 'disturbance handler'. These roles are often based upon experience and intuition

rather than the application of logically based research findings.

- When managers engage in decision-making there are parts of the process which often involve the use of intuition. The manager uses the right side of the brain in the diagnosis of what is going wrong and then designing customized solutions.
- There are aspects of the decision process where unpredictable factors have an impact. Issues such as the timing of a decision and the 'right atmosphere' for a change are often subject to intuitive but rather logical thought processes.
- When managers come to make a choice between options the method most used by managers is judgement. The application of rational analysis is less frequently used. The implication is that intuition and 'right brain thinking' plays a significant role.
- Managers confront not the stable and predictable world that planning would wish to cater for. Rather they have to deal with an unpredictable and turbulent environment. The strict application of logical thought is in itself not sufficient for a manager to survive.
- Mintzberg suggests that strategic vision in organizations is often located within one person.

Barriers to creative thought

The potential value in creative thinking in managers can be stifled because of obstacles.

These obstacles are:

Self-imposed

We have limits to our thinking which arise from constraints we consciously or unconsciously impose upon ourselves.

This is the person who searches for a lost object in the knowledge that they are looking in the wrong place but hopelessly tied to a different kind of logic. Hence the classic and oft-told story of the person looking for a dropped key under a street light when they dropped the key in the shadows. The reason for looking under the street light is that 'it is easier to see what you are looking for'.

This has been observed in managers who have found a particular solution to have worked in a past situation and therefore tend to cling to it even when it is less appropriate to the problem in hand. The effect is to limit the managers' search to particular areas.

As an example consider the following:

$$1 + 0 =$$

Most people would react immediately with '1'.

However, thinking creatively the option of '10' is also possible.

If the inclination to view 1 and 0 as numbers is resisted and + is viewed creatively the possibility of 'In and Out' occurs.

If 1 and 0 are simply seen as geometric shapes then a wide range of ways to combine them become apparent, making a range of both familiar and unfamiliar shapes (tree, child's spinning top, eye with eyelid, etc.).

Patterns

We often use particular patterns as a way of forming our thought process. Though useful these patterns can impede creativity.

As an example consider the following:

1, 4, 7, 11, 14, 17, ...

Which of the following is next in sequence: 21 or 41?

Many people opt for '21' by seeing the sequence as a mathematical progression.

However if the pattern is seen in terms of numbers made up only of straight lines then the next number in the sequence is 41 (only straight lines).

Consider the next letter in this sequence:

FGH ...

I or J?

Conformity

There is a natural tendency to avoid 'standing out from the crowd'. This can be an obstruction to creativity. A famous industrial manager, Alfred Sloan, had convened a meeting of his managers to review some proposals which had been made. He asked if any of the managers had any problems about the proposals and received a reply that none had. Whereupon he adjourned the meeting until such time as the managers had found some problems with the proposals.

Not challenging the obvious

The perception of a problem is often based upon an assumption that has to be challenged in order for a creative solution to emerge.

During the Second World War Barnes Wallis invented a number of new and highly effective bombs. One assumption which he challenged was that you had to hit the target in order to destroy it. Some of the fortifications in question were believed impregnable to direct hits. Wallis conceived of destroying them by near misses which would undermine the foundations.

Jump to judgement

There is often a willingness to rush to a solution before the various dimensions of the problem have been fully explored. In effect it involves 'closing off' the options at too early a stage.

The concern about meeting the needs of elderly people, for example, led to the rapid expansion of facilities such as residential homes, nursing homes and day centres. It was assumed that such provision would be the answer to the problem. Experience has shown that the needs of elderly people must be met by a range of resources and that indeed often it is the families of elderly people who need the resource as much as the elderly person.

Looking a fool

It is only natural to avoid potential embarrassment. The fear of seeming foolish often stifles creativity. The technique of classic brainstorming outlined later relies upon the suspension of judgement as to the wisdom or foolishness of the generated ideas.

Vertical and lateral thinking

Edward de Bono developed the concept of lateral thinking. He contrasted it with vertical thinking. He maintains that traditional education focuses upon the development of vertical thought processes. It is important to note that though they are two different and distinct types of thought process it does not necessarily follow that they always lead to different outcomes. He views both as important in problem-solving.

He distinguishes between lateral and vertical thinking in the following ways (see Figure 4.2):

Thus an example from De Bono's own younger days was when on

Lateral thinking	Vertical thinking
Seeks changes	Seeks judgement
Looks for difference	Looks for yes/no answers
Uses information to provoke new ideas	Uses information to analyse what works or doesn't
Uses intuitive leaps	Proceeds in logical steps
Welcomes distraction	Focuses on what is relevant
Follows unlikely avenues	Follows the most likely avenue
Open ended: no promise of a result	Closed: promises at least a minimal outcome

Figure 4.2 *Lateral versus vertical thinking*

an initiative exercise he was in a group of people tasked with using ropes and bits of wood to get across a water-filled hole. De Bono is reported to have suggested that the problem be solved by moving the hole.

Lateral and vertical thought is an extremely important concept to understand in problem-solving. Let us consider some examples.

You are going on holiday with your caravan and you arrive at Dover Harbour late at night to catch the early morning ferry. You have no alarm clock and know that you need to sleep. How will you wake up in time to catch the ferry?

A logical (vertical) approach would probably focus upon the possibility of obtaining an alarm clock or securing the help of someone to wake you up in time. The steps would be considered in logical sequence. Try local shops and supermarkets, service stations, etc. Failing that you could see if a local hotel might agree to wake you up for a fee.

Lateral thinking would open up a range of other possibilities. One solution was to scatter bread on the caravan roof so that birds would come and feed in the early morning. Why not park illegally so that you would be moved by the 'authorities'? Perhaps you could 'make' an alarm clock by using what you have. A canister dripping water onto another which when it becomes just so full will fall over making a noise. What businesses are likely to open up early and generate sufficient noise to awaken you ... perhaps the local dairy? Why park near the docks anyway? Why not drive out and park near a farm so that the farm animals will wake you up?

Special techniques to promote lateral thinking

Awareness

This is awareness of current ideas and what characterizes them. De Bono suggests that the following aspects of current ideas are useful in gaining this understanding.

Dominant ideas

These can determine how the problem or issue is viewed. Different people may hold different dominant ideas about the same issue. Attitude to trade-union recognition may vary but is often shaped by dominant ideas about the role of trade unions in society, etc.

Assumptions or tethering factors

Here people often have operating assumptions about the problem. De Bono uses the example that people assume that the longer you park your car the less it should cost per hour. However if traffic congestion is caused by parked rather than moving traffic then perhaps the per hour rate should increase the longer you park your car.

Convergent and divergent problem-solving strategies

Problems can generally be divided into two categories.

On the one hand there is a problem which shows itself because something which was expected to occur has not occurred the way in which it was expected to occur. Another way of expressing this is as a deviation from some standard or expected result. The nature of the problem can be described in terms of this deviation.

Then there are problems where something prevents what you want to happen from taking place. There is an obstacle in the way which has to be overcome. Typically it is associated with a desire to make some kind of change. Here the need is often to generate ideas and options.

Thus the recently issued (July 1992) Customer Charter for London Underground states: 'We aim to run 460 trains each peak period. Our target is to run not less than 97.5% of them at the busiest times. Last year we averaged 96.4%. We will show our performance line by line on a poster at every station.'

From this we can infer the following expected results:

1 There is a target of 460 trains each peak period.
2 There is a target of 449 trains during the busiest part of the peak period (97.5 per cent of 460).
3 There is a target of showing the performance of each tube line on a poster at every underground station.

These targets may represent desired changes (if they are targets which are not currently being met). If they are not currently capable of being met then they represent the second kind of problem. There may be obstacles such as insufficient trains, staffing problems or lack of space for posters at some stations.

Given the targets are currently being met, if one or more of these results fails to occur then it could be regarded as a 'deviation' from the expected. As such it will be amenable to a structured problem-solving approach. There are a variety of models to guide a manager on how to solve both kinds of problems.

John Adair has run courses on managerial decision-making and problem-solving. On these courses he asked managers what they actually did. From this John Adair suggests the following five stages which managers follow in problem-solving or in making a decision:

1 Define the objective

This involves recognizing that a problem exists which requires some kind of solution or decision.

2 Collect information

Here the manager gathers facts, opinions, etc. Some may need to be checked. It may also involve establishing what are the cause or causes of a problem. Time available and other resource constraints will be noted.

3 Develop options

The manager uses a range of devices to identify possible solutions. This may be as simple as just listing out the options. Colleagues and people affected may need to be consulted.

4 Evaluate and decide

The manager uses various devices to decide upon the most appropriate option. This will involve some kind of selection criteria.

5 Implement

The chosen option is then acted upon. The progress of the solution is monitored and reviewed.

There is a sixth stage which should usually take place but which is often missed out.

6 Learning and feedback

A post mortem may be conducted to ascertain whether the option was worth doing. This can be a source of learning for the future.

Adair suggests that this five-point plan can serve as a general model of how managers behave. It has strong validity and the virtue of simplicity.

Let's see how it might operate in everyday life. Most of us will have to move home at some stage. If we live with other people then it is a problem which affects more than just the individual. The way the process might operate is described below.

First of all you recognize that there is a problem over your current accommodation. Let us assume that you feel that it has become too small for your needs. You are aware that there is simply not enough space for your family and its possessions. Cupboards bulge and spill their contents. The bicycles rust outside because there is insufficient space indoors. The children need separate bedrooms. You realize that there is a problem and that you need to make a decision to resolve it.

The next stage is (in most households) to consult with partners to confirm the nature of the problem. Perhaps the cupboards are bulging because they are full of junk and a big 'clear-out' is all that is needed. The bikes may not be used at all. Do the children really need separate bedrooms? You also consider the implications of when you might wish to move. How urgent is the problem? Can you wait 6 months or even longer? The sensitive matter of money also rears up. Can you afford a higher mortgage or higher rent for a larger property? If so how much? Where might you be able to move to? Moving away from your current area may not be easy.

After gathering information you then consider what options are available. The option of moving to a larger property may be available. Alternatively you may consider it possible to extend your current property. If the issue is lack of storage for what you have you may consider building a shed or moving the car out of the garage. On a more radical note you might consider having a major clear-out of everything not essential to your current needs. Perhaps the children could move into the large bedroom and the bedroom could be partitioned to give separate living space for each child.

The options might then be considered. Some may immediately appear as impractical. The garden may be so small that a shed would overwhelm it. Perhaps the large bedroom is impractical for a partition. Here something will almost certainly become apparent. Moving may be favoured but not outside the area. The reasons why particular options are favoured or discounted have as much to do with subjective (emotional) reasons as objective (factual) ones. The partitioning of the bedroom may be feasible in practical terms but it does not resolve the emotional desire for a 'separate bedroom'. The wish to move locally may seem irrational given that other areas have more facilities but you like the local shops and feel comfortable. Eventually you will decide and that decision will bring implementation issues.

Assuming you have decided to move then there is the selling of your current property. If it is rented you negotiate with the landlord about leaving dates and return of any damages deposit. You have to locate a new property and secure it. Then you have to make arrangements to move and have gas, electricity and telephone connected. Probably you will end up with a checklist of tasks and dates by which things need to be done.

Does this seem familiar to you? Problem-solving and decision-making can and do affect people in their everyday life. The principles are not so very different when it comes to putting them into practice in management.

Convergent problem-solving

Charles H. Kepner and Benjamin B. Tregoe divide problem-solving and decision-making into two separate phases. They developed a technique for structured problem-solving which has been very widely taught around the world. Kepner Tregoe has a profitable consultancy operating in many countries based upon this problem-solving process. In the year ending 1990 they earned £2.9 million in fees in the UK.

Kepner and Tregoe's approach involves separating problem-solving and decision-making into two cycles. Each cycle has seven stages. The essence of the technique is that it is based upon a rational approach to problem-solving. A problem is seen as a deviation from an expected outcome.

The stages for the problem-solving cycle are as follows:

1. a description of the **deviation** from the expected;
2. an **is/is not** series of statements;
3. **distinctive** features which characterize the 'is statements';
4. whether each distinctive feature represents a **change**;
5. once all distinctions and changes have been identified to look for possible **causes**;
6. each cause is then **tested** to see if it explains the deviation in terms of the distinctions and is/is not statements;
7. finally the most probable cause is **verified** by testing it out in the work environment where possible.

These stages can be remembered by the phrase.

DiD Close Circuit TV (DIDCCTV)

Let's see how this technique can operate in practice. We'll use an example from a large bakery.

The bakery problem

The bakery took in the raw ingredients and manufactured bread. The dough was mixed on site by machine from the ingredients. The loaves were then formed by machine and placed on large trays to be baked in several ovens. After they had been baked in the oven the loaves were removed and the trays placed upon trolleys and left to cool. Once the loaves had cooled they were then taken to slicing and wrapping machines where they were sliced and wrapped according to customer requirements.

The loaves were then put back on trolleys and wheeled through to the van loading bays. They were then loaded onto the company's vans. The vans delivered the loaves to a wide range of customers.

Most of the customers were supermarkets and small shops who sold the bread directly to the individual customer.

The bakery ran on well-established lines. There were clear demarcation lines between management and bakery operatives. The operatives ran the machinery, handled the bread and loaded the vans. There was overall supervision by chargehands in the bakehouse and in the slice/wrap and loading areas. The chargehands adopted a free and easy attitude to supervision since the work was routine. More senior managers made occasional visits to the factory floor and when this happened operatives made a show of working hard.

However, management became concerned about quality issues. Customers would bring back loaves of bread because they had found a cigarette end embedded in the loaf between two slices of bread. In each case a manager saw the customer and an offer of compensation was made. Some customers were angry, others simply amazed at their find.

The company was understandably very concerned about these incidents. Quite aside from the customer relations impact there was the food hygiene concern. There were obvious health and safety implications.

The problem is one amenable to structured problem-solving using a schema such as that of Kepner and Tregoe. The way it would be handled would be as follows.

Stage one: the deviation statement

Kepner and Tregoe sees the problem as falling into several categories each of which needs to be explored.

1 Identity
What we are trying to explain.

2 Location
Where the problem is observed.

3 Timing
When the problem occurs.

4 Magnitude
How serious the problem is.

The principle is ask questions based upon the maxim taught to new journalists:

- **Why** questions: i.e. Why is it a problem?
- **What** questions: i.e. What is the nature of the problem?
- **Where** questions: i.e. Where does the problem occur?
- **When** questions: i.e. When does the problem occur?
- **How** questions: How often does it occur?

The result of applying this to the bakery problem would be as follows:

1 Identity

Some loaves are contaminated by foreign matter; namely cigarette ends.

2 Location

The problem is observed by customers when unwrapping sliced bread.

3 Timing

It is an infrequent occurrence which has recently been noticed.

4 Magnitude

The problem is potentially very serious for a food manufacturer.

Stage two: specification of what the problem 'is' and 'is not'

Here the concept is one of comparison. The aim is to compare where the problem 'is' to where the problem could be but 'is not'.
Hence the application of Kepner and Tregoe (1981) schema to the bakery problem might look as shown in Figure 4.3.

Stage three: what is distinctive about the 'is' data

With the availability of 'is not' comparisons can be made to furnish clues as to what distinguishes the 'is' data (see Figure 4.4).

Stage four: study distinctions to determine if a change has occurred

Here the aim is to ascertain whether anything has been altered or changed in respect of any of the distinctions which have been identified. Where there is such a change then it can give a clue to the possible cause (see Figure 4.5).

	'Is'	'Could be but is not'
Identity	Sliced bread	Unsliced bread or rolls
	Wrapped bread	Unwrapped bread
	Cigarette ends	Other items (such as coins)
Location	Customer observed	Noticed by retailers or own staff
Timing	Infrequent	Frequent
	Irregular	Regular
	Recent origin	Long standing
Magnitude	Serious	Minor
	Only few loaves	More loaves

Figure 4.3 *The bakery problem (1)*

	'Is'	What is distinctive
Identity	Sliced bread	Goes through a slicing machine
	Wrapped bread	Goes through a wrapping machine
	Cigarette ends	Implies a human cause
Location	Customer observed	Disturbed wrapping paper or disfigured bread would be noticed on dispatch or delivery to retailers
Timing	Infrequent	Likely to be a chance happening rather than deliberate sabotage
	Irregular	
	Recent origin	The slicing machines are due for major servicing
Magnitude	Serious	Smoking while working is a sackable offence but many staff are heavy smokers
	Only few loaves	Chance happening

Figure 4.4 *The bakery problem (2)*

	What is distinctive	Change
Identity	Goes through a slicing machine	No changes in machines
	Goes through a wrapping machine	
	Implies a human cause	
Location	Disturbed wrapping paper or disfigured bread would be noticed on dispatch or delivery to retailers	No delivery changes
Timing	Likely to be a chance happening rather than deliberate sabotage	
	One of the slicing machines is overdue for major servicing	Frequent machine stoppages
Magnitude	Smoking while working is a sackable offence but recent staff recruited are heavy smokers	Smokers recruited
	Chance happening	

Figure 4.5 *The bakery problem (3)*

Stage five: generate possible causes

Here the list of distinctions and changes are used to generate possible explanations for the cause. It is important to recognize that it may be more than one cause which may be the explanation for the problem.

- The problem clearly can be seen to affect only certain types of bread – the bread which has passed through one of the slicing and wrapping machines. This implies that the cause should be sought there rather than in the dough preparation or oven stages. To introduce cigarette ends into the bread after it has been wrapped would involve a high probability of disturbing the wrapper so that it would be noticed by the loader, delivery driver or retailer. Therefore that also suggests that the cause should be sought in a prior stage of the production process.
- The problem clearly has a human agency since cigarette ends are not part of the production process! Given the employment of smokers it is probable that a number of the machine operators smoke. The cigarette ends could also have been put in the bread by the customers who complained in order to secure compensation.
- The strong stricture against smoking while working – especially while working machinery – would mean that anyone doing so would be careful not to get caught. Dropping cigarette ends on the floor would amount to self-incrimination.
- Perhaps one or more of the machine operators has been smoking adjacent to the machine and has discarded the cigarette end into the machine where it would not be noticed by a passing supervisor.
- The most likely machine for this to apply to is the one overdue for a major service. The frequent stoppages may mean that one operative has been smoking while the other has been trying to fix the fault.

Stage six: test each possible cause against the specification

- The location of the problem with the slicing and wrapping machines matches the specification.
- The recent recruitment of heavy smokers onto the staff would account for the recency.
- The overdue maintenance of one of the machines might also account for idle staff smoking near the machine.
- The possibility of customers putting the cigarette ends into the bread themselves would not explain why it only happened to bread which had gone through the slicing and wrapping machines.

Stage seven: verification of the most probable cause

In this case the company could transfer non-smokers onto the slicing and wrapping machines for a trial period to see if the incidents ceased. They could also effect the major service on the one machine so that people were not tempted to stand idle by it.

Authors' note

In the actual case from which this was drawn the approach taken was to issue a further warning to staff about smoking on the factory floor. Further incidents of spoiled loaves occurred. The supervisor then endeavoured to track down the guilty party by asking for cigarettes from each of the machine operators and comparing them with those found in the loaves. The 'guilty operative', quite aware of the supervisor's intent, changed his brand of cigarettes.

Divergent problem-solving techniques

Here the objective is to 'open up wider possibilities'. It is the idea to get woken up for the Dover ferry by putting bird seed on the roof, parking illegally or across a factory gate.

There are some general principles which usefully apply to such techniques:

- Suspend judgement − get the ideas out before evaluating them.
- Get as many ideas as possible.
- Risky ideas are OK − after all thought is not a crime.
- Seek to join ideas together to build new ones.
- Creative thinking is hard mental exercise − take breaks and don't try to push yourself or others into long stints at it.

The first question is whether you are 'alone' or working with a group. If you are alone it is still possible to think creatively! Most artists work that way. Let us briefly outline a few techniques to enhance creativity when 'on your own'. It should be stressed that these techniques are quite capable of being used in teams as well.

1 Checklists

Here you use a list of items which might help to clarify aspects of the problem or generate a range of possible solutions. It is often used to invent new products or services. The four 'Ps' in marketing (Product, Price, Place and Promotion) is a basic checklist which can be used to generate ideas.

Another list was developed by Eberle (1972) under the acronym of SCAMPER:

- **S**ubstitute;
- **C**ombine;
- **A**dapt;
- **M**agnify (or minimize);
- **P**ut to other uses;
- **E**liminate;
- **R**everse.

The use of checklists has the advantage of simplicity but the disadvantage that they generate ideas in the particular direction associated with the item on the checklist. Would a checklist have given rise to the 'invention' of a product like Polo mints where the key product characteristic is a hole in the middle?

2 Problem division

It may be that the problem can be divided into two or more dimensions and that each of these can be divided into categories which can be compared. As an example consider problems in communication within an organization. Figure 4.6 shows how this might be considered along two dimensions.

The 3 × 3 matrix gives nine possible areas to generate improvements in communication within the organization. Obviously further dimensions could also be added (seniority, department, location are possibilities). These would give rise to far more possible areas to consider.

3 The use of analogies

An analogy is an observation which links one item to another in some kind of compared relationship.

So you may be concerned with quality of recruitment in your organization.

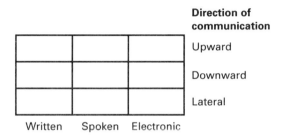

Figure 4.6 *Communication problem in an organization*

You would generate analogies drawing on the concept of quality. A list of analogies might be the following:

- finish of product,
- attention to detail,
- amount of thought,
- checked carefully,
- assurance that it has been produced to best of one's ability,
- won't let me down,
- don't mind paying extra for it,
- five-star hotel,
- reliability,
- focus on design,
- time spent in conceptual stage,
- conscientious about work and standards,
- caring for customer.

The analogies are then considered and ones which seem applicable can be, in turn, developed further.

Perhaps the analogy of caring for the customer seems useful. Maybe that can be developed into the conception of regarding potential staff as customers. This could give rise to such ideas as:

- personalized letters,
- better reception arrangements,
- interviews arranged at their convenience,
- providing lunch for interviewees,
- demonstrating the company's products to interviewees,
- a senior manager greeting potential recruits.

4 Brainstorming

If you are working with a group then you may find it helpful to use brainstorming as an idea generating device.

This is a technique developed by Alex Osbourne. It is widely practised and has taken on a number of forms. The principles which underlie it have already been identified above as applying to divergent problem-solving techniques. The avoidance of early judgement and aiming for as many ideas as possible are central.

The general form taken in a brainstorming session is as follows:

- Identify the problem and have it written down in question form, e.g. How can we ensure quality recruitment?

  It is important to have the problem couched as a 'how' style question
- Bring together a group of the right size and composition (ideally between five and twelve people). They should have been given the problem statement beforehand.

- Outline the format of the session (sequence of events and time frame).
- Outline the rules of brainstorming:
    - no criticism of other people's ideas;
    - all ideas are OK − the wilder the better;
    - the aim is maximum numbers of ideas;
    - 'hitch-hiking' onto or amending other people's ideas is great.
- Sometimes (especially with a new group) it helps to conduct a warm-up. One of the authors takes off a shoe and asks the group to think of uses for just one shoe. This warm-up need only take 5−10 minutes.
- Display the problem statement for all to see.
- When the brainstorming session starts one person writes down all the ideas as they are offered.
        The session should aim at about 25−40 minutes duration.
- A subgroup of odd number (say five) then evaluates the ideas generated and picks the best.
- The selected ideas are reported back to the main group.

It is important to remember that brainstorming itself is about producing ideas, not evaluating them. The leader must be careful to facilitate the production of as many ideas as possible.

Brainstorming promotes 'wild and offbeat' ideas. When people of different seniority are involved this can inhibit free-ranging ideas. The more junior staff are often reluctant to suggest things which more senior people may disparage. More senior people may feel suggesting apparently foolish things might cause them to 'lose face'.

Brainstorming is best used:

- when the problem in question can be stated in fairly simple terms;
- when the leader (manager) feels comfortable about using it;
- when those involved are of a similar seniority (or seniority is not an issue).

5 Card writing

Where the group is not comfortable or suitable for brainstorming then a writing technique to generate ideas can be used. People write ideas on cards (which can be anonymous). The cards are circulated or displayed and other group members then develop further ideas from them or seek to improve on the ideas.

The principle of having a clear and simple problem statement applies here as with brainstorming. It is also important to brief the group and give time for discussion of the statement to ensure it is understood.

The process thus involves the following stages:

- Problem statement,

- Group briefing and discussion,
- Idea generation,
- Ideas evaluation (often by seeking to 'group' ideas in some logical way by moving cards around on a table or pinboard).

Using techniques to deal with complex data

A high level of numeracy is not usually needed to resolve managerial problems but what is often required is an ability to deal with a large amount of information.

There are several considerations to bear in mind when dealing with large amounts of data:

1   First, it is worth considering the value to be gained by summarizing the information in order to get a general picture.

   Therefore when the newspapers report that inflation has been 5 per cent in the past year they are giving an overall picture based upon the average rise in prices of a range of items. You accept this and recognize that it does not mean that a specific item (the newspaper, for example) has gone up in price by 5 per cent. Think of the difficulty you would have getting an overall picture of inflation if the newspaper instead just listed the individual price rise of every item you might buy and left it to you to get a picture.

2   Second, it is useful to bear in mind that in a large set of data, usually a relatively small number of the items of information, account for a large part of the total amount of information.

Therefore, returning to the inflation example, you would perhaps be less troubled by a price rise in caviar than you would by a rise in the mortgage interest rate. The reason for this is that (for the vast majority of people) far more of their income is spent on mortgage repayments than on caviar. An economist called Pareto noted this effect and coined what he described as the 80:20 rule. According to this rule about 80 per cent of the problem can be accounted for by about 20 per cent of the possible causes.

Let us consider a fairly typical problem confronting a manager. Here is a list of forty members of staff and beside each person is the number of days which they have been absent from work in the past year (see Figure 4.7).

Let us assume that the manager is concerned about absence from work and wishes to quantify the problem.

One way would be simply to start at the top of the list with Adams and ascertain reasons for Adams's absences. Then you proceed alphabetically down the list to Wilson identifying in each case what reasons for absence exist and whether they can be tackled.

There is an advantage that there is certainly a clear methodology behind it and if you had to break off from the task you could return

Name	Days absent in past year
Adams	0
Akran	0
Ahmed	2
Bolt	9
Boston	65
Buck	1
Carson	5
Chung	10
Churchill	180
Comfort	1
Crawford	1
Crosby	2
Cummings	7
Davis	10
Duncker	50
Dunnett	2
Fallon	50
Field	2
Fulmer	4
Gesch	6
Gordon	45
Hamilton	7
Hicks	55
Jenson	9
Kempner	5
Khalid	5
Maguire	2
McIlroy	4
Miller	4
Osborne	10
Prince	25
Simons	5
Summers	8
Taylor	120
Timpson	2
Torvill	4
Van Oss	6
Vickers	6
Williams	9
Wilson	12

Figure 4.7 *A staff sickness problem (1)*

to where you left off. It is also 'easy' in the sense that you are not setting yourself the task of rearranging the data.

Can you think of any reasons why this strategy may not be the most appropriate?

Summarize the data

Another method may be to endeavour to summarize the data in order to get an idea of what the 'average' amount of absence was.

The total of days absent for the forty staff is 750 days. If you divide 627 by 40 you get an average of nearly 19 days absent per member of staff.

You could then pick out those members of staff who had more than the average amount of absence and look into the reasons for it.

This method has an advantage in that it enables you to focus initially upon the staff who account for most of the absence. If necessary you could then go on to look at the absence of the rest of the staff.

However, the average is affected by a small number of staff with very high absence. You do not get a picture of the absence pattern for the rest of the staff.

Use the 80/20 rule

However, it is also possible to analyse the problem in more detail and look at the proportion of absence accounted for by the 'worst 10 per cent or 20 per cent' of staff (see Figure 4.8).

As you can see from the breakdown the 'top' 20 per cent of the staff account for 80 per cent of the absence. This illustrates Pareto's 80/20 rule. It may possibly be one of the most simple and effective rules for a manager in effective analysis of data.

The best way to illustrate it practically for yourself is to try it out. You can try it out on a number of everyday matters. What about looking at your monthly household expenses. Keep the supermarket till receipts and look at your monthly outgoings (mortgage, loan repayments, utilities, etc.) See what proportion of the total is accounted for by the most expensive items. It probably won't work out to be exactly 80 per cent of the bill is found in only 20 per cent of the items but you may be surprised.

Experienced managers use Pareto even though they may never have heard his name. When the board (or the director) says 10 per cent cuts are required the responsible manager knows that it is the larger budgets which are the ones most likely to give the basis for meeting it. Hence in health authorities or in education expenditure cuts of any consequence will involve looking at staff since staff salaries constitute such a high proportion of the budget.

When a 10 per cent increase in sales is required the sales manager knows most of it is likely to be secured from focusing sales efforts at the top 20 per cent of customers.

There is the old management dictum that 80 per cent of the work is done by 20 per cent of the employees. If you are one of those 20 per cent perhaps you can understand why it is that your manager keeps coming to you for that little bit extra.

Name of staff	Days absent	Subtotal	% of absence
Adams	0		
Akran	0		
Buck	1		
Comfort	1	2	0.3
Crawford	1		
Crosby	2		
Dunnett	2		
Timpson	2	7	0.9
Maguire	2		
Ahmcd	2		
Field	2		
McIlroy	4	10	1.3
Miller	4		
Torvill	4		
Fulmer	4		
Kempner	5	17	2.3
Carson	5		
Khalid	5		
Simons	5		
Van Oss	6	21	2.8
Vickers	6		
Gesch	6		
Cummings	7		
Hamilton	7	26	3.5
Summers	8		
Williams	9		
Jenson	9		
Bolt	9	35	4.7
Chung	10		
Davis	10		
Osborne	10		
Wilson	12	42	5.6
Prince	25		
Gordon	45		
Duncker	50		
Fallon	50	170	22.7
Hicks	55		
Boston	65		
Taylor	120		
Churchill	180	420	56.0
Total days absent		750	100
Average days absent		18.8	

Figure 4.8 *A staff sickness problem (2)*

Use a diagram to illustrate possible cause

Diagrams can be extremely useful in understanding the nature of a problem. If we consider the staff sickness example then we might identify a range of possible causes or factors associated with it. These could be simply listed out. However they could also be shown on a diagram such as in Figure 4.9. This sort of causal diagram is often known as a 'fishbone diagram' for obvious reasons. The advantage of using this format of representation is that it enables you to add and amend information in a way that is not so easy when you have a conventional form of notes.

Another form of diagram which is often of considerable value in understanding why something has happened (or has failed to happen) is a 'force field diagram'. This depicts the opposing pressures involved in a situation. This returning again to the staff sickness problem Figure 4.10 shows the forces involved.

Elsewhere in this book (Chapter 3) there are examples of the use of diagrams to facilitate presentation of information.

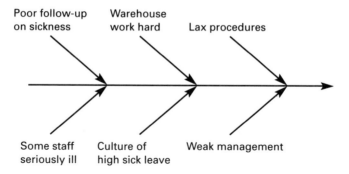

Figure 4.9 *A staff sickness problem (3)*

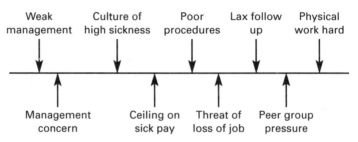

Figure 4.10 *A staff sickness problem (4)*

Characteristics of group process

You will have noticed that problem-solving (and decision-making) is often a group activity. To function effectively in groups a manager needs to understand something about the process and life of groups.

One simple way to understand group process is to think in terms of the difference between task and maintenance roles. In most groups both these roles appear. Without a task focus the group often fails to achieve its purpose. If there is no maintenance focus then the group may prove to be a fraught and unpleasant experience for those involved.

Task roles

- concern with content;
- get the job done;
- appearance of being 'tough';
- related to rationale for group.

Maintenance roles

- give cohesion;
- awareness of individual emotional needs;
- related to the emotional life of the group.

These two roles complement each other. Task roles are necessary to get the job done. Maintenance roles promote communication and co-operation.

Group process model

A well-known and tested model of group process is the following:

Forming→Storming→Norming→Performing→Ending

Forming
Anxiety, dependence on leader, search for 'code of conduct', testing out behaviour — 'what shall we do'.

Storming
Conflict, rebel against leader, resist task ('it's impossible'), test out leadership, work out implications of task.

Norming

Group cohesion emerges, resistance reduces, mutual support emerges, resolve to complete task ('we can do it').

Performing

Performance of task, flexible and functional roles, energy high, solutions emerge ('we're getting there').

Ending

Discussion moves away from task — members disengage — often desire to continue and not stop.

A failure to recognize the need to go through these stages can impede the successful operation of a group. Frequently the manager (group leader) displays impatience and tries to 'press on' to the performing part of the process. However, the group needs to go through the earlier stages in order to engage successfully in the performing stage.

Ending is also an issue sometimes for project groups. Having dealt with the particular problem which brought them together, the group is often reluctant to disband. Effective problem-solving groups usually have a definite and limited life cycle.

Roles in groups

It is helpful for you as a manager to be aware of different roles which people might play in groups. There is not the scope here to go into a great deal of detail. However the following role descriptions are useful.

The initiator

Starts things off — usually falls to person who brought group together. Also important in changing group direction — giving new impetus.

The clarifier

Draws out the precise meaning of individual contributions in relation to the group task. Encourages people to be specific and puts generalizations in more concrete terms.

The information giver

May have the information to hand or offers to locate it. May be technical or 'understanding' information. May be superficial or profound but is always relevant to the group task.

The questioner

Asks the fundamental questions about group task. These help define nature of task and challenges assumptions being made. Questioner helps group take a step back.

The summarizer

Pulls the contributions together. Does not add further information but allows a check on progress. Sometimes formalized (minute taker) but may be informal. Provides breathing space and allows for reflection thus separating out stages of the groups work.

The supporter

Demonstrates warmth between individuals by supporting contributions or by later including them. Support may be non-verbal.

The joker

Obvious – provides light relief and let off steam – can be destructive to individual or group but can also be positive and creative.

Sharing experience

Makes personal statements about general issue relating to the group task. Allows group to move to deeper level. Prevents 'over professionalism' of group.

Process observer

Appears when group is stuck. Reflects on reason for blockage 'why are we going around in circles?'

Sometimes as a manager you are able to select the group you would like to assist you; sometimes the team is already there. Considerable research has been done to assist the manager in identifying the characteristics of an effective team.

Meredith Belbin (1991) has conducted such research for many years and as a result he considers that the 'perfect team' is one which includes people able to undertake certain crucial roles. These are described below.

Belbin's 8 team roles

1 The co-ordinator

The chairperson or enabler. He/she need not be brilliant or creative, but would rather be called disciplined, focused and balanced. He/she talks and listens well, is a good judge of people and things; a person who works through others.

2 The shaper

Highly strung, outgoing and dominant. He/she is the task leader and in the absence of the chairperson would leap into that role even though he/she might not do it very well. His/her strength lies in the drive and passion for the task but he/she can be over sensitive, irritable and impatient. He/she is needed as a spur to action.

3 The plant

Unlike the shaper, the plant is introverted but is intellectually dominant. He/she is the source of original ideas and proposals being the most imaginative as well as the most intelligent member of the team. He/she can, however, be careless of details and may resent criticism. He/she needs to be drawn out or he/she will switch off.

4 The monitor–evaluator

He/she is also intelligent but it is an analytic rather than a creative intelligence. His/her contribution is the careful dissection of ideas and the ability to see the flaw in an argument. He/she is often less involved than the others, tucked away with the data, aloof from the team, but always necessary as a quality check. He/she is dependable but can be tactless and cold.

5 The resource investigator

This is the popular member of the team, extrovert, sociable and relaxed. He/she brings new contacts, ideas and developments to the group, the salesperson, diplomat or liaison officer. He/she is not especially original or a driver and needs the team to pick up on their contribution.

6 The specialist

The person who possesses the particular knowledge or skill. Often a solitary 'boffin' type who functions best alone. Contributions made often represent the necessary breakthrough which overcomes an obstacle which has been holding up the team.

7 The team worker

He/she holds the team together by being supportive to others, by listening, encouraging, harmonizing and understanding. Likeable and popular but uncompetitive, he/she is the sort of person you do not notice when there but miss when absent.

8 The completer–finisher

Without which the team might never meet its deadline. This is the person who checks the details, worries about schedules and chivvies the others with a sense of urgency. His/her relentless follow through is important but not always popular.

Note: In teams a person may perform more than one role. The full set of roles is most important where rapid change is involved. More stable groups can get by without the full set of roles.

Examples of problem-solving drawn from managers in various organizations

David Tait, Manager, Woolwich Building Society

At the start of a project we set up a controls workshop. We get together a representative from each area. We have a brainstorming session. We think about all the things which could go wrong.

We then group like-minded comments together under 'key risk areas'. We then have a benchmark for where controls should be placed. We've found it to be quick and effective.

In all the workshops which we have had the majority of people have been complimentary and said that areas were identified that they had never considered. They were given an opportunity to see the system from a different perspective. It has shown people from branches that if they did not do certain things correctly then there would be problems.

Flow charts are helpful as a way of sequencing events and you can use them to establish control points. If a report takes up a number of pages people sometimes have problems following the sequence of events. Whereas if you put things down in a flow chart then people can follow the logic of what's happening.

Nigel Wright, Manager, Woolwich Building Society

We've just gone through a merger with Town & Country Building Society. We had a fairly major exercise in systems conversions and co-ordination. It went extremely well through meticulous planning. We had a problem on a part of the system of day two of the merger. It was a part of the system which enabled us to get account numbers. The system went down. It took us three days to get it resolved.

In the end someone came up with someting which wasn't obvious but enabled us to get around it.

There were a number of interested parties in the problem. What happened was that we were in communication with the interested parties. But when I said 'have you got the people around a table'; the answer was 'no'. There had been some one-to-one meetings but otherwise it had all been telephone conversations. They needed to look at the paper reports and see why there was a problem with the account numbers. They had spent two-and-a-half days trying unsuccessfully to sort it out. There had been misunderstandings. We got the people together and the problem was solved in half an hour. The solution was to use a slightly different system environment which would produce the information.

The lesson is common sense − some problems you can solve at arm's length but some you can't especially when they are multidisciplinary and there is no collective responsibility.

Richard Hooper, Training Manager, London Borough of Enfield Social Services Department

I find brainstorming is pretty endemic. The other day at a meeting about joint assessment for community care it was suggested that we did brainstorming and everyone seemed to know how to do it. I was quite surprised how widespread it is.

It depends on whether you are working in a group or on your own. A lot of what I do is working in teams. So chairing skills become important. It's about shutting up noisy people and bringing out quiet people. It's more the manager as a facilitator of a group which means sometimes taking a dilemma to a group without any real idea of how things might turn out. It's different when you're taking something to a group where the solution is quite clear and you're trying to sell something to them.

If a group is not coming up with a solution the first question is will I notice it. Maybe someone else will and point it out. So I'd bring whatever process is going on to a halt. I'd look for a way out − maybe summarizing or asking other people for a way out.

As an example there was a project implementation group where we were at a stage where we knew what we were aiming for and we were trying to work out a critical path. We were looking at setting up National Vocational Qualifications. We got as far as describing what kind of assessor training we might need. But then we had some real blocks and we got lost. We were trying to sort out the difference between what we were as a project group and as a group trying to implement it. I felt that I had lost the chair of the meeting a few times. It was like a free for all. I was getting confused over my chairing.

Learning points

- What ways can you categorize problems at work?
- What is the difference between analytical and creative thought?
- What is the difference between 'left and right brain thinking'?
- What are the barriers to creative thought?
- What is 'vertical and lateral thinking'?
- What is divergent and convergent problem-solving?

- What are the stages in problem-solving which John Adair suggests managers use?
- What is?
  - Kepner and Tregoe problem analysis,
  - checklisting,
  - problem division,
  - use of analogies,
  - brainstorming,
  - card writing?
- What are the following techniques to deal with complex data:
  - summarizing,
  - 80/20 rule,
  - diagrams?
- What are the differences between task and maintenance roles in groups?
- What are the stages in group process?
- What are the key roles group members hold?

Action planning

1 Identify at least two different work problems.

2 Describe them using at least five different dimensions.

3 Draw a diagram comparing them on each dimension.

4 Identify what problem-solving techniques would be appropriate (whether you would need the involvement of others).

5 Use the techniques to try and solve the problems.

6 Identify further opportunities to practise problem-solving.

5 Decision-making

Introduction

This chapter is linked closely with Chapter 4 on problem-solving. The aim of this chapter is to explore the ways in which managers make decisions and communicate them. Techniques to assist decision-making will be explained and demonstrated.

At the conclusion of this chapter you should be able to understand:

- the nature of the decision-making process;
- how managers make and take decisions;
- some commonly used decision-making techniques;
- factors associated with effective decision-making.

The nature of the decision-making process

Sir John Harvey Jones wrote a book entitled *Making It Happen* in which he sets out his views on management and leadership. He notes that in his view management and industrial leadership is an art not a science. Scientists confronted with a research dilemma will often use a tried and tested approach to resolving it. Science is international and shares a common language and set of assumptions. 'Good scientific practice' can often be agreed and recognized across language, cultural, racial and political boundaries.

On the other hand management owes much to the particular experience, background, training and environment of the individual manager. Different managers in different settings may arrive at different decisions when confronted by the same situation. John Harvey Jones comments that 'prescribed systems of management are seldom transferable'. However, one factor he observes is that managers generally have a preference for action. This action orientation is inherent in the nature of the management function. It is, in the title of his book, 'making it happen'.

Lee Iacocca, a famous American manager in the Ford and Chrysler car companies expressed same attitude. He said:

> If I had to sum up in one word the qualities that make a good manager, I'd say it all comes down to decisiveness. You can use the fanciest computers in the world and you can gather all the charts and numbers, but in the end you have to bring all your information together, set up a timetable, and *act*.

Therefore, decisions are at the heart of what a manager does. In 1976, 200 top industrial managers were surveyed and as a part of that survey they were asked to put twenty-five attributes of top managers in order of importance. Figure 5.1 shows a list of these attributes. As an exercise in decision-making to start you off decide what order of importance you would put them in.

As you make your decisions reflect upon the process you are using. You will notice that we have not given you any time limit. When this exercise is used with management students we find that the time required depends upon whether the students are working on it as individuals or as a group. Which requires more time? We find that a group of students will need at least three times as long as an individual student. There is an immediate lesson there in terms of the length of time that group decision-making requires.

Let us consider how you decided to rank the management attributes. Our experience has shown that several methods are possible:

Willingness to work long hours
Willingness to work hard
Willingness to take risks
Understanding of others
Skill with numbers
Single-mindedness
Open-mindedness
Leadership
Integrity
Imagination
Enthusiasm
Enterprise
Curiosity
Capacity to speak lucidly
Capacity for lucid writing
Capacity for abstract thought
Astuteness
Analytical ability
Ambition
Ability to spot opportunities
Ability to meet unpleasant situations
Ability to administer efficiently
Ability to adapt quickly to change
Ability to 'stick it'
Ability to take decisions

Figure 5.1 *Attributes of a top manager*

Start at the highest and work down

Here you decide what you consider the most important is − write '1' by it and then consider the next most important and so on.

Start at the lowest and work up

This is the reverse of the above − you start with the one you consider least important and write '25' by it and then consider the next least important and so on.

Use some form of grouping

Here you might try to consider the attributes in terms of what are the most/least important three, five or what ever grouping you have chosen to use.

Whichever method you used (and most people use a combination) you would also have had in mind some kind of 'decision criteria'. This is one of the reasons why individual managers take less time than groups. Usually an individual will quickly adopt some kind of criteria which serves as a mechanism to decide on importance. It might be what the manager feels their own organization regards as important. It may be their recollection of management theories. (This is unlikely in our experience!) It may be based upon some 'ideal' image of the perfect manager she or he has in their mind. You may have realized that the last item on the list was likely to be first priority (ability to take decisions)! Figure 5.2 shows the top ranking managers gave.

A group of managers, on the other hand, are unlikely to share initially the same view on either the decision process or the judgement criteria. Therefore a lot of the time will be spent on deciding how to decide and what criteria to adopt. This has been shown to be a characteristic of decisions made in groups. It can apply even where the decision is quite straightforward. One example is that of the jury where the decision is usually simply 'guilty or not guilty' (Scotland allows the additional possibility of 'not proven'). Perhaps you have served on a jury and may recall your experience of the process in the jury room? Research has shown that jurys spend much of their time not actually deciding guilt or innocence but rather discussing and agreeing the decision-making process. Should each charge be considered in turn; should each juror have a say in turn; should the jury 'vote' and if so should it be a 'secret ballot', show of hands or written ballot; should each juror be required to justify their view in turn or not?

So why not get rid of group decision-making? Decisions will be made far more quickly and less time will be wasted. The answer is that many decisions are improved by group involvement. How would you feel if you were on trial and the jury consisted of one

1	Ability to take decisions
2	Leadership
3	Integrity
4	Enthusiasm
5	Imagination
6	Willingness to work hard
7	Analytical ability
8	Understanding of others
9	Ability to spot opportunities
10	Ability to meet unpleasant situations
11	Ability to adapt quickly to change
12	Willingness to take risks
13	Enterprise
14	Capacity to speak lucidly
15	Astuteness
16	Ability to administer efficiently
17	Open-mindedness
18	Ability to 'stick it'
19	Willingness to work long hours
20	Ambition
21	Single-mindedness
22	Capacity for lucid writing
23	Curiosity
24	Skill with numbers
25	Capacity for abstract thought

Figure 5.2 *Ranking of attributes most valuable at the top level of management*

person? Nevertheless decisions made by managers are frequently made by the manager in relative isolation and without a great deal of consultation. Sometimes this is right and appropriate. But sometimes it is not. We will return to the issue of involvement of others in decisions later in this chapter.

There are some widespread beliefs about the ways in which managers make decisions. Let's consider just two of these.

Rational weighing up of the alternatives

The belief is that the manager makes a decision by carefully and dispassionately considering the various alternatives. The alternatives are measured against whatever tangible success criteria the organization uses. In the case of a business it could be profit; in the public sector the criteria might be cost reduction or service efficiency. The manager then makes a rational decision using these organizational criteria. The alternative which offers the most benefit is the one the manager chooses.

The decision-making is a conscious process where evaluation is followed by choice

A model of problem-solving and decision-making where there are a series of deliberate steps guide the manager. The manager considers each option carefully before making a choice. The choice is based upon a prior evaluation.

Now no doubt there are some decisions which managers make which do conform to the beliefs about rationality and a step-wise process. However, there are many situations where one or both of these beliefs do not appear to guide the decision which a manager makes.

There are a number of factors which influence managers and which affect the decision process. These include the following:

- *The effect of the past*: If you consider the way in which many organizational budgets are set then you can see the effect of past decisions. Let us say your budget for item Y was £X this year. Many organizations use £X as a basis for looking at what your budget for item Y should be next year. It is called 'incremental budgeting'. Rational decision-making would be to review whether item Y is in fact the best way to spend your money. Alternatives would be considered and a decision made on the budget based on the ability of item Y to contribute to the organization objectives. The past spending on item Y would only be one factor in many.
- *The politics of the organization and its environment*: Some decisions are not amenable to the simple application of logic. The routing of the Channel Tunnel rail link to London is a case which illustrates this. If the rational factors of material cost, time and speed of construction determined the decision then, we could argue, the Government should have pressed ahead with the 'Southern route' and furthermore should have looked at the route being overground for almost all of its length. Instead the Eastern route which is less direct is being considered. The reasons for this are to be found in the politics of the decision. The example of the Channel Tunnel rail link can be repeated on a smaller scale in virtually every organization. Decisions may be influenced by the need to appease certain powerful individuals in the organization. A decision may be delayed or even not taken.
- *The 'importance' of the decision*: We all make decisions all the time. Some are almost instinctive and involve little conscious thought. Managers make many decisions and some (many?) of them are seen as important in the fact that they are made rather than in the rational and stepwise process involved.
- *The amount and quality of information available*: The information

environment in which a manager works is imperfect. Information comes from a variety of sources and is frequently sketchy and not precise. Rational decision-making and a stepwise evaluation process imply that the manager accumulates all the information necessary for a rational decision. But time is often of the essence and a decision tomorrow is not acceptable to the organization. Therefore the manager engages in a 'balancing act' where sufficiency of information is weighed against speed of decision.

- *'Rightness' of decision*:   A scientist or engineer who made wrong decisions 50 per cent of the time would very probably be regarded as incompetent or worse. Yet a widespread view in management is that the success rate of decisions is rarely more than 50 per cent.

Factors associated with effective and ineffective decision-making

A first and key factor is to recognize that there are different types of decision. One way of grouping them is based on that used by John Adair in *The Action Centred Leader*:

1   Routine decisions which are:
    - predictable,
    - obvious,
    - unlikely to cause much disagreement;
2   Crisis decisions which are:
    - highly time-constrained,
    - caused by an emergency,
    - where managers are often 'on their own';
3   Non-routine decisions which are:
    - not crisis-driven as above,
    - thought through,
    - carefully evaluated.

The first group of decisions are made all the time by people. Some of the people are managers! There is generally a good basis for making such routine decisions in organizations. The Department of Social Security employs a large number of staff who have to decide on whether people are eligible for various benefits. The staff have to see many people each working day and the claimants (or customers as they are now being called) expect a swift and clear response. The decisions are largely routine and based upon clear criteria.

Where a manager is concerned the main sources for making correct routine decisions are:

1   previous personal experience of making similar decisions;
2   knowledge of 'how such things are decided in this organization';

3 organization directives, guidelines or procedures manuals;
4 legal requirements;
5 clear specialist advice from a colleague;
6 general personal experience (i.e. maturity and understanding of people).

The second group of problems are crisis-driven and most managers have to deal with them from time to time. Sometimes managers are seen as 'crisis prone'. This may be associated with a problem in making decisions so that by procrastination every decision eventually becomes a crisis one. This is not a model you would wish to aspire to!

An example of a crisis-driven decision from the Department of Social Security might be the situation where large groups of 'New Age Travellers' descended upon a particular area and set up camp. The local population were concerned and the police wanted to move them on quickly. However the 'New Age Travellers' were for the large part claiming social security payments and were not willing or able to move until these had been made. The local social security office staff met this crisis by setting up a temporary office at the site and making immediate payments. This represented a clear departure from the normal routine involved in assessing and meeting social security benefit claims. There may have been some limited consultation but the speed with which the operation was set up suggests that it did not go through any period of major Civil Service deliberation!

An example of a private sector company's response to crisis is the reaction of Perrier on finding out that some of its product was contaminated by benzene.

Perrier UK

In February 1990 Perrier, a supplier of 'designer water', had 32 per cent of the market and was the market leader for the product. It seemed secure and safe from competition and threat. Its product was acknowledged as pure and of high quality.

But a control test carried out in the USA found traces of benzene in samples of Perrier mineral water. Benzene was regarded as possibly carcinogenic and Perrier's US subsidiary took action to remove the affected product from the US market.

In the UK the news was received on a Saturday morning and the UK management held a crisis meeting that Saturday evening. They were able to make use of a previously prepared crisis plan.

Ten crisis emergency telephone lines were set up and meetings were held with the Ministry of Agriculture, Fisheries and Food (MAFF) to arrange testing of UK samples of Perrier water.

Meanwhile a French spokesperson for Perrier speculated on the cause of the impurity. This was widely reported in the Press and Perrier's reputation for quality was jeopardized. Then the UK tests showed Perrier in the UK was also affected by benzene.

The crisis plan included the immediate withdrawal of all products from sale. The French parent company deferred taking this step until they had made a public statement at a Paris press conference. The UK subsidiary took the precaution of communicating with all the major supermarkets and warned them that the product was likely to be withdrawn.

The Paris press conference was besieged by far more reporters than the company had expected. The organizational arrangements broke down under the weight of numbers.

Meanwhile the UK subsidiary adopted a different strategy. The Chief Executive briefed individual journalists and explained the situation and the intended company response. The press coverage was generally sympathetic as a result. On the Thursday of that week (following the Saturday of the crisis meeting) Perrier UK ran newspaper adverts informing customers about the withdrawal of the product and explaining how to return bottles and get refunds. The emergency phone lines were kept very busy.

The overall picture then was of the UK part of the Perrier organization responding to a major crisis quickly and effectively. The planning for such an eventuality which they had undertaken was a key factor in enabling such a response.

The third group of problems are the ones involving time and much thought. You can recognize this in the Perrier example. The crisis could be handled effectively because there was a plan for such an eventuality. There is a simple shortcut to thinking about such decisions. It is called the 5 'Cs':

1 Consider,
2 Consult,
3 Crunch,
4 Communicate,
5 Check.

The first of these involves considering the nature of the decision and what it might involve.

- Is it routine, crisis or non-routine?
- What information is available?
- What information is required?
- How much time is available?
- How important is the decision?
- Who do you need to discuss it with; in fact can you make the decision yourself anyway?

Consultation is not the same as participation but some decisions might best be made by groups. The issue of the extent of management consultation about decisions is partly about management style.

Management style is in part influenced by the organizational context and in part by the kind of person the manager is. Some managers tend to be autocratic and others are more participative. As an example you might want to think about the difference in style between Margaret (now Baroness) Thatcher and John Major.

The context of the organization is also important. One of the authors discussed a senior management position in the Health Service with one of the recruiters. The recruiter dwelled at some length upon the management style which the job required. She explained that the reason for this was that former senior military officers had been appointed in the Health Service. Their management experience had been in organizations where the hierarchy was clear and orders were obeyed. The reality of the Health Service (at that time) was a different one where decisions involved discussion and negotiation. There were powerful special interest groups (such as the British Medical Association) who were not prepared to accept without question a non-medical managerial hierarchy.

Therefore, as a manager you need to consider the extent to which you need to consult and share involvement in the decision.

Vroom and Yetton (1973) developed a series of rules to guide the extent to which managers should involve others in the decision process. The rules ask the manager a series of questions about different aspects of the decision (see Figure 5.3).

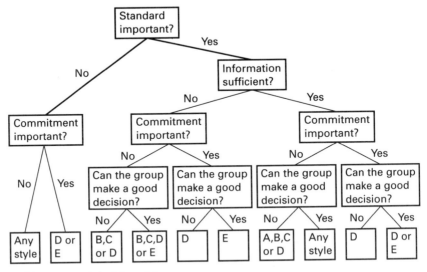

Management decision styles

A Personal decision using currently held information
B Involve others in provision of information then personally decide
C Discuss the decision with other individuals then personally decide
D Discuss the decision as a group then personally decide
E Discuss and decide collectively

Figure 5.3 *Criteria for group decision-making*

Depending on the answers to the key questions the manager selects an appropriate style from the following:

A personal decision using currently held information;
B involve others in provision of information then personally decide;
C discuss the decision with other individuals then personally decide;
D discuss the decision as a group then personally decide;
E discuss and decide collectively.

The key questions which the manager needs to resolve are described below.

How important is the standard or quality of the decision? Many decisions made in everyday life are more important in the actual making than in the outcome. The important thing is that the decision is made rather than the choice of any particular option. An example which comes to mind is the one off dispatch of non-valuable items by courier service. If the manager has no particular experience to draw on in the selection of courier service then she or he could involve others in a discussion over which one to select. Alternatively the manager could simply call several courier services and pick the cheapest one able to deliver within the required time frame. If other staff were involved in the decision it may well be that a slightly better courier service may be chosen. However, if the decision is not sensitive to that then there is little point in involving others.

In many cases, even though it is not necessary to involve others in making the decision, their involvement is essential in carrying it out. It may be advisable to involve people in the decision in order to gain their commitment to it. This is frequently overlooked by managers. The consequence is shown by problems in implementation. People who had not been involved in the decision process but who are crucial to carrying it out fail to do what is expected of them.

An example of this is to be found in Local Authority Social Services Departments. The Social Services Department hold what is called a 'case conference' when there is evidence of concern about the care of a child. These used to involve senior managers and professionals such as doctors, health visitors and police officers. In the past parents were often not involved but informed of the decisions afterwards. Their views were put on their behalf to the case conference by one or more of the professionals. The problem with this approach was that the agreement of the parents to any plan of action was crucial given that removal of the child from the parents was always seen as a drastic step. Somewhat understandably parents frequently resented putting decisions into effect that had been made without their involvement. The same applied to other people directly responsible for implementing case conference decisions such as foster parents and home help staff.

Now the practice is increasingly to involve parents and direct support staff in such case conferences even though the responsibility for making decisions does not rest with them.

Information is key to many decisions. There is always the possibility of acquiring more information. But the question is not simply about the amount of information but its sufficiency. Some decisions can be made on the basis of the information the manager currently possesses. Other decisions require that the manager obtains further information.

Then there is the delicate matter of whether the people who might assist in the decision are in fact capable of making it. The reasons for this might not be just a matter of lack of expertise. There may be a conflict of interests. Thus trade unions are concerned when managers do not consult with them about proposed redundancies or lay-offs of staff. There could be a considerable problem if managers invited the trade unions to participate in selection of staff for redundancy or lay-off. The view of many trade unions is to use a general principle such as protecting the longest serving members rather than looking at individuals. The view of management is usually that they would wish to select the people who 'will be missed the least' by the organization.

Finally there are other factors which may enter into a choice of the decision style. These include:

1 *Time*: Some decisions are by their nature very time constrained. Consultation takes time and that time may not be available to allow it to take place even though it is desirable. An interesting view on time versus consultation was expressed by a company fire and safety officer as described below. Every time we have a fire drill I have no trouble getting the production staff to leave the building. They accept they have to stop what they are doing and there's no argument. But the training and personnel people are always the last out. It's because they are so used to sharing decisions. I think they'd burn to death while deciding among themselves whether it was serious enough to warrant leaving the building.

2 *Cost*: This is in part a function of time in that bringing people together costs money. However, information also can cost money and the question is then whether the cost of acquiring the information offers a worthwhile payback in terms of the likely improvement in the decision. An example may be the choice of courier company mentioned previously. Suppose the manager finds the cheapest quote is £10 after making five phone calls. Let's say making a further five phone calls produces a courier company able to do it for £9. You need to calculate the cost of the manager's time in making those further calls. If it is peak rate then the phone bill itself could easily add up to £1. Even if the manager delegates the work to an assistant the cost factor may simply not be worth the marginal saving on a one-off delivery.

3 *Security or confidentiality*:   Some decisions are made openly and with full disclosure to all concerned. However, many decisions are affected by commercial confidentiality. If Tottenham Hotspur Football Club engaged in full and open consultation with its fans to decide game tactics then the tactics would be known to rival clubs. Similarly, retailers need to safeguard their decisions over how to combat terrorism because full disclosure would render the plans of limited use. In the case conference example mentioned previously a balance has to be struck between involving more people and the need to protect the confidentiality of child and parents.

A manager who is able to apply appropriate decision styles is likely to be able to be more effective in both making and implementing decisions. However adaptability is difficult for many managers. The reasons are as follows:

- *Past experience often influences a choice of style*:   Whether a manager has been successful or not is a key factor.
- *Habit*:   Many managers become comfortable with just one or two styles and are reluctant to change.
- *Organizational norms*:   There may be a favoured style which is directly or indirectly encouraged. Hence the problems which managers who change company experience when they find the new company 'does things differently'.
- *An unwillingness to seek help*:   There is a natural but unfortunate tendency to avoid asking for help because it may imply the manager is not 'up to it'.
- *A lack of skills*:   The manager may not be able to identify which decisions would benefit from a particular style and may not be able to actually put that style into practice.
- *Subordinate and colleague expectations*:   Some managers may be unduly influenced in their choice of style by the fact that their staff or colleagues expect them to decide in a particular way.

Crunch: deciding between alternatives

There are a range of ways that a manager can decide between different alternatives. Here we will just explore several of the most commonly used ones. The ones which will be considered are:

- advantage/disadvantage,
- essential/desirable/unacceptable,
- weighting,
- decision trees,
- utility (risk preference).

Advantage/disadvantage

This is probably (after coin tossing) the simplest means of deciding between different alternatives. It is a method which you have almost certainly used repeatedly in making decisions in your own personal life.

The difference is in the way we are going to show you to use it. Let's take a decision about whether to have a company car, use a company loan scheme to buy a car or use your current car for work (and get mileage paid). We would stress that this example is used for the purpose of illustration of decision-making techniques only and should not be used as a basis for car tax planning!

The first step is to list the decision criteria which will be important to you in making the decision. You may use brainstorming or some other method (see Chapter 4) to generate these criteria. For the sake of example let's assume that you have come up with the following criteria:

1 choice of (new) car;
2 size of car;
3 repayments (on a loan);
4 running costs;
5 tax liability;
6 maintenance costs;
7 replacement vehicle (for when the car is 'off the road');
8 reliability;
9 spouse/partner able to drive;
10 children able to drive (you have an 18-year-old son/daughter).

You then list for each option whether the criteria represent an advantage or disadvantage (see Figure 5.4).

As you can see from our example the straightforward addition of advantages and disadvantages shows that taking a car loan comes out as being in front.

This method has the virtue of simplicity and is a useful way of initially assessing different possibilities. However, it has one obvious problem in that it does not distinguish between the importance attached to the different criteria. Furthermore in common with all decision-making techniques there is the possibility that it may overlook a criteria.

Essential/desirable/unacceptable

The second technique offers a basic measure of distinction between different criteria. It is a decision-making technique frequently used in staff selection and in planning negotiation strategies. Let us consider it in the case of the problem of the car decision.

The first requirement is to classify all the criteria needed to make

Use company car	Advantage	Disadvantage
1 Choice of car	1	
2 Size of car		1
3 Loan repayments	1	
4 Running costs	1	
5 Tax liability		1
6 Maintenance	1	
7 Replacement vehicle	1	
8 Reliability	1	
9 Spouse/partner able to drive	1	
10 Children able to drive		1
Totals	7	3

Take car loan	Advantage	Disadvantage
1 Choice of car	1	
2 Size of car	1	
3 Loan repayments		1
4 Running costs	1	
5 Tax liability	1	
6 Maintenance	1	
7 Replacement vehicle		1
8 Reliability	1	
9 Spouse/partner able to drive	1	
10 Children able to drive	1	
Totals	8	2

Use current car	Advantage	Disadvantage
1 Choice of car		1
2 Size of car		1
3 Loan repayments	1	
4 Running costs	1	
5 Tax liability	1	
6 Maintenance		1
7 Replacement vehicle		1
8 Reliability		1
9 Spouse/partner able to drive	1	
10 Children able to drive	1	
Totals	5	5

Figure 5.4 *Choice of car option (1)*

a good selection from those available. This may be done by looking at each criterion and deciding whether:

1 It is unacceptable and if an option possesses it then that option must be excluded.
2 It is absolutely essential and must be present in the selected option.
3 It is desirable and so as such is a useful 'tie breaker' if two or more options come out equal.

After consideration the following list emerges (see Figure 5.5).

Let us sort the list so that the unacceptable item comes first followed by the essential with the desirable listed last (see Figure 5.6).

If we look at the options now we can see that the following emerges:

1 The car loan option falls because we regard it as unacceptable to enter into loan repayments.
2 The company car option survives the unacceptable criterion and also meets the two essential criteria.
3 The own car option survives the unacceptable criterion but only meets one of the two essential criteria.

Therefore using this method you would select the company car option even though the straightforward listing of advantages/disadvantages puts it as second choice.

		Unacceptable (as disadvantage)	Essential (as advantage)	Desirable (as advantage)
1	Choice of car			1
2	Size of car			1
3	Loan repayments	1		
4	Running costs		1	
5	Tax liability			1
6	Maintenance		1	
7	Replacement vehicle			1
8	Reliability			1
9	Spouse/partner able to drive			1
				1
10	Children able to drive			

Figure 5.5 *Choice of car option (2)*

		Unacceptable (as disadvantage)	Essential (as advantage)	Desirable (as advantage)
3	Loan repayments	1		
4	Running costs		1	
6	Maintenance		1	
9	Spouse/partner able to drive			1
				1
1	Choice of car			1
2	Size of car			1
5	Tax liability			1
7	Replacement vehicle			1
8	Reliability			1
10	Children able to drive			1

Figure 5.6 *Choice of car option (3)*

Weighting

A more sophisticated approach to deciding between options is to use some form of weighting the criteria. Let us suppose that you have now got a list of available cars under the company car scheme. You are able to make a choice between three models of car. To avoid disputes over the merits of different manufacturers we will simply call them Car A, Car B and Car C.

None of the cars possesses any characteristic which would render it unacceptable and they meet your essential requirements. So you have to make a choice. You list out the criteria upon which you will decide between the three cars. Let us say you arrive at these criteria:

- acceleration;
- safety;
- smooth ride;
- luggage space;
- economy;
- ease of parking.

Then you decide on some numeric scale to rate each criteria in terms of its importance. The scale should be long enough to give you some range of choice. Usually a 5- or 7-point scale is suitable. For our example we will use a 5-point scale.

1 = not very important;
2 = somewhat important;
3 = quite important;
4 = important;
5 = very important.

You have probably used a scale like this in questionnaires which you have completed in magazines or possibly in assessment tests at work.

You then set up a table similar to that in Figure 5.7.

The object is first of all to judge the importance to you of each of the criterion you have listed. You do not consider the criteria relative to one another. Consider each criterion in isolation and write down in the first column of the table the number that corresponds to how important you think it is.

You then judge each car in terms of the extent to which you feel it meets that particular criterion using a similar 5-point scale:

1 = only limited satisfaction;
2 = some satisfaction;
3 = considerable satisfaction;
4 = mostly satisfies;
5 = fully satisfies.

Thus in Figure 5.7 the criteria of acceleration is seen as quite important and Car A is seen as fully satisfying the acceleration criterion.

The weighted score for each car on each criterion is a simple calculation. You multiply your 'importance' score by the 'satisfaction' score for the car. Thus for car A the weighted score on acceleration is $3 \times 5 = 15$.

After you have calculated the weighted score for each criterion for each car you can then add then up and you arrive at a total weighted

Criteria	Importance W	Car A is A	Car B is B	Car C is C	Car A A × W	Car B B × W	Car C C × W
					Weighted scores of:		
Acceleration	3	5	3	2	15	9	6
Safety	5	2	4	4	10	20	20
Smooth ride	4	5	2	3	20	8	12
Luggage space	2	3	3	5	6	6	10
Economy	1	5	4	2	5	4	2
Ease of parking	3	1	3	4	3	9	12
Totals					59	56	62

Figure 5.7 *Choice of car option (weighting)*

score for each car. As you can see from Figure 5.7 this gives option of Car C an edge over the other two options.

Decision trees

Decision trees are a means of dealing with a decision when there are points at which a decision may be made and the implications of the various alternatives can be spelled out. Sometimes the likelihood of which alternatives will happen may be unknown. At other times it might be possible to calculate the odds of something happening.

Let us use our example of the choice of car option (own, company or car loan) to try and estimate the likely costs of each option over the next year. We will ignore non-work mileage in order to simplify the calculations.

We will consider the implications of the following costs:

1   loan repayments;
2   running costs;
3   depreciation;
4   tax (please note this is not based on actual current company car tax);
5   reliability.

For the purpose of the example we will make assumptions about the annual (work related) mileage which we expect to do and the running costs (petrol, oil, routine servicing, insurance and road tax, etc.) associated with that mileage (see Figure 5.8). The company car is assumed to have the running costs met but attracts a tax penalty.

You will note that the cost of the company car scheme comes out worst and that the option of using our own (current) car comes out best of all in cost terms.

However, there is an item you will have noticed which does not have any figure attached to it on the 'own car' option. That is the reliability of the car. The difference between the 'own car' and 'car loan' in cost terms is £900. A major mechanical repair such as a new gearbox or engine would easily cost that.

Now this is where we can use decision trees to cope with uncertainty. We do not know that our current car is going to suffer a major mechanical problem in the next year. Indeed there is a possibility the car may not require any attention beyond routine servicing over the next year. We consult the garage and from our knowledge of the car, its age and history we break down the possibilities as follows:

10 per cent: The car will require no attention beyond routine servicing.
30 per cent: The car will require minor repairs (costing about £300).
60 per cent: The car will also require a new engine (cost about £1500).

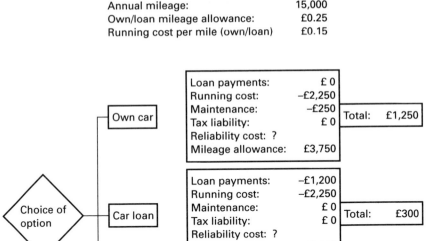

Assumptions
Annual mileage:	15,000
Own/loan mileage allowance:	£0.25
Running cost per mile (own/loan)	£0.15

Own car
Loan payments:	£ 0
Running cost:	–£2,250
Maintenance:	–£250
Tax liability:	£ 0
Reliability cost:	?
Mileage allowance:	£3,750

Total: £1,250

Car loan
Loan payments:	–£1,200
Running cost:	–£2,250
Maintenance:	£ 0
Tax liability:	£ 0
Reliability cost:	?
Mileage allowance:	£3,750

Total: £300

Company car
Loan payments:	£ 0
Running cost:	£ 0
Maintenance:	£ 0
Tax liability:	–£1000
Reliability cost:	£ 0
Mileage allowance:	£ 0

Total: –£1,000

Choice of option

Figure 5.8 *Choice of car option (decision tree 1)*

However, our friendly local garage mechanic offers to give the car a major overhaul which will cost £500. Again using best information available we estimate that this overhaul will change the possibilities as follows:

50 per cent: The car will require no attention beyond routine servicing. 40 per cent: The car will require minor repairs (costing about £300). 10 per cent: The car will also require a new engine (cost about £1500).

Figure 5.9 represents both these options as a decision tree. We now have enough information to calculate the expected outcome for each option. It is evident that having the car overhauled enables us to predict an expected outcome of £770 as opposed to £990 if we do not have the car overhauled.

The value of decision trees is that it enables you to handle a situation where there is uncertainty but there is enough information to make an 'informed guess'. This is not uncommon in management. They are particularly useful when it comes to calculating the value of information which will reduce uncertainty. In our example of the

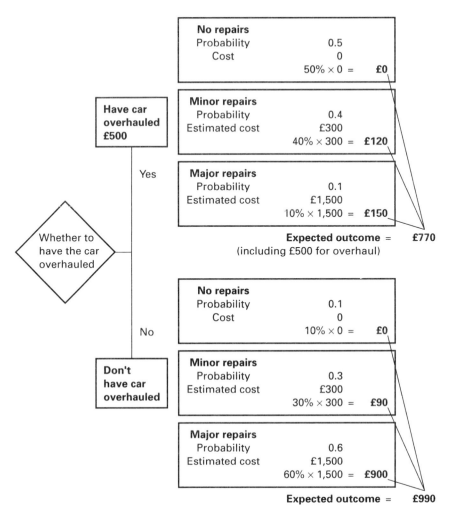

Figure 5.9 *Choice of car option (decision tree 2)*

decision over whether to use our own car or take a car loan anything which provides better information could be worth having. That is why people get a house survey report before making a final offer on purchase price.

Utility (risk preference)

The knowledge of the likelihood of possibilities is helpful. However the astute reader will point out that if in the example in Figure 5.9 we decide to pay £500 for the overhaul then we could lose out. How? Well the chances of having no expense on the car without the overhaul is 1 in 10 (10 per cent). The chances of repairs costing only £300 is 3 in 10 (30 per cent). So if we were happy with odds of 4 in 10 (2 to 5 against) then we could risk not having the overhaul.

People vary in the amount of risk which they are willing to accept. The extent to which you are risk averse as a manager depends on a number of factors. These include:

- The amount at stake is small. People are generally neutral for small amounts.
- Where the amount at stake is large. People are generally reluctant to accept risk here even if the gain is proportionally large.
- Where the risk to recoup previous loss. People tend to accept risk on the basis of trying to retrieve an earlier loss.
- Where winning enables an obstacle to be overcome. People will often accept risk to achieve some life ambition.
- Where losing would be catastrophic. People will generally pay a lot to avoid the risk.

If you use the concept of utility then you can get a picture of whether you are risk averse, risk neutral or risk seeking (see Figure 5.10). Let us consider the car example again. The two extreme outcomes are as follows:

1　We do not have the overhaul and get away with no outlay at all. This is the most preferred outcome and has a utility of 1.0.
2　We pay £500 for an overhaul yet still suffer an engine replacement cost of £1500. This is the least preferred outcome and has a utility of 0.

Figure 5.10 shows these plotted together with the straight line (risk neutral) running between the two least preferred and most preferred outcomes.

Next we assume that there is a 50/50 chance of either one of these extreme outcomes occurring. How much *certain* outlay on the car (say in terms of a cast iron mechanical warranty) would we accept to

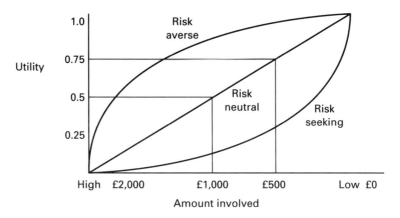

Figure 5.10 *Risk preference (utility)*

avoid this 50/50 gamble? The answer to this will give you a point to plot. £1000 represents the risk neutral answer (plotted on Figure 5.10). More is risk averse; less is risk seeking.

You can now plot a further point by making the assumption that the chances are 75/25 in favour of the most desirable outcome occurring. That it is 75 per cent likely there will be no cost as opposed to 25 per cent that there would be a cost of £2000. What certain amount would you give to avoid this. The risk neutral amount is £500 (plotted on Figure 5.10). If you would pay more than that to avoid the risk of a £2000 cost then you are risk averse.

Then you can plot the point where the chances are 75/25 in favour of the worst outcome (£2000 cost). How much would you pay to avoid having to take these odds? More than £1500 makes you risk averse; less is risk seeking.

The typical risk profile is shown in Figure 5.11. People are strongly risk averse where the possibility of a large loss is high. However, where the amounts are smaller then they are more inclined to take a gamble. Near the high loss end then the average person may take a gamble because the odds are against 'winning' anyway.

Winston Fletcher points out that risk taking in creative industries is related to the amount of investment at stake. In the music business it costs relatively little to produce a new record. Indeed some budding artists produce their own. On the other hand a major West End musical will cost a great deal to put on.

The cost-per-project is a key factor. If your investment is spread thinly across a large number of projects then you can afford to accept a higher degree of risk. On the other hand a company whose investment is substantially tied up in just a few projects is more risk averse.

Communication of decisions

This aspect is covered in Chapters 2, 3, 8 and 9. Effective communication of decisions is vital and readers are urged to review these

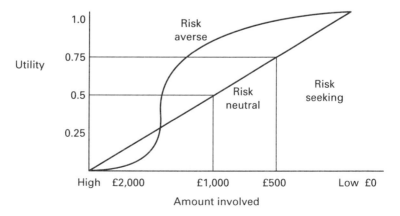

Figure 5.11 *Typical individual risk preference*

chapters. The selection of media (written, verbal and face-to-face) and the choice of available power bases are critical.

Checking

Managers need to monitor and review progress once decisions have been made. This is covered in Chapter 6 where goal setting is described.

Examples of decision-making drawn from managers in various organizations

David Tait, Manager, Woolwich Building Society

It's often the small decisions which can upset staff. You have to keep people informed. There's a natural assumption in all of us to assume decisions have been taken on things and if you don't hear you sometimes wonder why you've been kept in the dark. That often means that no decision has been taken. I think that there is an onus on you to communicate back that no decision has been taken − maybe you are waiting on additional information. When a decision has been taken you should communicate the results as quickly as possible. An example of this is described below.

Some years ago the Chief Internal Auditor had retired. At that time the society was facing the requirements of the 1986 Building Society Act. They decided that the internal audit had grown − partly because of merger. The Society decided rather than appointing someone immediately they wanted to have an idea of what the function was to achieve. They had consultants come in and carry out a review. This was done over a period of time and a report was produced. The report went to management. It was decided that the report would not be released to the staff but that changes were to be made.

It dragged on for some months without people knowing what the results of this review were. It was eventually decided to release some information. But there was only a potted version given out and this was before we had appointed a Chief Internal Auditor.

People were understandably concerned as to what was going to happen and how it was going to affect them. It did contribute to a certain amount of negative feelings. Management were in a difficult position because they hadn't appointed the Chief Internal Auditor who was then going to be charged with carrying out the recommendations and they didn't know whether he would agree with them. Before he arrived people were generally saying 'what's going on around here?'

After he arrived he took reasonably quick action and brought out a number of objectives. How we were going to be restructured and what we were going to be responsible for and how we were going to set about it. After that people noticeably relaxed once they were aware of the decisions that had been taken.

He actually took a different view and did not implement the consultants' report as was recommended. He implemented his own version. The thing was he took decisive action when he arrived. The circumstances were that no action could be taken before he arrived and it was a difficult position. But because the review had been commissioned people were obviously aware that things were going to change. It took them longer to recruit him than anticipated and as a result there was this period in the middle when staff knew that there was going to be changes but they didn't know what. For some people it was noticeable that they were not too happy with that.

People did not know what decisions had and hadn't been made. It is clear now that they had decided to make changes but were not in a position to implement them because the person hadn't been appointed. There wasn't a lot of communication (with staff) at that particular time. Looking back if the point had been made that the contents of the report would only be used as a guide to senior managers to the kind of person that they wanted to appoint and that the actual way things would be reorganized would be left until he had been appointed and had the opportunity to speak the people and make his own mind up it would have been easier. I'm sure that looking back with benefit of hindsight it was obvious what was happening. I'm sure that possibly senior managers never believed that they had to perhaps state the obvious. But knowing how people were reacting at the time, stating the obvious would not have been a bad thing.

Nigel Wright, Manager, Woolwich Building Society

We introduced some years ago 'performance-related pay' which I was part of. It became a huge exercise. It started off with management. It is interesting to note the length of the process which took us over 2 years from start to implementation.

The regional managers were on our side but then they were expressing concerns. There was a continuous series of barriers put up. Collectively they would say that the district managers were on our side but we then found that the district managers' opinions were not always in accord with their own (regional) managers.

There were never diametrically opposed views but instead of the overall comment 'don't worry' (about the district managers) from the regional managers we found that the district managers weren't on our wavelength. The lesson I draw is that you listen to your immediate managers but also tune into the ground floor as well. On major decisions you have to get a feel for what's going on. One of my early managers would say 'I hear your views and I think it's time to get on my bike' and he would get out there and go and look.

*Richard Hooper, Manager, London Borough of
Enfield Social Services Department*

Intuitive decisions for me are when loads of things are running short, like time or there's an opportunity where if a decision is not made then the opportunity is lost. There's things like 'can I get away with not talking to anyone about this decision, do I know what all these other people might think and how they might be affected by me making this decision?' Am I happy with living with that and having to sell it to people afterwards. It's intuitive in that loads of things come together at the same time and it's only afterwards that the rational aspects come out. The reasons are not immediately apparent.

Learning points

- What is rational decision-making?
- Why doesn't it always occur in organizations?
- What types of decision are there?
- What are the 5 'Cs' in decision-making?
- What are the elements of the following methods of selection?
  - Advantage/disadvantage,
  - Essential/desirable/unacceptable,
  - Weighting,
  - Decision trees,
  - Utility (risk preference).

Action planning

1 How will you evaluate how effective your decision-making is?

---

2 Identify opportunities to apply decision-making techniques in your work setting.

---

3 Identify non-work opportunities to apply decision-making techniques.

---

4 As an immediate practice you could consider the example of the car options outlined in this chapter:

- Go through each of the techniques again, only this time put yourself in the position of the Chief Executive of the organization. Do you come up with the same decision priorities and weighting?

---

6 Planning, goal setting and time management

The overall competency focus of this chapter is to:

1 develop teams, individuals and self to enhance your performance; and
2 plan, allocate and evaluate work carried out by teams, individuals and self.

which will be developed by the ability to:

- develop and improve teams through planning and activities;
- identify, review and improve development activities for individuals;
- develop oneself through the job role;
- set and update work objectives for individuals;
- plan activities and determine work methods to achieve objectives;
- allocate work and evaluate teams, individuals and self against objectives;
- provide feedback to teams and individuals on their performance.

involving the following dimensions of personal competence:

- showing concern for excellence;
- setting and prioritizing objectives;
- monitoring and responding to actual against planned activities;
- obtaining the commitment of others;
- managing personal learning and development;
- collecting and organizing information;
- identifying and applying concepts;
- taking decisions.

Introduction and objectives

Planning activities are a key part of management work. Planning is linked closely to both setting and prioritizing objectives. After examining these this chapter will look at the most precious commodity available to a manager in undertaking planning and goal setting. That commodity is time.

By the end of this chapter you should know how to:

- assess how you spend your time;
- be aware of ways in which you can use your time more effectively;
- understand what planning is in organizations;
- appreciate the stages of planning and their importance in management;
- understand how to set objectives;
- prioritize your activities and tasks.

Planning in organizations

Planning is an activity which frequently gets pushed aside in the hurly burly of everyday pressures. Nevertheless it is a key part of effective management. There is a link between the planning level and management level in the planning process. The more senior the manager the more likely that the planning undertaken will relate to the organizations' strategic as opposed to operational objectives. The relationship between the planning level and management level is shown in Figure 6.1.

The differences between planning day-to-day tasks, operational and strategic activities primarily relate to the extent the plans affect the way the organization operates.

A salesman plans the order of visiting customers as a day-to-day activity. The Sales Manager may plan that the customers in the Birmingham area should be the target of a particular sales drive. The Sales Director may plan to change the whole sales strategy for the company's products.

It is important to note that the distinctions are sometimes not always clear. Recently there has been press publicity about conditions and practices in certain secure hospitals staffed by prison officers. It

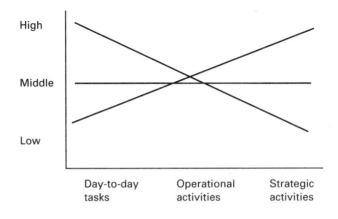

Planning level

Figure 6.1 *Amount of time spent on planning*

was reported that the prison officer staff brought a custodial as opposed to a caring approach to their duties. Clearly the kind of approach adopted to patients in these hospitals is at least an operational if not a strategic planning decision. Yet it would appear that it had been decided, possibly by default, by relatively junior staff.

Planning is important to managers in a number of ways:

1 It enables the organization to achieve its objectives. Without the concept of direction which planning requires then organizations are akin to the drunk staggering from lamp post to lamp post. The drunk has little plan beyond the short-term goal of reaching the next pool of light.
2 Planning, as Figure 6.1 shows, is a part of the managerial task irrespective of the level of the manager. Even relatively junior managers plan their activities. The main differences are the time frame and scope. The more senior the manager the longer the time frame and the greater the scope.
3 Planning is arguably the managerial activity which occurs before other activities. In order to organize resources the manager, at whatever level of seniority, needs to plan. Sometimes the planning can have a macabre aspect to it. During the Falklands War part of the planning before the major battles of Goose Green and Port Stanley involved supplying the body bags for burying the dead.
4 Finally planning is inextricably linked to effectiveness and efficiency. Cost effectiveness has to be a key factor. The organizational world is full of examples of plans conceived at a cost far in excess of any possible savings which they could achieve. There is often a fine calculation over how much to invest in planning given the likely return.

During the Second World War a large number of allied military personnel were captured by the Germans and became prisoners of war. They were housed in well-guarded camps and a number of prisoners sought to escape. Initially a large number of attempts failed and in part this was due to a lack of co-ordination and planning. In several of the larger camps this led to escape organizations being set up. If a prisoner wished to have the support of the organization he had to present a plan to a committee. The committee would then decide which plans to support.

The success of these escape organizations was considerable despite the fact that they had no formal authority to forbid escape attempts. The plans prisoners had to submit were akin to 'business plans' which bid for the limited resources available (food, tools, 'civilian' clothing, documentation, outside contacts and prisoners' skills).

There is a hierarchy of planning which operates in organizations of any size (Figure 6.2). At the top of the hierarchy is the mission or purpose of the organization. Sometimes it is described as the 'mission

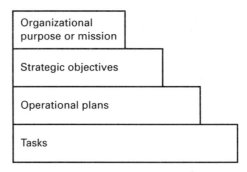

Figure 6.2 *Hierarchy of planning*

statement'. Possibly one of the simplest was that given to NASA (North American Space Administration) after the USSR was the first to put a man into space. President Kennedy told NASA that they were to beat the Russians in getting to the moon. The clear and straightforward nature of that objective certainly fostered its success. It is possible that the current lack of an objective of such clarity is creating a strategic problem for NASA.

Any well-run organization needs to be able to draw up a planned strategy for achieving the organizational mission. This will commit the resources of the organization and will involve making choices. For example over the next year (1992–93) British Aerospace will have to decide whether to sell or retain the Rover Group. Objectives are almost certainly in place to guide the company. These would be at a strategic level. They are likely to be based upon a view of where the company sees its future: What mix of products? What customers? What market sectors or segments should be targeted? It will also be based upon the company's assessment of what is likely to be happening in the economy. Possibly most important of all, the company will have a keen eye to the expectations of its shareholders.

Then there are operational plans which serve to direct the everyday running of the organization. For example currently there are two large companies, IBM and BT, who have reduced their workforce. For IBM this represented a major change in the ethos of the company since security of employment has been a key belief held by the company and its employees. IBM planned the workforce reductions in four phases in the UK aimed at careful targeting of particular staff sectors. Extensive counselling was provided and the severance terms were not just presented in terms of cash. Employees were encouraged to set up in business with work contracts with IBM.

For BT the process was less drawn out and it was reported that about 19,500 left in a single day representing one of the largest one-off workforce reductions in UK industrial history. The incentive offered was primarily financial and the redundancy offer was strongly marketed to staff. The demand for the offer was such that unions described BT's policy as one of compulsory retention with many people applying being refused redundancy.

The operational plans drawn up by the two organizations led to two quite different outcomes. The human resources plans of both organizations probably included the following planning elements

1 recruitment plan,
2 training plan,
3 re-development plan,
4 productivity plan,
5 redundancy plan,
6 retention plan.

Operational plans create a hierarchy of tasks which need to occur in order to meet the plans' objectives. These tasks often imply a planning activity in order to ensure that they are carried out. Thus if we consider just one of the operational plans above, the redundancy plan, we can list out some of the activities which need to take place.

Redundancy plan

- workforce audit (age, sex, seniority, skills, etc.);
- consultation;
- nature of redundancy offer;
- costing and budget;
- preparation of redundancy offer;
- communication of redundancy offer;
- decisions and any negotiation/appeal process;
- communication of results;
- implementation of payments/severance.

The above list is only a basic guide. Some items may be directed by company procedures or rules. Some may be the subject of legal requirements. However if we take just one item, communication of redundancy offer, we can see that it too might break down into a further subgroup of tasks/activities.

Communication of redundancy offer

- Media of message? (verbal, individual letter, poster, leaflet, etc.)
- Wording?
- Timing?
- Messenger (who delivers the offer)?
- Printing?
- Costing and budget?

Each of these tasks or activities has a planning component. The old saying is applicable that 'for the want of a nail a shoe was lost, for the want of a shoe a horse was lost, for the want of a horse a soldier was lost, for the want of a soldier a battle was lost'. Consider the effect of a postal strike on a redundancy offer which has been communicated by letter to the employees' home address. If all the letters have been sent out it is possible many employees will not receive them until the postal strike is over.

Most organizations will, as part of their planning process identify possible problems in implementation. They will then take preventative action to reduce the possibility of the problem affecting implementation. In circumstances where the problem is a serious one then there will be a back-up facility or contingency plan. Thus it is probable that the car you drive or (or whatever public transport you use) will have a contingency device to ensure that a leak of the brake fluid will not deprive the vehicle of all braking power.

Preventative action is cheaper than contingency plans. It is cheaper to have office equipment regularly serviced than to have a back-up for each item of equipment. Besides there is always the residual possibility that the 'back-up' may fail to work!

However, there is a trade-off between risk and the cost of a contingency plan. The loss of company records through a fire would generally be very serious. Research suggests that many companies fail to survive such a calamity. Therefore, back-ups of computer data and perhaps having a back-up computer facility available are usually worthwhile expenses. The likelihood of the fire occurring is small but the implications of a fire are great. Therefore a company would be quite averse to taking the risk (see Chapter 5).

On the other hand if a company is contracting with an advertiser for all households in an area to be leafleted about a new product there is a high likelihood that some households may not receive the leaflets. They may not be delivered or may be picked up by other people, etc. The implications of this happening are probably not serious. A contingency plan to send out further leaflets would be costly and inappropriate. Preventative action would be a better way to deal with it perhaps through arranging a check on a sample of households to ensure that leaflets were delivered (and letting the advertiser know you will be doing it). The advertiser, knowing that the company would be checking up, would be careful.

Goal setting and analysis

This can be seen as a process which has a number of logical stages. Figure 6.3 shows these.

The process begins with establishing objectives. If we look back to the example of the company wishing to circulate product information to households in an area then let's assume the objective was: 'To increase public awareness of Product Z in the area'.

This might have in turn have led to the following action plans:

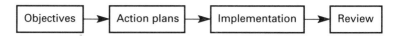

Figure 6.3 *The goal-setting process. Reproduced by permission of the Institute of Management*

1 advertising in the press;
2 advertising on radio;
3 poster advertising on billboards;
4 leaflet delivery to local households.

Implementation would involve the preparation of the advertising copy and placing it in the appropriate media. The leaflet distribution would probably require a contract with an experienced organization familiar with the area.

Review is the stage when the nature of the original objective becomes crucial. We used the term 'increase public awareness of Product Z'. How do we review how well our four action plans have done this? We could go out and ask people but how do we know that their awareness afterwards is any greater than it was before?

In Chapter 1 we pointed out that all goals should be SMART:

- **Specific,**
- **Measurable,**
- **Assignable,**
- **Realistic,**
- **Time-related.**

The original objective does not lend itself to being SMART. It is not specific (what is public awareness and in what area?). How do you measure an increase in public awareness? It does not specify responsibility for carrying it out. It may not be realistic depending upon what Product Z is (no size of increase is mentioned). No time is specified.

So let us re-examine the objective. This will involve a certain amount of analysis.

Robert Mager (1991) in his book, *Goal Analysis,* offers a 5-step process for analysing goals. The steps consist of the following:

1 Write down the goal.
2 Write down a list of what achievement of the goal would represent in terms of actions or speech.
3 Review what you have written down. Check for duplications and what Robert Mager described as 'fuzzies'.
4 Write a sentence which describes each item on the list.
5 Check to make sure everything is covered.

If we take Robert Mager's steps to analyse the situation we might come up with the following. Assuming that the company is profit-oriented then what is really at issue is sales of Product Z. This does lend itself to specific measurement. Therefore what we might write down as achieving this goal would be:

- A substantial increase in sales of Product Z over a period of time in an area which can be attributed to advertising.

If we examine this statement we see some words which are clear in their meaning:

- increase,
- sales,
- Product Z.

There are some words which Robert Mager might describe as 'fuzzies' such as:

- substantial;
- period of time;
- in an area;
- can be attributed to advertising.

'Fuzzies' are things which are abstractions. They do not lend themselves to general agreement over whether or not they have happened. Thus there would be little problem in gaining general agreement over whether there has been an increase in sales or Product Z. However, whether that increase is substantial or not may be subject to disagreement.

The aim is to identify the 'fuzzies' and, as far as possible, turn them into performance-related statements. Therefore we might do this as follows:

- substantial = an increase of over 20 per cent;
- period of time = a period of 3 months;
- in an area = Corby, Northamptonshire;
- can be attributed to advertising = following an advertising campaign in Corby.

Our objective thus becomes:

- an increase of over 20 per cent in sales of Product Z over a period of 3 months in Corby, Northamptonshire following an advertising campaign in Corby.

If Product Z was sold elsewhere we could make the goal relate to an increase in sales in Corby compared to average sales elsewhere.

The reworded goal is specific, measurable and time-related. The question of whether it is realistic is only answerable in terms of the market and the product. If the market is very slow growing then 20 per cent over 3 months may be very unrealistic. The goal is assignable in that the Sales Manager (or whoever) can be tasked with carrying it out.

The objective can then be turned into an action plan or rather a series of action plans. Thus the plan to leaflet households might include elements aimed at:

- identifying suitable leafleting contractors;
- drawing up and agreeing contract specifications;
- soliciting bids for the work;
- awarding the contract;
- monitoring contract performance;
- evaluating the impact and reporting back.

Prioritizing objectives

Setting priorities is inevitable in any situation where the resources are insufficient to meet all the demands placed upon them. Some managers have no system to work out priorities. They may rely upon the guidance of other managers or staff. They may simply adopt the old engineers' maxim that 'the wheel that squeaks gets the oil' and simply focus effort on those objectives where the clamour for action is the loudest.

However, there are several simple ways to set priorities. If used and communicated these can enable a manager to target resources in a way which puts the manager in the driving seat. It is important to check that the priorities identified by the manager are agreed by the organization as appropriate. Therefore, priority setting should be a joint activity between managers and subordinates.

The ABC approach

This represents possibly the simplest method of setting priorities. Let us suppose that you have a list of tasks which may require your attention. You cannot do them all at once. You must find some way of establishing which ones are more urgent. Let us suppose the list runs as follows:

- prepare monthly sales returns;
- arrange staff appraisals;
- conduct fire drill;
- visit northern region customers;
- draft new sales brochure;
- test new product;
- negotiate maintenance contract;

- review disciplinary code;
- recruit clerk;
- prepare budget.

You could then categorize the list in terms of:

A: highest priority − cannot wait;
B: next priority;
C: do it if possible after A and B.

It is a simple system which only requires a basic categorization of priorities. The resulting list might look as follows:

A   prepare monthly sales returns;
B   arrange staff appraisals;
A   conduct fire drill;
C   visit northern region customers;
C   draft new sales brochure;
A   test new product;
A   negotiate maintenance contract;
A   review disciplinary code;
B   recruit clerk;
A   prepare budget.

The list is then sorted according to priority:

A   prepare monthly sales returns;
A   conduct fire drill;
A   test new product;
A   negotiate maintenance contract;
A   review disciplinary code;
A   prepare budget;
B   arrange staff appraisals;
B   recruit clerk;
C   visit northern region customers;
C   draft new sales brochure.

The disadvantage is that sometimes it can prove difficult if many (or most) of the tasks are seen as of the highest priority. Then the manager has to use some other criteria to prioritize the 'A' group.

Prioritizing by paired comparison

This is a more sophisticated method which takes more time and thought. Therefore it would not be appropriate for looking at your objectives for the next few weeks. It is useful in looking at longer-term objective setting.

Let us consider an example of a Training Manager in an organization. The manager has established that there is a priority need for training in the following areas:

1 equal opportunities,
2 appraisal,
3 budgeting,
4 negotiating,
5 sales,
6 assertion.

The problem the manager confronts is how to prioritize these six areas in terms of both managerial time and training resources. The ABC method is seen as insufficiently sensitive since all the areas have high priority.

Paired comparison is a way of developing a priority ranking. The easiest way to do it is to set up a matrix so that each item can be compared with every other item. This is done in Figure 6.4.

The manager (or perhaps the management or staff group) then consider the first training item ('equal opportunities'). They compare it with each alternative item in turn and decide whether:

1 equal opportunities is more important – give it 2 points (and the other item 0 points);
2 equal opportunities is less important – give it 0 points (and the other item 2 points);
3 equal opportunities is equally important – give it 1 point (and the other item 1 point).

Thus 'equal opportunities' is seen as equally important as 'appraisal' but more important than 'budgeting' in this example.

After you have completed all the paired comparisons then you add up the totals and have a point score for each item:

equal opportunities   6
appraisal   4
budgeting   1
negotiating   5
sales   6
assertion   8

The method is useful in establishing priorities between a number of objectives which all seem equally favoured. If using the alternatives of 2, 1 or 0 still lead to deadlock then the alternate choices could be widened (3, 2, 1 or 0). Alternatively a forced choice rule could be used to prevent the allocation of 50 per cent of the points to each item. A computerized variety of this method was developed by Jimmy Algie at Brunel University to enable Social Services Departments to rank order their priorities.

	Equal Opportunities	Appraisal	Budgeting	Negotiating	Sales	Assertion
Equal opportunities	X	1	0	1	1	1
Appraisal	1	X	1	1	2	1
Budgeting	2	1	X	2	2	2
Negotiating	1	1	0	X	1·	2
Sales	1	0	0	1	X	2
Assertion	1	1	0	0	0	X
Totals	5	4	1	5	6	8

Figure 6.4 Training priorities for an organization

Management by Objectives (MBO)

Management by Objectives has been described as a:

1 strategy;
2 process of planning and control;
3 process of participation;
4 system for getting results;
5 attitude of management;
6 time orientation.

Paul Mali, a leading American expert on MBO, has defined it as:

a participative system . . . in which managers look ahead for improvements, think strategically, set performance stretch objectives at the beginning of a time period, develop action . . . plans, and ensure accountability for results at the end of the time period. (Paul Mali (1986) p. 35)

MBO contrasts with 'traditional' management practices in that it involves the worker in objective setting. To do this the organizational purpose has to be made clearer. If responsibility is pushed down the hierarchy as far as possible then knowledge and understanding must also be encouraged.

The focus moves from effort to accomplishment. Individuals and teams agree targets which are measurable and which are reviewed. There is a future orientation in planning. The stress is not upon examination of the past but rather upon where things are going in the future. The progress made towards objectives is tied strongly into assessment at time intervals. Time is a vital component not just in MBO but for managerial effectiveness and it is considered at greater length later in this chapter.

Strategy and planning have been covered previously and the comments are relevant to MBO.

Participation and MBO

The participation of staff in objective setting is central to MBO. If you have contributed in, or better still been responsible for, the agreed target then you are far more likely to be committed to achieving it. The 'R' (Realistic) factor in SMART is addressed by getting people to set their own targets rather than imposing ones on them.

You may comment that letting someone set their own target will mean that they set one which is 'too easy' or insufficiently challenging. The evidence is that given encouragement and support people will usually set themselves challenging targets and work hard to accomplish them. Clearly the excuse that the target was 'handed down' is not available when the individual had a major say in setting the goal.

Communication, both verbal and written, is central to achieving participation. Chapters 2 and 3 have given you the basic understanding to enable effective communication.

Getting results through MDO

Earlier in this chapter we discussed how to express goals in the form of measurable desired outcomes. MBO has a similar focus upon measurable results. Organizations which are 'for profit' have a number of obvious result measures (sales, costs, profit margin, gross profit, etc.). These are explained in greater detail in other books in the series.

Even organizations which do not have a tangible 'product' or which are 'not-for-profit' have result measures which can be used in MBO. A charity might look at the percentage of administrative costs, the effect of fund raising drives, the speed of response to requests for help, and so on.

In fact we would argue that anyone working in an organizational context can set objectives which are measurable. There may be an issue around how well the measures reflect the organizational mission. How well does church attendance show that the church is promoting the gospel for example?

The concept of time

There is an oft-repeated story in which a person advises another to invest their money in land. When asked why the response is: 'Because they are not making any more of it'. Time is a commodity which, for you as an individual, is similar to land. You only have so much of it. Unless science comes up with a magic potion which enables you to work without sleep or beyond the current limits of our biological span you have to confront the reality that the only option you have is to improve on your management of your time.

Thus time is different from many other resources available to the manager. The ways it differs are crucial to understanding its importance.

- It cannot be stored up like a charge in a battery.
- For each person the amount of time available is limited.

Some professionals, such as lawyers, charge for the use of their time and thus have to record it in order to bill the client. Tradespeople such as plumbers or electricians also usually charge an hourly rate. Do you know what you cost per hour? It may come as a surprise to you. Let us assume that your salary is £18,000 p.a.

What you actually cost your employer is more than this. For professional, managerial and administrative staff the 'on-cost' of pension, national insurance contributions, etc. is often about a third of salary. This added on makes your annual cost £24,000.

Let say you take three weeks annual leave and there is another week which is counted out because of statutory holidays. This makes your weekly cost £500 (£24,000/48 weeks).

Your working week is 36 hours but there is about 6 hours in total spent at lunch to be taken off. This leaves 30 hours. Then you have to allow for other 'dead time' such as tea breaks or waiting for something. Let's say conservatively about another hour per day. So this leaves you 25 hours effective working time per week. You cost your employer £20 per hour.

That does not include all the support services (office rent, equipment, company car, electricity, secretarial help) without which you probably couldn't function. Depending on your office location, position, work and other factors this could double or even quadruple your hourly cost.

As an exercise to focus your mind you may wish to calculate your hourly cost to your employer.

The usage and wastage of time

Sir John Harvey Jones offers these thoughts on the use of time:

> I suppose the most essential part of this struggle is the management of one's time, and here there are a number of key things that can be done. I have always believed that when I am at work I should work as hard and effectively as I can, all the time that I am there, but that equally, when I am not working, there should be a clear line between the two experiences. In order to cover the sheer amounts of work, of contact, reading and writing and so on, it really is necessary to use every moment of enforced working time to the best effect.
> (*Making It Happen*, p. 288)

Sir John offers various personal suggestions for the use of time. These include being in a position to work when travelling by carrying portable dictaphones and suitable reading matter and visiting people in their offices rather than asking them to come and see you. His comments upon the cost effectiveness of private aircraft and chauffeurs are unlikely to apply to more than a small proportion of managers!

In 1750 Edward Young said 'procrastination is the thief of time'. Procrastination is putting things off to a later day or time. It is not simply resolved by 'knee jerk' reactions and trying to do everything immediately. Rather it is a syndrome characterized by a willingness to defer action or a decision which has become a habitual form of behaviour. The question asked by someone 'suffering' from this syndrome is 'Can I put it off?' as opposed to 'Why can't I do it now?'

Problems in use of time

The indicators of time management problems have been described as the following:

- having to work long hours;
- insufficient time for planning;
- frequent interruptions from people in person;
- frequent telephone interruptions;
- resolving subordinates' problems.

Managers describe the following ways to address these problems:

- set goals and priorities;
- make time to plan;
- delegate;
- focus time on the key activities.

Research has identified particular kinds of people who are prone to use their own or others' time ineffectively. These are people who are:

- recognition seeking;
- complainers;
- resentful;
- spontaneous;
- fearful;
- indifferent;
- over-organized;
- activity-driven;
- time-obsessed.

We can consider these types in terms of brief pictures of the behaviours involved.

Recognition seeking

Everyone knows how much work Lee does. Lee is at pains to let them know. Whatever the task Lee rushes around struggling to make deadlines with the sweat pouring out. However planning is a low priority. The recognition of the pressure is vital to Lee. People comment on how Lee always takes too much on.

Complainers

Sam is never short of a reason for why the job can't be done. 'The organization is badly set up, the people are incompetent and nothing can be done.' Certainly Sam is not going to sort out the problems. Telling everyone about them takes up all the time available!

Resentful

If you want co-operation and support don't go to Pat. Pat is nursing such a grudge about the organization. The basis of the resentment may be short lived or long standing. The effect is that Pat has no desire to do anything to help the objectives of the organization.

Spontaneous

Beverly hates predictability. Planning and work diaries smack of regimentation. Beverly likes to 'go with the flow' and take each day as it comes. There is little point for staff asking Beverly for deadlines or boundaries.

Fearful

Jo never makes a wrong decision. Jo rarely makes any decision at all. Jo feels that the organization is always blaming people for wrong decisions. All possible risks have to be thoroughly explored and discounted first. This takes a lot of time.

Indifferent

Lesley is a real 'jobsworth'. When asked to do anything Lesley's most likely response is: 'It's more than my job's worth'. Lesley is indifferent to whether projects are finished on time. Lesley is bored with the job and the only exciting day is payday.

Over-organized

Nikki is a 'list person'. There is a list for everything and they cover every eventuality. Nikki spends most of the time updating the lists. The one list Nikki doesn't have is a list of things actually achieved.

Activity-driven

Mel is a real dynamo. Mel organizes everyone and is a constant source of energy. However whether the activities relate to the real world is another matter. Mel would have been great at arranging deck chairs on the sinking Titanic.

Time-obsessed

Karel has the biggest diary in the office. It is full of appointments and every minute is fully accounted for. At every meeting Karel becomes anxious as soon as any delay to (Karel's) timetable seems likely to occur. Karel has worked out a faster way to go to the bathroom. It may even save 30 seconds a day. Karel never has enough time for all the things in the big diary!

Do you recognize yourself or a colleague in any of these descriptions of (mythical!) people? If so do not despair for there are certain simple things you can do to manage your time more effectively.

Knowledge essential to good time management

There is an old proverb which says 'know thyself'. This is particularly true of time management. Before you can set about improving your use of time you need to know how you currently use it and what attitudes affect how you structure this, your most precious resource.

This involves undertaking a certain amount of personal research. Usually this is through completing what is called a 'time log'. A time log is a record of how you spend your work time.

There is no form of time log precisely suitable to everyone. However, the model offered (Figure 6.5) may give you some ideas to use. The principles which should guide the time log are as follows:

- It should be completed over a reasonable length of time. For most people a period of 2 or 3 weeks is suggested. Obviously you need to be aware of whether this time period is 'typical' of your work pattern. A period covering the Christmas and New Year holidays may not be representative of how you spent the rest of the year.
- It should enable you to record the kind of activity quickly and in sufficient detail to analyse how you use your time. Therefore, you should develop some kind of list of your activities. Here is a simple form one manager used:
  - outgoing telephone call,
  - incoming telephone call,
  - meeting (planned),
  - meeting (unplanned),
  - routine paperwork,
  - non-routine paperwork,
  - travelling.

  In recording which activity was happening during each 15 minutes the manager also used an arrow to show whether the activity was

  → = self-initiated;
  ← = responding to someone else.

  The manager also used a shorthand to show who (if anyone) was involved in the activity.

  B = Boss,
  C = Customer,

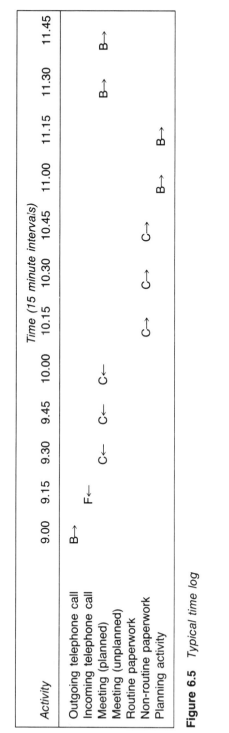

Figure 6.5 *Typical time log*

S = Subordinate,
A = Administration,
F = Finance.

● It should use intervals of short enough duration to pick up activities
which 'interrupt' your planned activities. With management students
we use intervals of 10 or 15 minutes.

From this you can see that if you record your main activity every
15 minutes over some 100 hours of work (3 weeks) you will end
up with 400 pieces of data. Making useful sense of the data is the
next step.

As an example Figure 6.5 shows a morning from the time log of
the manager. That day the manager came in at 9.00 a.m.; made a
phone call to her boss confirming agenda items for a meeting later
that day; received a phone call from someone in Finance; held a
planned meeting that a customer had asked for; spent time writing
up aspects of that meeting; planned for the meeting with her boss
which she then went to.

The manager who keeps up the faithful and accurate recording on
this basis over a period of 3 weeks will be able to look at the 400
(approx) entries and analyse them according to:

1 proportion of time spent undertaking various activities;
2 proportion of time spent on self-initiated activities;
3 proportion of time spent on activities associated with different
people in the work setting;
4 sequences or patterns of activity;
5 duration of individual activities (or the extent you change from one
activity to another).

Now how you draw up a time log is your decision. But the
categories of activities which you use must make sense to you. It is
often useful to include items to record interruptions to ongoing
activities. Otherwise it is easy to lose track of the number of times
someone 'drops in' while you are trying to get through your in-tray.

Measuring your use of time is not in itself sufficient. You also
need to think about your approach to time management.

1 Do you set priorities and deadlines for yourself and do you review
them regularly? This is dealt with elsewhere in this chapter. However, it is an integral part of successful time management.
2 What about delegation which is also dealt with elsewhere in
Chapter 2?
3 How easily are you able to say 'no'? You may wish to reconsider
the section on assertiveness in Chapter 2.
4 How much time do you spend on unnecessary detail? Perhaps you
are the sort of person who tries to be accurate to five decimal
places when one is quite sufficient?

Sources of improvement in time management

Routine paperwork

Few managers enjoy handling routine in tray items. Henry Mintzberg, a well-known writer on managerial work, suggested from his research that often managers desire to be interrupted and fight shy of routine humdrum activity.

However routine paperwork is a 'necessary evil'. In some cases it is essential to accomplishing managerial targets. Paperwork can be categorized as follows:

- writing,
- reading,
- calculating,
- searching,
- scheduling,
- file-retrieving,
- delegating,
- proof-reading,
- filing.

There is an acronym which can be used to describe the possible ways of responding to a piece of paper arriving on your desk. It can be summarized as the 'four Fs'.

Follow it up;
Forward it;
File it;
Forget it (i.e. use the 'round filing cabinet' under your desk).

The chosen action is best undertaken immediately. A speedy follow-up almost invariably saves time later on. The more times that you handle the same piece of paper the less efficient the use of time.

How the follow-up happens is often important in the use of your (and others) time. Consider the implications of the following responses to an internal memo.

1 Dictate a reply to your secretary.
2 Draft a reply to be typed up.
3 Write a memo back yourself.
4 Write a response on the memo itself and send it back (keeping a photocopy if necessary).
5 Telephone the sender with any information required.

Obviously the circumstances may rule out some of these options. However, the options are listed in order of the total time they would probably take (including the time of the person receiving your reply). If you only use the first option then you should review whether this is the most effective use of your time.

Forwarding items for action is a skill in itself. Winston Churchill reportedly distinguished items for quick response by writing on them 'action today'. You may wish to review Chapters 2 and 3 to see if your skills in delegation are making the most effective use of your time. The use of 'post it' style notes can be a useful device if it is not suitable to write upon the paperwork itself. However, there is always the risk of the note becoming detached from the associated document.

Filing information is a task many managers are able to delegate. However, in these days of leaner organizations and computerized information systems a secretary per manager is likely to become a thing of the past. The test of any filing system has to be the extent to which it helps you do your job.

The increasing use of computers offers both benefits and risks. The benefits comes from the sophisticated techniques for searching the memory for that memo you recall writing sometime in 1991 and the vast storage capacity available compared to 'paper-based' systems. (This whole book can fit on just one computer disk the size of a drinks mat.) The risks come from the possibility of system/disk failure or theft of the actual computer itself. You also need to be sensitive to the provisions of the Data Protection Act! Recent research suggests that many people recall where information is by cues which are not usually incorporated on computer filing systems. They might remember the colour or thickness of the document or where it is geographically (in the top drawer).

Forgetting or getting rid of pieces of information is sometimes the hardest thing for a manager to do. It is often quite surprising how much information you file which, like the clutter in your attic or garden shed, serves no useful purpose. Rather it actively impedes you by slowing up the retrieval of documents which are essential.

A piece of advice was offered by a very successful (and paper averse) manager to one of the authors who, as a manager, inherited a huge paper mountain. It ran roughly as follows: 'I suggest that you put it all in a large cupboard. Throw out anything you haven't had occasion to refer to within 3 months.'

Use of meetings

Meeting and chairing skills are covered elsewhere (Chapter 2). However, your analysis of how you use time may well reveal that you spend a lot of it in scheduled or unscheduled meetings. Meetings cost organizations a lot. So as a manager you should ask:

1 'Is this meeting really necessary?' Perhaps a telephone call or a memo would suffice.
2 'Is there a clear purpose for the meeting?' It does not follow that

every meeting has to have a formal agenda. Many meetings (and organizations) are not like that. However if you do not know why you are going to a meeting and you are chairing it then we would suggest there is a problem. It is also hard to prepare for a meeting whose purpose is unclear. A subsidiary question which often helps is 'How will I know if the meeting has been successful?'

3   'What do I need to bring to the meeting?' Sometimes it may be something tangible, such as a report or an item. At other times it may be an opinion or informed comment which you need to think through beforehand.

4   'How much time will the meeting need?' The calculation of how much to fit into an agenda and in what order is the art of a good chair. However, if you are not the chair you can often help by identifying what time your items will need and how important they are.

5   'What records will be kept?' Meeting minutes do not (usually) need to record matters in great detail. However, they do need to record decisions and actions. If names are attached to actions then it assists the communication of decisions and later follow-up. Records made at the time, even if brief, are usually far more useful than more lengthy records made at a much later date.

Handling interruptions

As we have noted elsewhere managers are subject to frequent interruption. Sometimes these are 'self-inflicted'. A proper time log will reveal the extent to which you are so affected. There is no lack of good advice for handling interruptions.

1   Avoid people coming to your office. Instead go to see them and then you control the length of the discussion.

2   If people do interrupt you be firm but polite with them. Go straight to the point rather than engaging in small talk.

3   Stand up and sit on the edge of your desk when someone comes in. This shows you do not wish a long interruption.

4   Offer to call back.

5   Give a clear indication of how much time you have — and stick to it or the word gets around that 'one minute means up to half an hour'.

6   Display a clock prominently where a visitor can see it.

One of the authors used to have two rules which staff all were aware of:

1   If the door was shut then no interruptions.

2   If the door was open then interruptions were OK as long as the duration was agreed to be no more than 5 minutes. Beyond that required an appointment via the manager's secretary.

This enabled staff to feel comfortable about approaching the manager directly. It also provided the manager with the opportunity to both control the length of interruption or to stop all interruptions without the use of 'do not disturb' signs.

Use of the telephone

It is a source of some surprise that telephone skills have not been normally taught to managers until recently Telephonists, receptionists and secretaries have had training provided yet the manager is a late starter.

Increasingly business is done by distance using the telephone. Managers spend a lot of time 'on the phone'. Sometimes there is some kind of perceived status attached to being the one 'receiving' the call. Yet if you can make the call at a time of your choice then you control the time not the recipient.

Therefore analysis of telephone usage can pay dividends in time efficiency. The following guidelines are useful:

1   Plan telephone calls. Treat them as mini-meetings. Time the length of calls using that clock or a watch.
2   Set time aside for making calls in blocks rather than making them in a sporadic fashion.
3   If you are subject to frequent telephone interruptions which disrupt your work then try to have calls 'fielded'. If you have no secretary or receptionist to do this then it is often possible to come to reciprocal arrangements with a colleague.

Use slack time

Sir John Harvey Jones is a strong advocate of making the best use of travelling or waiting time. He apparently carried several dictaphones and plenty of spare tapes and batteries when travelling.

Though you may plan your time well it is inevitable that often circumstances may force you to wait to see someone or you may have to undertake a long trip. Being prepared for such eventualities is a sign of effective time management. Non-essential, but important reading, can be kept in a folder in order to provide a ready source of material.

In our time calculation of the work cost above we allowed a total of 11 hours each week for breaks and meals. Often this time can be used very effectively for something similar to what the Americans call 'working breakfasts'. If there is someone who you need to talk to informally then rather than scheduling a meeting in one of your offices why not join them for coffee or a walk at lunchtime? Hewlett Packard and other companies often encourage such informal association. One local authority set up coffee areas throughout the civic centre for staff to meet informally.

Time dualling

This is related to the use of slack time. It involves trying to find a way in which you can use the same time for several purposes. For example, maybe you have to meet a group of new staff and also you have to get some views on how staff feel about the cafeteria for the next management meeting. Why not combine the two?

Use of routine

This last point is in many ways the most important. Managers like to think that they manage by exception and delegate all the routine work. But the reality is that virtually all managers have a substantial amount of their work which is routine — such as the paperwork referred to previously.

The development of work habits which effectively and speedily handle the routine aspects of your job makes a major contribution to both freeing up time and minimizing stress.

Some suggestions are:

1   Set aside blocks of time for routine work.
2   Have a simple diary system which your staff and colleagues understand.
3   Try to get routine aspects of your work as habitual as brushing your teeth. Then you might even be able to do other things simultaneously!

Examples of objective setting and prioritization drawn from managers in various organizations

Setting objectives – David Tait, Manager, Woolwich Building Society

We have performance-related pay and the guidelines say that there should be a quarterly review. We discuss their objectives and have a personal development plan for every member of staff. Every member of staff has their own job description and also a skills matrix which sets out all the skills which are necessary or desirable and staff are encouraged to plan their own career. They are always aware that there is a limited budget in terms of time and money for people to undertake their training.

Project realignment – Geri Mitchell, Advisor, London Borough of Enfield

The organization had decided to reduce the number of organizational layers and a large number of employees would be affected. Work patterns needed to change to meet a new concept of service delivery. This would involve a different contract for a group of the employees. Staff were concerned and the trade union was resistant to the proposed change. Relatively junior trade union representatives were bypassing normal consultation machinery and going direct to the Director. The project was widely seen as 'stalled' and not progressing. There was a sense of disbelief. The trade union had organized a large meeting to discuss the perceived threat to the current service.

Geri and her colleague took on the task of communicating the project to staff in order to get it moving again. They undertook a 'road show'. This had the aim of giving the same message to the staff. Every member of staff had a personal invitation to attend. The trade union were invited to be involved without any commitment to its objectives. The road show aimed to take the message of the project out to staff and visual aids (flip charts) were extensively used. There was a question and answer session afterwards. After that staff has an opportunity to discuss the project with the invited trade unions. The road show presenters deliberately withdrew to ensure free discussion took place.

After each session the presenters checked with the managers present and got feedback to inform future presentations.

After the road show a workshop was held to enable managers to share their experiences. There was still a level of anger and managers had wanted the road show to 'lay down the law' to get things moving. People were asked to identify issues and action plans. It enabled managers to share fears about the changes. It also enabled information to be picked up and issues identified. Regular consultation continued afterwards.

Managers said they were unclear about budget issues so training seminars and consultation sessions were set up.

The effectiveness of the road show was assisted by:

- the consistency of the message;
- the information was given to large groups of staff over a short time so minimizing the distorting effect of the 'grapevine';
- it was recognized that different groups of staff had different communication needs – hence the workshops for managers;
- the balance between supporting staff through change while conveying the reality of the change.

Since the road show staff have shown more willingness to discuss the changes and the new jobs involved. Staff are taking up new duties voluntarily and accepting changes in conditions of work. Staff are undertaking the training necessary for the adjustments. In some areas up to 80 per cent of the staff affected have moved to new contracts.

The trade union have reverted to using the normal communication channels (see Figure 6.6).

Goal setting − Nigel Wright, Woolwich Building Society

We are driven by PRP and we set quantifiable objectives for everyone down the line.

It isn't MBO like Humble which advocates bottom up objective-setting. It's very much more top-driven. In effect it's a performance management system which is linked to pay.

It falls into two categories.

1 There are quantified business objectives which come out of strategic plans.
2 There are qualitative objectives such as personnel ones.

They are all deadlined and quantifiable as far as possible and must meet the following criteria:

- measurable,
- achievable,
- relevant,
- controllable.

I spend most of my time setting objectives for line managers to achieve on a shorter sometimes daily basis. I tend to operate on the basis that people develop plans. The plans need to be clear with itemized action points and deadlines which are clear and acceptable to me.

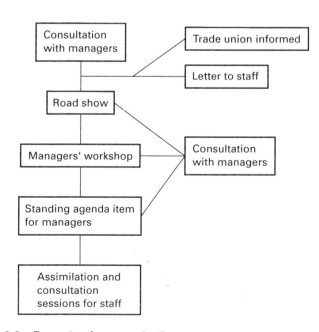

Figure 6.6 *Example of communication*

I want to see one sheet of paper with action points — task-related. I believe if you develop a plan which is a decent one and you monitor progress against it then there are only a couple of reasons why it doesn't work. Perhaps the plan was wrong in the first place. Maybe someone didn't fight for a principle or was pressured into something sooner than they should. If so they should bloody well have said so. Or implementation failed somewhere along the line. Perhaps circumstances changed. Were they circumstances we could have foreseen and done something about? Or is it simply that you are not putting into practice what you put on paper.

If you are talking task-oriented things then this is a good way to operate. I find it is very successful. You can be flexible within it. If you are very clear with your managers. You say I want a plan. I want it to have bullet points. I put it in my diary system and monitor it. Something arrives on my desk. I can then say I've either got the response which says 'yes, I've done it, it's OK' and I can check the quality and I can delve underneath and go and sample the work and say: 'Oh well, you say you've done it but I don't think much of this' or I can say: 'That was super, I've got some very good feedback on that'. It works very well.

Goal setting — a senior manager in a retail organization

It is a large store in the top 15 with 180 staff and 4 sales managers. The pharmacy manager also covers other areas. P found that the junior manager(B) operating the dispensary was ineffective. He was disorganized and struggling. P had to cover the pharmacy to help him cope. P's impression was that B was disorganized. There was a massive queue and staff didn't seem to know what to do. P felt B clearly needed to improve. Though B knew what his job entailed, the problems P found hadn't been raised with him. So B needed to have this discussed with him. This P did by:

- involving other members of the management team in looking at best practice elements to work with;
- looking at reorganizing the layout and customer flow (labelling, dispensing, checking and reception);
- moving equipment;
- relocating stock;
- most importantly in getting B to see he had a problem with the pharmacist who was poor at managing reception.

They involved the area operations expert who produced a report. B received personal feedback — he was told he was 'too laid back' and did not put theory into practice.

B spent some time looking at another (well-run) department. After about 4 weeks B could see the problems and began to look at solutions.

It was important to persuade B that the problems were immediate and needed a quick solution. P used B's appraisal to point this out. P indicated that B was not measuring up against performance criteria. B didn't like hearing this but accepted the criticism.

After this progress began. The area ops expert made another visit and goals for change were set.

Measures for change used were:

- the time P had to spend in the dispensary;
- the ops expert report;
- measures of customer flow;
- a performance check list which covered ten different aspects of the work (this latter was completed by B then by P);
- long-term measures – payback in terms of improved customer service and growth in prescription volumes.

Prioritization and goal-setting – Richard Hooper, London Borough of Enfield

I run several things at once, like a computer running programs which has several loaded up at one time. For example, if something needs checking out with a management team or involves a committee report then those events have their own time cycle. Something else may be more personal and be more flexible.

Everytime I pick up my in tray at the other end of the office I find a couple of days' work sitting there waiting for me. I manage that by avoiding going down to that end of the office. In terms of my own mail I think I'm fairly good with most letters that come in. Quite a lot of them I ignore or throw away. If I'm in at work just after Christmas and there's not a lot of people around or over the summer when things go quiet I have obsessional phases when I decide to deal with everything. I'm surprised then to find out that quite a lot of memos (sent to me) they've forgotten about. I do find that a lot of time as a manager is reactive. It's a bit of the job I could do without. About every 2 months our training unit will have an attack of cockroaches or the solicitor will try and evict us from it. On those sort of things I'll drop everything.

We do have an MBO system. It's called the business process. It's meant to be that everyone can point to it and say, 'that's my job there'. It got a bit messy in social services because our job is about development – this project and that project.

The business process is structured in a task analysis kind of way. There is an aim which is called a committee aim which is then broken down into key result areas of which we have about fifteen. Each result area has several action plans and then each action plan has several key tasks. When you get to a key task it is written in such a way that you'd know whether it was down or not. Every year from about February to May people review themselves against key result areas and action plans. For people who can't do that you write a report about what the hell you've been doing. The idea is that everyone should be involved — even social services clients.

The director would cream out headline news and feed it back to the councillors to show whether the committee aim is being met or not. Things are also used internally. We are asked to identify areas for cutting back or for growth. These are used in the annual budgeting cycle and in appraisal of managers. I use the review as a way of generating another year's work for the trainers.

Prioritization and goal-setting — Vickie Golding, Area Manager, London Borough of Enfield

I was asked to set up a Quality Assurance (QA) group. I was given a vague outline and was unsure over how to go about it. We were very busy and QA seemed a bit of a luxury. I found it hard to understand what QA was about.

I read up a bit about it and then wrote a report which I sent around to staff. I asked for comments and suggestions. There were none. So I held a staff meeting and 'nobbled people' beforehand.

At the area meeting I aimed to put it across in a simple way. I asked for help and ideas. I stressed that only attendance and a contribution to the QA group was required. I told them that the QA group would only run for a limited time with a set number of meetings.

I got names of people who might be interested. I had to sell them the idea. I was aiming for a mixture of staff to get involved in the QA group. Sometimes it involved using someone to find others who might be interested. I was looking for creative people. The administrative staff showed an interest so I involved them. Some carers became involved and I put in a lot myself.

It changed for me once the group was up and running. It was the attitude.

For the first meeting of the QA group I prepared an agenda and I spent a lot of time setting it up. I discussed what was involved with several people and provided some simple reading for the people attending. We split into two groups. Why? Mainly because I felt that the size of the group was such that dividing it would enable people to contribute.

The QA group produced a report on standards. I then wrote a short article for a local magazine. It was about attitude.

It was a learning experience setting up that group. It helped when later I had to set up a community forum.

Why didn't people respond when you wrote to them initially?

It was seen as a luxury when we had had so much unallocated work

What did you say at the meeting to change this?

Talking about it ... by simplifying it. The original document wasn't very good. I explained that we needed to look at the services we offered and the standards we were meeting. I made it sound interesting and different from what we normally do. Someone suggested a questionnaire. I was able to put it across more simply.

I caught their imagination. How? I suppose I had a very good relationship with some people and because I was asking for help. The names came from people who knew me or from specialist workers. It was looking to something in the future.

I also emphasized that people wouldn't have to do any work – take minutes or whatever – all I was asking for was their time.

Writing vs. Talking – What I did was to send just one sheet – saying I wanted volunteers and we'd be meeting over 3 months and that there wouldn't be any need to take minutes or whatever. The end product was to be the report which I wrote.

How did the operation of the group help this?

I spent a lot of time setting up the first meeting and how to operate it. I discussed it with people. I decided that we needed to review the service and we split into two groups to discuss this. I found someone to lead the groups and the groups were given the same task. We split the group for a couple of meetings. I split the group – the only criteria was that there was staff in each group. But in one group there was very litte sw representation.

The main reason was to encourage people to contribute – carers and clients would find it hard to contribute in the larger group.

Afterwards people said that the group had affected their attitudes and had enabled them to listen to others.

What has happened to the report?

Standards are being set as a result of this and other reports. Within the office there has been a continuing impact. One of the admin people and one of the OT's are following up on QA. One of the problems is getting information out to people. Managers have a copy and all those taking part; there is a copy on the notice board. People were excited when they got their copy.

I tried to make the report interesting by using sample questionnaires at the end.

Learning points

- How does planning affect managers at different levels of seniority?
- Why is planning important in management?
- How do tasks, operational plans, strategic objectives and organizational purpose fit together?
- What is the goal setting process?

- What is meant by SMART?
- What is a 'fuzzy' as opposed to a performance aspect of a goal?
- How can you prioritize objectives
  - by ABC?
  - by paired comparison?
- What is Management by Objectives (MBO)?
- What characterizes 'time' from most other resources?
- What sorts of problems do managers encounter in managing their time?
- What kinds of people waste time?
- What do you need to know in order to improve your time management?
- What ways can time management be improved?

Action planning

1   Identify the planning process in your organization.

2   Ascertain where your contribution comes in.

3   List out the work and non-work objectives which you have over:

- the next month;
- the next year;
- the next 5 years.

4   Try to set them up so they are SMART.

5   Use a prioritizing system to identify the ones which are most important.

6   Develop action plans to implement them.

7   Analyse the way you spend your work time over a period of at least 3 weeks.

8   Identify ways to improve on your time management.

9   Turn these into goals which are actionable and measurable and implement them.

7 Stress and the manager

What is stress, how does it affect people, how can people cope with it. The overall competency focus of this chapter is to:

- develop teams, individuals and self to enhance performance.

which will be developed by the ability to:

- develop and improve teams through planning and other activities;
- identify, review and improve development activities for individuals;
- develop oneself within the job role.

involving the following dimensions of personal competence:

- showing self-confidence and personal drive;
- managing personal emotions and stress,
- managing personal learning and development;
- collecting and organizing information;
- identifying and applying concepts.

Introduction

This chapter sets out to examine the nature of stress and assertiveness. Stress is a problem for many people not just managers. Assertiveness can be a highly effective way of managing actual and potential stress. After you have read this chapter you should have an understanding of:

- what stress is;
- why managers and organizations should be concerned about it;
- what causes stress;
- what are the signs of stress in yourself and others;
- what you can do about controlling and reducing stress both for yourself and for people you work with;
- why behaving assertively can improve your effectiveness and reduce stress.

What is stress?

A mismatch between perceived demands and perceived ability to cope. It is the balance between how we view demands and how we think we can cope with those demands that determines whether we feel no stress, distressed or ... challenged in a way we feel we can handle. (Adapted from Looker and Gregson (1989) p. 29)

Almost everyone has a view about stress. You do not have to be a manager or even in work to feel stressed. Concern is expressed about the stress associated with such things as:

- unemployment;
- raising a family;
- illness
- caring for a dependent relative;
- moving house;
- death of a relative;
- relationship or marital problems.

In order to start you thinking about stress try to list at least three different sources of stress (other than those already listed above) in the everyday life of yourself or a person familiar to you.

1 _____
2 _____
3 _____
Further?:　　4 _____　　　　5 _____　　　　6 _____

- The things you listed may have been associated with particular life events or changes − a holiday or someone leaving home.
- They may have been environmentally related − 'it's not safe to go out at night on my own'.
- Perhaps they were linked to particular people − 'my boss is a stress factor'.
- They may have touched upon how you (or the person you had in mind) managed their life − 'I can never say "no" to anything so I end up doing too much'.

People express a wide range of views about the causes of stress. The sorts of comments you hear reveal a great deal about the views of everyday managers and staff. Cast your mind back using your own work and life experience. Recall the comments which either you or your friends, family or colleagues have made on the subject.

Now on a sheet of paper complete the following sentences. There is no right or wrong answer. Photocopy the page to make it easier.

1　I find I get most stressed when ...
2　The last time I felt under stress was because of ...
3　The most stressful thing about my particular job is ...
4　The most stressful aspect of working in my organization is ...
4a　I think this is because ...

5   Of all occupations I think the most stressful is . . .
5a I think this is because . . .
6   The sort of person who copes best with stress is . . .
7   The sort of person who copes worst with stress is . . .
8   What I find stressful in my work surroundings is . . .
9   What my colleagues find stressful in their work surroundings is . . .
10 What I find most stressful in my home (i.e. non-work) life is . . .
11 The single thing my spouse/partner/best friend (choose as appropriate) could do which would most reduce my stress is . . .
12 The single thing my manager could do which would most reduce my stress is . . .
13 The single thing my organization could do which would most reduce my stress is . . .
14 The single thing the government could do which would most reduce my stress is . . .

The answers which you have given provide a picture of how you, as an individual, see stress in your own life and work. It is a brief and oversimplified picture. It does not provide any indication of how much stress you might be under.

However, you may find it helpful to compare your responses with the following multiple-cause diagram provided (see Figure 7. 1).

Stress can be seen from three perspectives.

Cause

Stress can be seen as the cause of problems. On an individual level we associate stress with a wide range of illnesses such as coronary (heart) disease, high blood pressure, migraine, asthma, ulcers, etc. Importantly we also see stress as having an effect upon a person's behaviour. How often have you felt a person's erratic or angry behaviour is down to 'stress'?

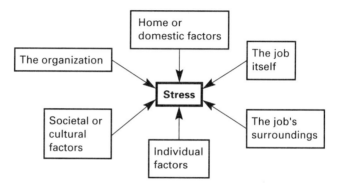

Figure 7.1 *Factors associated with stress*

Effect of a problem

Here the view is that stress results from other problems. Therefore the pressure of modern day life, long work hours, the high rate of relationship breakup, etc. are factors which are the cause of stress.

A problem itself

Perhaps stress is a function of how we react to pressure. Some occurrences people can cope with stress better than others. Therefore, we should look at the actual nature of the stress people feel and help them to develop better coping mechanisms.

Stress can be seen, according to Looker and Gregson (1989), as 'good', 'bad' or 'ugly'.

- It is 'good' in the sense that it can be associated with excitement, stimulation, creativity, success, achievement and increased productivity.
- It is 'bad' in the sense that it can be associated with boredom, frustration, distress, pressure, poor performance, unhappy and disharmonious relationships, failure and illness.
- It is 'ugly' in that it is associated with specific health (and sometimes life threatening) concerns such as ulcers, heart attacks, depression, etc.

Stress is a word of many facets. It conjures up a notion of a strain and indeed in the engineering industry has a technical meaning associated with the amount of pressure a material can resist before deforming. The meaning of stress becomes enriched when applied to people because, unlike concrete, balanced people have some choice over reactions. Unlike the motorway bridge they can engage in a range of behaviours.

Thus when applied to human behaviour stress is part of an interactive system. People vary in their make-up, experience and motivation and so the same amount of stress applied to different people is likely to have different results.

Cooper and Cummings (1988) offer a way of looking at stress in terms of a process. They suggest that people aim generally for a steady state in the way they relate to the world. This suggestion is based upon models used in a range of fields (biology, physics and social science) which seek to explain behaviour as aimed at correcting a disturbance. You can see this happening in the way your own body tries to adjust when outside temperature rises or falls. If it is hot your body sweats in order to lose heat. If it is very cold then shivering is an adjustment process to enable the body to increase temperature. Both are 'involuntary behaviours' which you have little control over.

Cooper and Cummings suggest that this model can apply to how we react to disturbance in our outside world. They see each person as having a range of stability within which they feel comfortable. When this stability is threatened by an outside force then the person tries to restore the position to one of comfort. Thus stress can be seen as a feedback cycle (see Figure 7.2).

We could suggest that everyone has a certain part of their life which is stable and does not change much over time. Though a person's life may appear chaotic and constantly moving the argument is that there are 'zones of stability' which each person needs and jealously guards. You may like to try this out on yourself. List all the changes which have happened to you in the past 5 years. You may find the following categories helpful as a guide. Simply note where there has been a change and where there has not.

- job;
- house;
- partner/spouse;
- close friends;
- pet;
- car;
- where you go on holiday;
- leisure pursuits;
- how you spend weekends.

If all of these have had change in the past 5 years then think of what has not changed. It may seem inconsequential – perhaps you have the same briefcase (or handbag). Perhaps you always have the same lunch or breakfast?

Think carefully about the meaning for you of these areas of relative stability. It could be that they have an importance in anchoring you in the face of potential stress in other areas of your life.

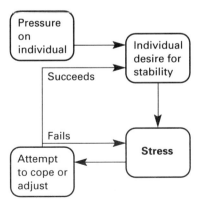

Figure 7.2 *The adjustment/coping cycle. Adapted from Cooper, Cooper and Eaker (1988)*

Stress can be seen as a process which some people cope with better than others do. Cooper, Cooper and Eaker (1988) offer this diagrammatic representation of the stress process (see Figure 7.3).

The physiology of pressure or threat

Pressure or threat has effects upon people in terms of their actual bodily reactions. Some of these are quite noticeable to others. Some of the effects are hormonal. They are natural and in many ways functional. Our ancestors relied upon heightened awareness at times of danger in order to survive. Animals, even domesticated ones, still rely on this.

The immediate physiological effects can include:

1 enlarging of pupils;
2 faster breathing;
3 faster heart rate;
4 'paleness';
5 sweating;
6 trembling;
7 sickness/bowel effects.

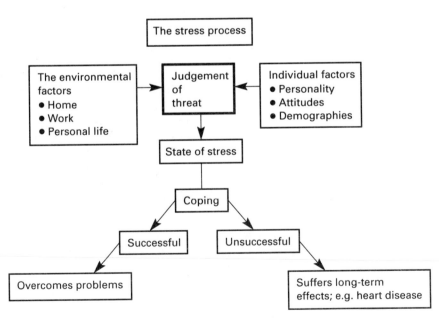

Figure 7.3 *The stress process. Adapted from Cooper, Cooper and Eaker (1988)*

Signs of stress at work

In the short term:

1 fight instead of flight — the short, sharp row;
2 fight — taking it out on others;
3 flight — going sick, leaving, retiring;
4 internal flight — slow down, reduce commitment;

In the long term:

1 illness or predisposition to illness;
2 absenteeism;
3 indecision;
4 arbitrary decisions;
5 excessive eating/drinking/smoking;
6 theft;
7 workaholism;
8 avoidance or overreaction;

How many of these signs do you recognize in yourself or others in you workplace?

Costs of stress at work

Stress obviously has a range of costs. One often quoted figure is that in the UK £5 billion is lost each year as a result of stress affecting people at work. This figure was based upon sickness statistics where the sickness was diagnosed as anxiety or depression.

Clearly that figure only represents a part of the stress-related costs. There are other effects of stress which are harder to quantify (see Figure 7.4). But it would be a useful exercise to consider those possible areas of cost. Take a moment and see if you can list the possible sources of cost arising directly or indirectly from work-related stress. You should be able to come up with at least five. More than ten and you can claim success from the benefits of the earlier chapters on problem-solving!

There are in fact as many costs as your imagination can cope with.

If you look at the costs simply in terms of the staff-related costs there are the costs of:

• covering for people on sick leave as a result of stress;
• replacing people who leave as a result of stress;
• training new people to do the job;
• other people leaving before they suffer stress related illness;

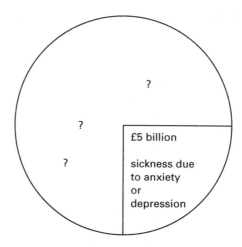

Figure 7.4 *The other costs of stress?*

- paying higher salaries and benefits to 'compensate' people for stress;
- early retirement costs for people who retire early for stress-related reasons.

In terms of the operations of the organization there are stress-related costs arising from:

- mistakes being made leading to loss of business efficiency;
- accidents leading to damage to persons, equipment and buildings;
- fines imposed as a result of avoidable industrial accidents;
- disciplining and cautioning staff.

In industrial relations terms there are stress-related costs arising from:

- the residue of ill feeling harboured by stressed staff;
- industrial disputes leading to loss of business;
- a lack of commitment to the organization's aims and values.

Indirectly we could attribute a stress-related cost to:

- actual theft from the employer by staff who feel aggrieved because of the stress they are suffering;
- deliberate negligence at time verging on sabotage by staff who feel aggrieved because of the stress they are suffering.

Arguably we could also apportion stress-related costs arising from:

- the cost to the NHS (and thus the tax system) of treating work stress related illness;
- the cost of non-contributory benefits paid as a result of work related stress;
- the loss of tax receipts from people who cease work for stress-related reasons (though these may be part compensated by the tax receipts from people who take their jobs);
- any increase in insurance premiums arising from compensation for stress-related incidents.

We should also not forget to add in the stress-related cost arising from:

- staff absence which is stress-related but which is not recorded as such in official statistics;
- the cost of official investigations of accidents and incidents of theft or sabotage;

There is an old maxim which says that people who feel exploited or aggrieved will seek to get even. This results in negligence or theft being not only tolerated but even expected. Ask yourself whether you would buy a car knowing it had come from a company which put staff under stress.

If your organization put you under stress which you felt unreasonable but you could not leave in the near future would you seek to get even by:

- excessive expense claims;
- misuse or abuse of equipment;
- 'working to rule' so that the company incurred loss of business or increased cost of doing business;
- taking things from work which you thought you could get away with.

The diagram is not sophisticated. It does not break down aspects of your job. You may have included such items as noisy or difficult neighbours, the recession, problems with your work colleagues and so forth which might seem to merit further categories.

However, it provides an indication of the main sources of stress which we can now explore further.

Individual factors associated with stress

Much has been written about individual factors which might be associated with stress – or rather a predisposition to experiencing the effects of pressure as stress.

Personality

A frequently mentioned factor is that of personality. In the early 1960s research into coronary heart disease patients suggested that they had similarities in their behaviour and personality. The term 'Type A' personality was used to describe these people. They were contrasted with people who did not possess these behaviours or personality characteristics. This latter group were described as 'Type B' personalities.

The theory which research set out to establish was that Type A personalities were more prone to coronary heart disease. Some of the research is most interesting in that the researchers looked at people who did not show any indication of coronary heart disease. They then examined whether later development of such disease was associated with the person being a Type A or Type B personality. Some research studies have followed the same people over a period of more than 10 years.

The findings suggest that Type A personalities are at substantially greater risk of developing heart disease than Type B ones are. The estimates vary between twice as much and six times as much depending upon the research. The higher risk factors are associated in particular with younger age groups which suggest that there may be an age-related factor operating.

So let's look at what constitutes a Type A as opposed to a Type B personality.

Type A behaviour consists of:

- trying to do several things at the same time;
- inability to relax;
- cramming more and more into your time;
- aggressive reactions or a desire to challenge others;
- fast speaking;
- inconsiderate listening (particularly shown by a tendency to interrupt or complete what someone else is saying);
- impatience with what is seen to be a lack of progress on the part of others;
- deadlines as an obsession;
- adding up numbers to measure everything;
- ambition for advancement and recognition (though the precise goals may be poorly thought out).

Type B personalities on the other hand do not possess the above characteristics. They also are:

- not obsessed with:
  - impressing others;
  - time as a governing factor in their lives;

- able to play and enjoy non-competitive leisure pursuits;
- relaxed when at work.

There is considerable discussion over the implications of Type A and B personalities and stress-related illness. It is a little reminiscent of the debate over which came first; the chicken or the egg. Does a Type A person take on a high stress job or do high stress jobs (or companies) foster Type A people and Type A behaviour? Some research suggests that some companies, especially expanding ones, tend to have a high proportion of Type A managers.

The hardy personality

Some people who are Type A personalities seem to be able to cope better and do not display high stress levels. A theory of 'hardy personality' has been put forward to explain this. Suzanne Kobasa looked at middle and senior managers who had been subject to highly stressful life events in the previous 3 years. Over half of the group had not suffered any stress-related illness. Kobasa looked at the differences between the executives who had become ill and those who had not. She suggests that those who had not become ill (whom she called 'hardy' executives) had the following differences in their approach to stressful life events:

- a clear sense of their values, goals and capabilities;
- a positive attitude to change.

The 'hardy personality' is someone who believes that they have some influence or control over what happens. External pressures are seen as something which are capable of being turned to the individual's advantage.

Age

Personality is not the only individual factor associated with stress. Characteristics such as age, sex and race are also involved.

Age is important because there are changes, both mental and physical, which affect an individual's ability to handle changes and threat. Age is a factor sometimes linked to occupation. Thus armed forces personnel particularly those in demanding positions are required to retire earlier than their civilian counterparts. For a younger employee the prospect of a major work reorganization may offer opportunities and welcome challenges. For a more senior and established person the possibility of a change in work location and responsibilities might be profoundly stressful.

The government policy of moving departments out of London and setting them up as 'next steps' agencies came as a profound shock to some groups of staff. Many, in their late 40s or 50s, could not envisage the upheaval associated with a relocation (usually to a place they were unfamiliar with) and the loss of job security associated with the change to agency status.

Sex

Women enjoy a longer life expectancy than men do. The difference may be likely to reduce if more women adopt, through choice or circumstance, the patterns of Type A behaviour and engage in a higher consumption of cigarettes and alcohol as a response to stress.

The pressures of 'dual career' households and the associated conflicts of work and family bring particular stresses for women. Research findings show that for men the presence of a spouse and children can be a career asset which adds to the c.v. Women, especially when applying for senior jobs, often omit spouse and children from their c.v. or application details. Research suggests that employers still tend to see a woman's family as a potential liability. The relatively limited childbearing years available to a woman (as opposed to the man's ability to father children into his dotage) can also cause stress of a particularly fraught nature.

Race

(The term 'black' is used below as a shorthand for all groups subject to discrimination on grounds of race or colour.)

The effect of racial discrimination can be extremely stressful. This is recognized separately by tribunals when making compensation awards. However, for every case which comes to such a tribunal there are many others which do not. The Mental Health Act Commission has expressed concern about the number of black people diagnosed as suffering from psychiatric illness and the treatment they receive as a result. Black people have higher levels of unemployment than white people. When they are employed then they are more likely to be employed in positions below that to similarly educated white people.

The effect of positive action to correct discrimination can also be stressful for the black person. Sometimes it can lead to the person being promoted into a position for which they have not yet acquired the necessary skills or experience. It can also mean that the black person is under pressure to 'perform' at all times in a way that the equivalent white person would not be.

Education

Stress-related diseases such as coronary heart disease are generally lower the higher the level of education. Education is associated with a greater awareness of the reasons for stress. Education also helps people to develop a range of interests which can help in coping with stress. A person who is well informed about the values of exercise and a balanced diet is in a better position than the person who is not so informed.

Home and domestic factors

Changes in a person's life − even changes for the better can be stressful.

One of the authors worked as a manager in social services for a number of years. During that time he was involved in introducing improvements in residential care for elderly people. He found to his surprise that improving the conditions in residential care homes usually led, in the short term, to a higher mortality rate among elderly residents. The changes (often required by legislation) represented a stressful life event for the elderly people concerned.

Some life changes are obviously associated with stress. Such occurrences as loss of a close family member, divorce or a major house move are familiar and need little explanation. However, stress can be associated with the birth of a grandchild, becoming engaged, etc. Research suggests that the more changes that you experience over a period of time the greater the susceptibility to stress. It is the amount of change and not simply whether it is seen as 'bad or good' which is crucial.

You should treat this 'life event' approach with some caution. It is not as straightforward as a kind of driving offence 'totting up' points system. Rather the individual factors mentioned previously serve to modify the effect of life changes. The same life events may have different significance for different people. You may be devastated by the death of your pet cat. Your partner may not regard the cat as being of particular emotional significance.

There are other individual factors which influence how well a person can handle stress. People who enjoy good social and emotional relationships with friends and family are better equipped to handle stressful situations. It seems that it is not the quantity of such relationships which is important but rather the extent to which the other person is seen as a source of help and support. The so-called stiff upper lip is a factor which makes it harder for men in the UK to share personal worries. Women are more accustomed to sharing feelings and fears. If you are a man reading this then you may wonder why there are so few 'men's magazines' while the newsagents has several shelves of magazines catering for women.

The job itself

Charles Handy (1985) has listed a number of factors associated with the job which contribute to stress:

1 responsibility for the work of others;
2 responsibility for innovation;
3 co-ordination/liaison roles;
4 relationship problems with colleagues;
5 career uncertainty.

In addition to domestic or individual factors Cooper suggests the following sources of work-related stress:

1 factors associated with the job;
2 aspects of the individual's work role;
3 work-based relationships;
4 career issues;
5 the structure and climate of the organization.

You may find it helpful at this point to review the answers you wrote to the earlier questions. Can you fit your answers into the categories which have been identified?

Organization factors

Recent television programmes have identified the varying responses of organizations to stress. Generally major companies in the USA had recognized stress as a problem and had instituted measures to respond to it. The programmes highlighted the work of some UK organizations such as the Post Office. But they also showed that some UK employers were reluctant to accept that stress was a problem in the work place.

Some organizations operate in a way which inevitably is stress inducing. Where the organization is strongly sales-driven and a manager or employee is only as good as his/her last achievement the stress factor can be quite high. You often may hear 'it's a young person's company' to describe such a situation. Advertising agencies are stressful settings and are characterized by young staff profile.

The nature of the organization is often a direct result of the nature of its industrial environment. It is evident that the pressure of change and the need to work increasingly more efficiently and effectively will have an effect upon the level of organizational stress.

As an example of this we offer the situation of a local authority refuse collection service. Prior to the introduction of compulsory competitive tendering the service had employed a proportion of mentally handicapped operatives. After the change the dustcart crews and managers realized the implications of higher performance targets. Suddenly the mentally handicapped operatives were no longer welcome on the crews. One manager explained: 'Contract tendering places the crew under great stress to meet targets. We don't feel it is right to put mentally handicapped people in that situation.'

Occupational factors

The older reader may recall a comic sketch by Peter Cook and Dudley Moore. In the sketch Peter Cook explains to Dudley Moore why it is better to be a judge than a coal miner. He observes that when miners get too old to dig the coal then they lose their jobs whereas judges can go on and on.

The reality is that a judge is likely to be in better health than a coal miner of the same age. Indeed the judge is likely to outlive the coal miner by many years.

There is a relationship between illness and occupation and between life expectancy and occupation. If we look at illness first then we can identify aspects relating to both physical and mental ill-health.

In Britain occupations are divided into six categories. These categories may be familiar to you if you cast your mind back to the last election as election commentators make frequent use of them:

A   Professional
B   Intermediate
C1 Non-manual skilled
C2 Manual skilled
D   Partly skilled
E   Unskilled

The basis of this classification is the amount of skill required to do the job. Generally evidence indicates that the higher a person is up the occupational scale the less likely they are to have significant ill-health.

This evidence holds true for both physical and mental ill-health. It also applies within organizations. A major study carried out over 7 years compared the risk of coronary heart disease with civil service grade. The higher the civil service grade the person had the lower the medical risk indicators of coronary heart disease (high blood pressure, obesity, smoking, etc.).

The amount of stress associated with different occupations has been researched. Generally the most stressful occupations are those which are described as 'uniformed'. Occupations such as the police, ambulance or prison service rate highly. Cooper reported the following overall stress ratings for different classifications of occupations. The figures represent an average of each different group of jobs.

Uniformed professions	6.4
Management	5.8
Industrial production	5.1
Caring professions	4.7
Health	4.6
Public administration	4.2
Financial areas	4.0

Environment	3.9
Technical specialities	3.7

(Source: Cooper, Cooper and Eaker, (1988) pp. 81–3)

What may strike you, the reader, is that moving into management is likely to be associated with a move into a higher stress rating: There are occupations which rate higher than management but management is above average for stress.

Many people, perhaps you are one of them, move into management from a background of technical expertise. If so then it is probable that the move will involve a considerable increase in occupational stress.

However, it should not be assumed that the occupation is sufficient to explain the level of stress. As the previous model has shown the sources of stress are numerous. It is not generally possible to put stress down to one particular cause.

Job-related factors

Frederick Herzberg (1959), an industrial psychologist, suggested that the aspects of a job which motivated people were different from those factors which were associated with dissatisfaction. These factors, which Herzberg identified as 'hygiene' factors, are similar to those which are associated with stress.

Occupations which require long hours, changing shift patterns and where the work setting is noisy, dirty or cramped are generally more stressful where such factors do not apply. You can compare for yourself the occupational stress factors associated with being an industrial scientist and being a shift worker in the traditional 'metal bashing' industry. Alternatively, compare a basic grade emergency ward nurse with a librarian.

In each case the comparison shows shift work (often not under the control of the worker) and longer scheduled hours as opposed to regular hours or hours under the control of the job holder. The work settings themselves can be contrasted with the general calm and quiet of the laboratory or library on the one hand and the noise and clamour of the factory or hospital emergency room.

The nature of the work task itself can be a stress factor. Repetitive and time-pressured work is associated with stress. One author worked for a period of time in a packaging factory. The repetitive and boring nature of the work led to occasions of deliberate sabotage of machinery. When the assembly belt stopped there was a cheer from the workforce. During the break periods the younger workers retired behind the canteen and smoked marijuana. The older workers made for the pub and alcoholic relief.

Shift work has a stressful effect which is increased by:

1   The length of the shift. Workers on oil rigs often spend considerable

lengths of time offshore. There are often considerable adjustment problems particularly when there are family ties.

2 The rotation of the shift: Typically there is a pattern which means a worker changes shift every week or 2 weeks. The disturbance to normal metabolism is considerable. It affects sleep and digestion.

3 Long-term night shifts. Here the disruption is less than shift rotation but nevertheless there is an impact. Social activities are disrupted. Normal sleep is often difficult because of the noises and intrusions of everyday life (road traffic, meter readers, aircraft noise, etc.).

Longer hours as a stress factor

There has recently been considerable public debate about European Community (EC) expectations regarding the 'normal working week'. The official United Kingdom response has been to resist the call for a shorter working week. However, links are established between long working hours and coronary heart disease. There is little doubt that beyond a certain point performance tails off and all the longer hours do is establish 'brownie points' with the organization.

One of the authors is familiar with a city institution where extremely long hours are expected. Some employees realized that it was evidence of presence rather than actual work which was required. They bought extra suit jackets and would discreetly go home leaving the jackets hung conspicuously over the back of their office chairs. The 24-hour worker had arrived.

Work overload is a stress factor. This can consist of either the amount of work required or the standard of work expected given the ability of the individual.

In the industrial setting where there is an assembly line the phrase 'speed up' is often used to describe increasing the speed of the assembly line. The effect of this can be very stressful if the worker is unable to cope with the increase of work. The rate of faulty work is likely to increase.

There are a number of factors which promote work overload. Typically these factors are:

* time (the end of year accounts or budget cycle);
* seasonal (your product is more in demand at some time of the year);
* skill (there is a shortage of trained staff);
* resources (insufficient to do the job properly);
* demand (your customers all arrive at the same time).

Some work settings are more predictable. You can imagine the typical dairy farm where the cows are all milked at regular intervals and the milk is guaranteed a market price because of milk quotas. Other settings as far less so. A major political demonstration in

London may require heavy policing. Often you read in the press that 'police leave was cancelled'.

One of the skills of effective management is minimizing the likelihood of work overload. You may find it helpful to list out the factors associated with work overload in your organization. What can managers do to minimize them? What can you do to minimize them?

Work underload is a source of potential work stress. It is a factor associated with insufficient challenge. When an organization wants to get rid of someone then depriving them of any meaningful work is an effective way. (Though it raises ethical questions!) Work underload is a problem which confronts the emergency and armed forces. What do firefighters do when there is no fire to fight? The answer is to engage in training exercises aimed at preparation for the fire when it occurs. For those of us who live in London the presence of fire engines at major underground stations has become an everyday reality. Many of the call outs are hoaxes. However, they enable the fire service to develop and practise the skills for the real thing.

Similarly the armed forces engage in frequent war exercises and we hope that their skills will never be required.

Work role factors

Clarity should guide the writing of every job description. Work roles should be allocated to avoid conflict. Notice the use of the word 'should'. The reality is more frequently something like this:

'Sam, your job description says you are responsible for providing sales figures. Why haven't you done them for me?'
'Well Robin, I've asked Jo for the information but s/he says that the figures go straight to head office and head office says I'm not entitled to receive them until the Sales Director has seen them.'
'Look Sam, I don't care how you do it but get me those figures.'

Obviously there is considerable potential for uncertainty and conflict in such a situation. The presumption is that Sam works for Robin. However, this may not be the case. If so then Robin may have to intercede with Sam's manager. Jo clearly believes that the figures in question go directly to Head Office. Head Office have their own view about how the figures get handled.

Stress is linked to uncertainty about what the job requires. Stress is also associated with conflicting job demands.

The potential for stress in these two areas is considerable and probably increasing. Why? The world of work and organizations is undergoing a faster rate of change. Some organizations have recognized that job descriptions become out of date too quickly. Updating them is seen as a fruitless and increasingly meaningless task. Therefore, they are getting rid of job descriptions. Instead employees will be managed by targets and objectives which are periodically reviewed. But managers used to job descriptions are often inexperienced in managing people by objectives and targets.

In such organizations there is considerable potential for role uncertainty unless the targets and objectives are clearly set. Lines of accountability can become easily blurred.

Both authors have worked in and with organizations where accountability has moved downwards (the term 'decentralization' is often used). A common phenomena in such situations is that, though the transfer of responsibility has been clearly agreed and communicated, the Head Office still believes that the authority is centrally held. The managers are treated is if they do not have the delegated authority. This can prove very frustrating especially when key decisions are not acted upon.

There are particular phenomena which can cause uncertainty over job role:

- *A promotion*: Alice was very happy about being promoted. She enjoyed working with her colleagues and saw them as friends. But after moving into the supervisor's job she found that light conversation at the lunch table became harder. She didn't feel able to share confidences with her team in the way she had in the past. Her colleagues, on the other hand, seemed to regard her as still one of the team. They were quite taken aback when she commented on the need to improve timekeeping. The Alice they knew 'shouldn't be saying that'.
- *A new job*: Lesley worked for a commercial manufacturing company. He was used to being set clear targets and was expected to meet them efficiently and without discussion. He moved to work for a voluntary organization and set about his new job in his accustomed fashion. He was surprised when colleagues upbraided him for failing to consult sufficiently and being insufficiently sensitive to the politics of the Management Committee.
- *A transfer within the company*: Riaz welcomed the opportunity to work with the sales department. He felt that his experience in production had equipped him to move into a sales role. However, when he asked what time people finished work in sales he was surprised to get no clear answer.
- *A change in the structure of the organization (i.e. decentralization – see above)*
- *A change in procedures*: A local authority conducted an audit of the forms in current usage. They found that many of them were duplicating information held on other forms. The senior managers agreed to simplify and reduce the number of forms. The clerical staff found the new forms hard to understand and began photocopying the older versions of the forms. The new forms piled up unused.
- *A change in the law*: The government increasingly requires local

authorities to put services out to contract. In order to meet this legislation local authorities had to set up separate purchasing and contractors' departments. People who had worked together harmoniously suddenly began to develop 'them and us' attitudes. Distrust and suspicion grew.

Managing people to reduce stress

The following list is drawn from Dr Vernon Coleman's suggestions to managers. They are aimed at reducing stress in subordinates:

- Give people as much responsibility as they can safely handle.
- Say thank you.
- Know when to push people – and when to stop.
- Smile at people.
- Remember that boredom is also a source of stress.
- Help people to accept change.
- Avoid getting obsessed with administration.
- Show people how to recognize signs of stress in themselves.
- Remember that responsibility and authority go together.
- Treat people as individuals and personalize the work setting.
- Help people to say 'no'.
- Ensure people know how to operate machinery they use in their work.
- Help people prepare for retirement.
- Encourage staff participation and welcome suggestions.
- Promote an atmosphere of forgiveness and caring.
- Encourage people to be independent but also to ask for help when they need it.
- Encourage people to relax and take holidays due to them.

Coping strategies

Some aspects of stress are more controllable than others. If your main source of stress is the nature of the occupation you find yourself in and you regard the stress as unacceptable then your choice is obvious – find another and less stressful occupation.

However, for most people stress is an amalgam of many factors of which occupation is but one. Most of these factors can be influenced by you. Some can be controlled by you though you may not realize it.

The way you respond to stress at work may be appropriate or inappropriate. Appropriate responses enable you to cope successfully.

Stress associated with work role and work environment can often be eased by behaving assertively as opposed to non-assertively or aggressively. You will find this described in more detail in Chapter 2.

You might find it helpful to think of in terms of 'rights'. The rights which you feel you possess and the rights of the other person in an exchange.

If you are behaving non-assertively you are in effect saying that the other person has rights but you do not. If you behave aggressively then you are saying that you have rights but the other person has not. Assertive behaviour is recognizing that you both have rights. Let's see how this behaviour operates in a potentially stressful situation.

Your line manager asks you to work late. The request is not unreasonable because of an unexpected backlog of work but you have promised your partner/spouse that you will be home at the usual time tonight.

You might respond by saying:

1 'I promised I'd be home by seven but I suppose I could stay on if I have to ....'
2 'You must be joking — no way.'
3 'I appreciate you have a problem but I can't stay on late tonight.'

The first response is non-assertive. Even though you are indicating a pressure elsewhere you are indicating that you are accepting the right of the other person takes precedence.

The second response is aggressive. It is not simply a statement of your own rights but also a denial of the right of your manager to even suggest that you work late.

The third response is assertive. You are acknowledging your manager's right to ask but are clearly stating that you yourself have a right.

Let's try it again only this time apply it to something which you felt uncomfortable about. Here are several suggestions in case you find it hard to think of a situation.

- You are asked to take on a new job responsibility but you feel that you have not had sufficient training or preparation.
- You are asked to clear up a mess which is not of your making.
- You feel that there is some part of your pay and benefits which has fallen behind what you regard as the going rate for your job.

Find a friend or colleague to assist you. If none is available then face a mirror as you say the words which you would use with your manager.

Then review what you said. You may find it helpful to write down what you said. Ask yourself (and your friend or colleague) the following questions.

1 What 'right(s)' was I stating for myself?
2 What 'right(s)' was I accepting that my manager had?
3 How did my tone of voice support or detract from what I said?
4 How did my facial expression support or detract from what I said?
5 How did my body posture support or detract from what I said?
6 (If you had a friend or colleague) How was my message received?

Some experts suggest that it is worth keeping a diary in which you record stressful events, who was associated with them and how you handled them. The purpose of such a diary is not simply to have a factual record but rather to enable you to adopt appropriate (i.e. assertive) behaviour. It is a learning aid.

The ability to use assertive behaviour is probably the single most effective strategy available to you. It is something within your control. It gives you a means to deal with the various aspects of stress not just in your work but in your life generally.

Using assertion you can then move on to apply it to implement such strategies as:

1 delegation – to your staff and colleagues;
2 participation – in establishing work objectives;
3 prioritization – of tasks;
4 control over your use of time.

Mervyn Eastman, Deputy Director of Social Services for the London Borough of Enfield has put forward the following method for dealing with stress.

- The most effective methods of managing my own stress I have found is in the framework of transactional analysis.
- Simply put, I have found the following very useful:
  1 I am *responsible* for how I feel (angry, frustrated, anxious). Nobody has the power to make me feel ... boss, staff, events, change.
  2 Recognizing that how I perceive and use authority has been determined by previous life experiences – but that I am in *control* of myself.
  3 Poor/bad behaviour of others is probably motivated by 'good intent'.
  4 I am able to *confront* (sensitively) the actions/words of those around me.
  5 Use the word 'I' and owning what I say/do:
    – Knowing the difference between 'I won't' and 'I can't'.
    – Saying 'I don't know' when I mean 'I do know'.
    – Avoid hedging.
    – Doing not trying.
- Recognizing that 'things don't happen to me' – I make things happen. How I deal with a 'charismatic boss' (which I presently have here in Enfield) is determined and controlled by me!

- Sleepless nights, smoking, taking my anger and frustration out on people at home, getting fed up, getting angry − belong to me, nobody else.
- If in doubt I read Abe Wagner!

Learning points

- What is stress?
- What are the signs of stress?
- How can it be seen as a process?
- How does it cause costs at work?
- What are the physical effects of it in a person?
- What are the main factors associated with stress at work?
- What is a 'Type A' personality?
- What is a 'hardy personality'?
- What sorts of occupations have higher stress?
- What is it about a job which might make it stressful?
- What is assertive, non-assertive and aggressive behaviour?
- How can assertiveness be used in coping with stress?
- What is a 'stability zone' and how might it be important in coping with stress?

Action planning

1   What are the main stress factors for you?

− individual;
− home/domestic;
− occupation;
− employer;
− work role;
− work setting.

2   How do you plan to manage each of these?

− over the next month;
− over the next 6 months.

3   How will you measure whether or not you have succeeded?

8 Creating and fostering effective workplace relationships

The overall competence focus of this chapter is to:

● create, maintain and enhance effective working relationships.

which will be developed by the ability to:

− establish and maintain the trust and support of one's subordinates;
− establish and maintain the support of one's immediate manager;
− establish and maintain relationships with colleagues;
− identify and minimize interpersonal conflict;

involving the following dimensions of personal competence:

− showing sensitivity to the needs of others;
− relating to others;
− obtaining the commitment of others;
− presenting oneself positively to others;
− showing self-confidence and personal drive.

Objectives of this chapter

● to understand how effective workplace relationships are created and fostered;
● to understand the nature of power and influence;
● to understand the use of negotiation and apply appropriate techniques;
● to know and practise the skills of seeking agreement to maximum advantage;
● to handle disagreement and conflict;
● to understand the role of leadership and apply appropriate styles to varying situations in the development of effective working relationships.

Introduction

The writers have often heard people comment that 'one can choose one's friends, but not one's relatives'. We have all had experiences in private life around the issues of developing relationships with parents, grandparents, siblings, our children and so on. These develop informally and are more or less effective depending upon how we, as the central individuals in such role sets, approach the whole idea of positive and constructive relationships with those whom we are supposed to love.

The workplace is not so different. Here again we are unable to choose those with whom we 'work'. Sometimes, as managers, we have some control over whom we recruit but our effectiveness as interviewers and ultimate selectors of personnel will determine how appropriate these final choices will be. We are, whatever the outcome, presented with a group of people with whom we must interrelate and, hopefully, influence the way they interrelate with each other.

Once more, the effectiveness of these interrelationships begins with us not only as managers but also as individuals who wish to gain the most trust, support, respect and co-operation between all individuals in the role set. (Just like love really, only we would not normally call it that at work!)

Leadership

As a definition for leadership, one could state that it is a dynamic process whereby one individual provides the wherewithal for those s/he is leading to influence each other to contribute voluntarily to the achievement of group tasks in a given situation.

Another perpetual debate among practitioners is whether leadership can be separated from the role of management. It is obvious that there are effective leaders who do not necessarily have the authority of management; it is therefore impossible for them to implement certain activities without referring to the relevant authority. The question which remains then is 'can a manager be effective without also being an effective leader?' It may be possible for a manager to 'delegate' leadership, but how might this be achieved?

To meet the objectives of effective workplace relationships, leaders must first endow the trust, support, respect and co-operation onto others within the role set in order to fulfil the group objectives. This will then become mutually 'enabling'; people who feel trusted will then trust in return. It is often difficult for managers to see how they can let go in this way and maintain what they perceive to be the vital prerogative of management: to manage.

One does not require the title of manager in order to manage and the less obvious the process of management is, the more effective it appears be. This is a debate which is likely to continue for some time yet and which requires a group of 'managers' to develop the idea, together with what implications the varying styles of leadership might have for differing organizational cultures.

The role of leaders

John Adair (1985), identified the functions of a leader into three basic common organization needs: those of the group; those of the individual and those of the task (see Figure 8.1).

This model could be developed to show that a leader's function is to provide the key role in identifying organizational objectives, which defines the needs of the task(s) to be performed and then link them to the individual departments or units of operation, at the same time as linking individual and group needs to those of the whole.

Difficulties arise where individual and group objectives do not match those of the organization. It is inevitable that they will not coincide completely as individuals and groups bring their own particular needs to the workplace. The leader then has the 'task' of balancing all these needs and creating synergy between them (where measured outcomes are more than the sum of all the parts); to optimize the outcomes.

Types of leadership

There are various views of what constitutes 'type' in terms of leadership, these include:

- charismatic – based upon the personality of a leader;
- traditional – based upon birthright;
- situational – based on being in the right place at the right time;
- appointed – based on bureaucratic authority;
- functional – based on behaviour or actions expected.

What makes you a leader?

Anyone can become a leader if s/he can persuade others to follow. People follow for a variety of reasons:

- the fear of criticism and/or punishment;
- the need to obey rules and procedures;

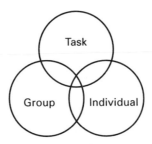

Figure 8.1 *Action-centred leadership*

- respect for a leader's accepted position;
- the leader has gained credibility over time and so on.

These reasons are not mutually exclusive, for example followers may both respect their leader and fear the consequences of disobedience. Current organizational thinking leans towards the respect and trust model of leadership. Where the former is more reliant upon systems and procedures, the latter requires flexible approaches, creative thinking and effective interpersonal communication.

Leadership of working teams

If the formally recognized leader is to become the genuinely accepted leader of his/her working team, that 'following' must be earned. Leaders constantly find themselves in competition with informal leaders who can exercise certain powers (length of service; the ear of a director and so on) and it would, therefore, be unwise for the formal leader to rely on the negative forces of fear and convention. In the long run, a team's respect and trust are likely to produce more effective results.

The formal leader's aim is not to depose the informal leaders; but more positively to gain the support of the informal groupings in order to meet organizational objectives. Informal leaders will cause fewer problems if the leader shows that s/he merits respect and proves capable of being trusted. This can take time, patience and personal sacrifice.

One of the authors of this book has had considerable experience in this area and one incident in particular deserves a closer look. As a senior female manager of professional consultants (male and female) in a small consultancy firm several years ago, a major difficulty occurred when she was promoted to company director. The competition did not exist as regards the directorship so much as the equalizing of status, and this from another woman who was promoted into the vacated management position!

The person concerned, who believed she should have held a directorship herself, had gained informal support from the consultancy team with whom she worked. The newly appointed director, believing her established credibility would hold firm, did not only avoid dealing with the problem directly, but thought that through the delegation of authority and responsibility to this and other managers (not previously allowed by the managing director) instead of earning respect and credibility for herself at the more senior level, would eventually resolve the problem.

However, through the director not proving her own competence in the new role, the manager was able to prove to the managing director, despite his previous support of the director, that she was in fact operating at a level similar to, and even beyond, the director herself.

Since the business was small and there was nowhere else to go in terms of career moves, the director decided it was time to move on. While this resolution may sound extreme, it in fact proved to be the right one, ultimately. Although the detailed problems themselves were difficult to resolve, the 3 months notice served by the director allowed her to develop and support the managers in their claims for more autonomy which thus created a complete swing around of everyone's views and opinions of the director, including the opposing manager (by now a director herself) and the director was able to leave on a positive note.

It must be understood that this is not the answer to all informal leadership bids, and with hindsight the director concerned now understands the importance of earning respect and credibility at every stage of development. However, where there is truth in the claim (ironically, the director herself provided the evidence) and especially where the company is very small, there are times when such evaluation is relevant and decisions such as this must be considered.

Leadership styles

When a problem or demand occurs on which teams or individuals have to act, the leader is often presented with the dilemma of the choice of leadership style. Should the approach be authoritarian (at one extreme) or would the democratic involvement of the team be more appropriate (at the other)? The choice is not simple; in any given situation, a wide range of possibilities present themselves, according to Tannenbaum and Schmidt (1958) these include:

- the leader gives the orders – the feelings and opinions of the team may or may not be taken into consideration, but they are expected to obey;
- the leader 'sells' his/her decisions – as well as giving the orders, the group are persuaded to accept them and the leader recognizes that there may be resistance;
- the leader explains his/her decisions – the group are given the opportunity to discuss the leader's intentions and thinking, allowing the exploration of the implications of decisions and to develop the instructions for implementation more fully;
- the leader's decisions are open to change – still taking the initial decision, the leader is prepared to hear other ideas and modify/change the decision before taking further action;
- the leader chooses between the ideas of individuals within the group(s) – having defined the problem or need, the leader allows group members to suggest ways of tackling it, providing the leader with a range of alternatives and who then selects the most promising;
- the leader states the problem and the group decides – the leader still defines the problem and then states parameters within which

the decisions must be made, but the group decides together what should be done;
- the leader defines the limits within which the group has total freedom – within the specified limits, the group define and analyse problems as the individuals perceive them and decide together what should be done. The leader commits in advance to help implement whatever the group decides.

Styles of a leader

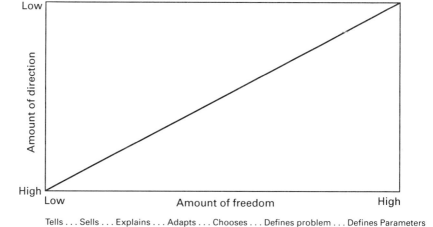

Tells . . . Sells . . . Explains . . . Adapts . . . Chooses . . . Defines problem . . . Defines Parameters

Figure 8.2 *Leadership styles. Derived from Tannenbaum and Schmidt model (1958)*

The forces deciding the choice

- Forces within the leader: the leader's own beliefs and inclinations. Some people are more comfortable as directive leaders. They may argue that they are paid to take responsibility for taking decisions and producing results.
- The leader's confidence in the workgroup/subordinates: a leader's view of subordinates is coloured by the amount of trust endowed upon people in general. This varies considerably between leaders which in turn affects their willingness to accept people's competence and good intentions.
- The leader's tolerance of uncertainty: where leaders involve their subordinates, it is implicit that outcomes are less predictable than their own decision-taking. Where some leaders have low tolerance of such uncertainty, others thrive on it as a challenge.

Forces within the subordinates/workgroups

- The strength of their need for independence: where some individuals want to take responsibility for their own behaviour seeing it as a challenge and tribute to their competence, the self-confidence of others may not yet be sufficiently developed to accept responsibility and they may need to know that someone else is accountable. Their defence may be that they see delegation as 'buck passing'.

- Tolerance of uncertainty: while some people prefer clear-cut directives, others prefer to accept the risks of greater self-direction.
- Expectations about leadership style: those used to strong directives may perceive involvement as a threat; those used to involvement will resent authoritarian decision-takers.
- Pressure of time: while often less a pressure than perceived by either leaders or followers, this is perhaps the greatest pressure of all. The more urgent the need for action, the more difficult it is for leaders to involve others and for others to accept involvement.

Making the right choices

There is no one best style for all situations and the able leader is not likely to be consistently autocratic or consistently democratic. Style will depend upon the situation, the problem and the subordinates involved. Upon each issue, s/he accurately assesses his/her own need and those of others in the organization likely to be affected by his/her methods of leadership; superiors, colleagues, people in other departments. An able leader also takes into account the needs of subordinates and their readiness for growth and development. If direction is appropriate, the leader directs; if involvement is relevant, the leader involves.

When assessing and measuring the effectiveness of decisions made by subordinates, it is important to remember that it is not the number of decisions they help make, but the significance of each decision made!

It is also necessary to remember that, whatever the level of involvement of subordinates in decision-making, the leader must accept the positive and negative outcomes of all decisions made, because delegation is not passing on the responsibility and accountability of achieving the organization's/department's objectives, but sharing responsibility for the actions employed in attaining them.

To reiterate the question posed at the beginning of this section, 'can leadership be divorced from the role of management?', what do you think?

The nature of power and influence

This section is based upon the concepts developed by Charles B. Handy (1985) in his book *Understanding Organizations*.

In defining power, it can be said that it relates to the capacity to affect the behaviour of others or the actual ability to do something.

In defining authority in relation to power, it can be termed as the 'status' which legitimizes the use of power.

Influence is the application and the effect of power and authority.

Power/authority does not only apply in hierarchies, but also in different ways in all work and social environments. Everyone is influenced by external power sources in some way. For example:

- when a baby cries – it demands feeding;
- governments demand taxes;
- the boss asks for work to be done;
- a friend asks you for a favour.

All four instances exert some kind of power over the individual. Charles Handy (1985) distinguishes between power and influence. He says that the difference lies in the fact that influence is an active process and that power is a resource providing the ability to influence. Recourse to any source of power is likely to provoke different kinds of response in those over whom it is exercised.

Power as a source of influence

Sources of power

1 Physical: a superior physical force using coercion to make people 'work'; e.g. the bully, tyrant or commander in the armed forces (threats are often sufficient). This is seen as the power of the last resort.
2 Resource: possession of a valued reward is often a useful basis for influence. It is calculative and in order to be effective:

   - there must be control of the resources; and
   - those resources must be desired by the potential recipient (links to expectancy theory of motivation).

   Conflicts of power occur where physical power in the form of laws affecting picketing, industrial action, etc. resulting in imprisonment for those convicted of infringement of these laws, versus resource power in the form of trade unions' ability to withdraw labour.

   Bureaucratization of power reduces individual power, for example, in the public sector the individual power of a manager to reward by increasing pay or promotion, etc. is reduced by corporate procedures and so on.
3 Position: this is present as the result of legal or legitimate power that comes as a result of the role or position of the individual in the organization; for example the role of manager allows him/her to give orders to staff. Power tends to reside in the position rather than the individual. This normally has to be supported by physical

and/or resource power; in other words the organization must back the manager or control the resources otherwise the manager's influence will fail.

Position power gives the occupant potential control over some Invisible assets:

- information;
- right of access to a variety of networks;
- the right to organize.

4   Expert: this form of power is vested in someone because of their acknowledged expertise. In meritocratic tradition people do not resent being influenced by 'experts'. It is often linked to occupations, e.g. doctors, lawyers, economists, etc.

As a power base, expert power requires no sanctions, but if expertise is questioned, it may be necessary for the holder to fall back onto other sources of power.

5   Personal: or referent/charismatic power resides in the person and his/her personality. It can be enhanced by position or expert power, success and self-confidence, but it can be seen to fade when an individual leaves a particular post, leaves a group or suffers defeat or failure. It is less resented than other power sources and comes from those over whom it is exercised. It is tied to the individual rather than the position. It operates mostly in informal power structures.

6   Negative or reflective power: if power is used in the agreed constituency, i.e. in its appropriate domain, it can be regarded as legitimate. If used contrary to accepted practice or outside the appropriate domain, power is regarded as disruptive and illegitimate, i.e. negative. Managers and all employees have the latent power to disrupt or stop work, distort, filter and confuse information. It is often practised at times of low morale, irritation or stress and so on.

Relativity of power

The power of person 'A', must have salience for person 'B' or it is ineffective. Bribes may sway some people but repulse others; prestige and threats may bring about similar reactions. The effective amount of power that anyone has will constantly ebb and flow as the constituency in which it is exercised changes its membership.

Balance of power

There is a power equation; power is seldom one-sided — even a prisoner can 'hit back'. Negative power is often practised at work, for example, the power to disrupt production. One type of power can offset another, for example money can overrule loyalty.

Domain of power

Few sources of power are universally valid over all constituencies. Some people wish to extend their domain, or scope of power and diminish the domain of others. For example, one manager may wish to exert control and influence over a particular department or project at the expense of another manager's control and influence. Legitimate power or influence means that managers' domains of power are prescribed and recognized by others; the conditions under which and over whom it can be exercised have been laid down.

It is not always necessary to officially sanction such power; custom is a strong legitimizer, since power is often regarded as legitimate until challenged. Once challenged the power may not necessarily be destroyed but simply restricted. For example, the computer expert, once an unquestioned organizational genius, has seen his/her domain progressively restricted over recent years, although their expertise is seldom called into question.

Power at Enfield Social Services has shown itself in various ways. For instance, one member of staff at a residential care home has been in the post for 20 years and has 'more power over some individuals' than the manager herself. This is a kind of 'time-served' legitimized power where an individual literally overpowers younger and weaker staff members. The manager is presented with some difficulty over this situation, because it has been allowed to grow over the years and makes it impossible to implement any sanctions. The woman's power and influence has become the 'custom' and meets the expectations of the wider group and will have to be eroded by the different expectations of new members.

On a different location within Enfield, the manager prefers to rotate staff between shifts and between units; she says that this prevents people from becoming 'stale and forming power bases'.

Influence

Methods of influence

According to Charles Handy (1985), influence can be overt (seen) or covert (unseen). For example, where individuals are in a negotiating situation it is not difficult for the parties concerned to determine the areas in which influencing attempts are being made. In contrast, however, one might take any other situation where two or more people are involved in discussion; an observer can often identify where the individuals concerned modify their views as a result of the discussion but this frequently happens without the awareness of those being influenced. How many times have you heard people say 'it was my idea in the beginning and it received little acknowledgement at the time, but an hour later it came back as the boss's idea with full commitment!'?

Individual responses to influence

1 Compliance: accepted because it is in the recipients' best interests to do so;
2 Identification: the recipient adopts the idea or proposal because s/he admires or identifies with the source, the initiator of influence;
3 Internalization: the recipient adopts the ideas of proposals as his/her own. S/he internalizes it so that it becomes one of his/her possessions.

The following three sections are based on ideas developed by Melrose Films (1991).

Common influencing problems and their solutions

These problems and simple rules for overcoming them are just as successful when dealing with influencing difficulties inside the organization as they are to outside selling situations:

- Overselling: people often 'oversell' their position in order to be heard at all. However, too many reasons put forward or too much emphasis placed upon advocating a particular idea or position, etc. will result in the disbelief of others; it could make them think something like '. . . the person doth protest too much!'
  Recognize the intelligence, reasonableness and logic of others by being realistic about the claims you are making.
- Diluting benefits: again too many benefits will dilute interest. Seeking many reasons why someone should 'buy' something, or accept claims being made, will make benefits appear multi-purpose with no clear focus and detract from the value of the more legitimate, specific claims.
  It is more advisable to make an impact with the most important benefits of your claims, by concentrating on the specific areas for which they are intended and are best at addressing.
- Irritating remarks: such words as 'fair', 'reasonable', 'generous' are more often used in emotional blackmail and effective relationships are not developed in this way.
  Be positive and keep to the real benefits of your arguments and issues surrounding them.

Dealing with excuses

- As with all organizational activity, adequate preparation is key to effective behaviour and results. Excuses can often cloud issues, but the well-prepared manager will not be distracted by those trying to excuse their behaviour or ideas.

However, it is important not to make people feel threatened by any clear understanding we might be displaying while they are trying to defend themselves. We must remain calm, helpful and assertive in order to help others identify the problems which are causing their anxieties and which make them react defensively.

- Be assertive when you know your arguments are just and do not scale down any requests you make in order to fit others' authority or willingness; it may not, on some occasions, be appropriate to compromise or modify your position, especially in dealing with organizational objectives or procedures such as discipline or grievance.
- Make allies not enemies. If the 'excuse' is genuine, it is often useful to enlist the person's help in approaching those who can really help, or in assisting the person to identify the means of overcoming difficulties, whether they are only perceived to be, or really are problems.
- In dealing with an ultimatum – do not panic and take your time. Test understanding and summarize often (the problem may not turn out to be as extreme as you at first thought); be firm but flexible, do not gain a reputation as a 'soft touch' (you must work out an agreement); widen the debate, employ lateral thinking and influence the thinking of others away from the ultimatum by proving that there may be alternatives to consider.

Coping with aggression

Do not respond in kind when confronting aggression, otherwise no one will be listening! If you back off altogether, the aggressor will not change his/her thinking and nothing will be achieved; the problem will only be unnecessarily prolonged.

You need to respond assertively by stating your own needs, wants, feelings and opinions, directly and honestly. Listen to the other person calmly, test your understanding and be flexible but, above all, the aggressor must have his/her approach redirected and be allowed to state his/her position despite the initial aggression. It is most usual for aggression to subside when dealt with assertively, and the person does not lose sight of what s/he wants. You will feel very positive yourself afterwards.

Acknowledge the aggressive person's determination or anger and state the affect the aggression is having on you, for example feeling nervous or becoming angry in return or whatever it may be.

Make suggestions and direct the conversation towards a goal. It is possible that you will have to go round the cycle a few times before achieving your aim.

The use of negotiation

Some people seem to have an inborn ability to get results in conversations and negotiations. This is usually because they are assertive (as opposed to aggressive), or they are natural diplomats.

Although negotiating is not the same as just getting our own way, we recognize that there are skills needed to increase the benefit to us in any particular situation.

Handling disagreements and conflict

Conflict exists everywhere, and often provides the basic context in which we need to negotiate.

We bring values, attitudes, beliefs, needs and perceptions to any situation and it is inevitable that these will be opposed by those people who have different ones. This then causes conflict. What is important is how we deal with conflict. We can ignore it, seek solutions, or seek to control it. An important element is whether it adversely affects relations within an organization.

However, we are used to and experienced in dealing with conflicts in our everyday lives; househunting, buying cars, how to be entertained, etc. It can create emotional reaction – anger, hostility, frustration, pain. We should recognize these and avoid them wherever possible.

There are also some important equal opportunities implications in the way we deal with conflict and from an interview held recently with a manager of a culturally diverse organization, it can be concluded that a lot of ignorance exists regarding the differences of opinion, attitudes and beliefs with conflicting results. The manager concerned believes there is the need for confrontation to promote awareness and education, but that unless it is handled carefully with extra firmness and precision over the rules governing sensitive issues like equal opportunities, unhealthy conflict and stress will result.

Negotiation then, is often needed to resolve conflict. Resolving conflict does not mean just 'winning'. It means satisfying the interests of all concerned. Satisfying interests on both sides of a conflict or negotiation situation is called a 'win–win' outcome. It can only be achieved by understanding the needs or interests of all concerned.

Negotiation is the art of seeking agreement to the maximum advantage of all concerned. This statement bears some analysis. Notice that it says 'seeking agreement'. This means that merely trying to bully someone into accepting our position is not negotiation. It is not very effective either. We should not confuse the notion of seeking agreement with the notion of changing someone's mind. It is not necessary to do the latter to achieve the former.

The definition also uses the phrase 'maximum advantage'. This is because it may not be necessary to achieve all that is desirable in order to achieve the most important goals. Sometimes an element of compromise on minor issues can secure agreement on the major issues more readily than may be apparent at the beginning. This suggests that we start out with a clear idea of what we want (and the distinction between what we must have, as well as what we would like to have). It also suggests that we use our efforts to find out what the other person also must have, and on what they are willing to compromise.

Fisher and Ury (1984) offer four basic principles for successful negotiating:

1 Separate the people from the problem: when self-esteem is threatened, then people react. This in turn can cause a reaction that threatens the other person. The swapping of such emotions and attitudes inhibits proper negotiating. It is important to recognize that the issue that causes the problem is distinct from the people themselves.
2 Focus on interests, not positions: positions are not the same as goals. We can take a position as a point of principle, and let the real issue go. So, for instance, although someone might insist on a colleague being moved to another department (the position taken), the issue might really be to prevent adverse criticism (the interest).
3 Generate a variety of possibilities before deciding what to do: active listening is all important. Do not accept positions at face value. Focus on possible areas of agreement – not of disagreement.
4 Base results on objective standards: these ought to be quantifiable criteria. They are easiest to understand in the context of financial negotiations. It is always legitimate to ask 'how did you arrive at that figure?'. However, objective standards can always be found, whether quantifiable or not.

Mediating

Mediating in a conflict is a task that often falls to managers and can be fraught with difficulty. It should be dealt with as the facilitation of the agreement-seeking process by a third party (the manager).

How to mediate successfully

- Acknowledge conflict: if conflict is ignored, it will become difficult to control. Healthy conflict, when acknowledged, used and ideas allowed to develop in so using, positive outcomes are likely. When potential conflict can be identified and deemed unnecessary, it should be 'nipped in the bud' and thus avoided.
- Be neutral in relation to people: if you appear to take any one particular side when trying to mediate, you will not be mediating at

all, but applying extra pressures to influence the behaviour of the other party. Allow each to have their say and facilitate the parties' agreement for a way forward.

- Keep to issues: do not allow personalities to be discussed or questioned. The issues surrounding the conflict should be discussed openly and objectively thus keeping emotions to a minimum. It should be noted that sometimes it is impossible to keep emotion out of situations and those who feel that strongly about the issues should not be dismissed by anyone as irrational because of it.
- Seek clarification: be sure that everyone really understands what is being said by clarifying understanding and summarizing frequently.
- Focus on agreement: agreeing a way forward is what you should be trying to achieve. Ensure the parties are positively trying to agree on ways that each can work with.
- Be facilitator not judge; a judge states the 'crime' and pronounces the 'sentence' or punishment; a facilitator allows discussion of issues, provides the wherewithal for agreement and allows the parties concerned to reach their own conclusions and decide upon methods for resolving the difficulties.

How to convince people

- tell people when you agree with them;
- admit when you are wrong;
- do not argue;
- put the case, quote the evidence;
- use rationality, not emotion;
- deal with objections.

Creating effective workgroups

Effective teamworking

In order to create effective teamwork, individuals should be encouraged to:

- be open and honest in their dealings with others in the group;
- use mistakes; eliminate fear of punishment, rejection, etc.;
- use competition and conflict to reach agreements and avoid the unhealthy aspects of extreme competition and conflict;
- use relationships to build support and trust; no one should feel isolated or threatened by their choice of behaviour, etc.;
- ensure activities are productive and stimulating, sessions without objectives will be frustrating and time-wasting;
- provide the wherewithal for all to own the group's decisions; every-

one must be involved in the processes, contributing to them in their own unique ways;

- enable the group to take risks, depending upon circumstances and situations;
- recognize, acknowledge and compliment personal development;
- have clear and agreed objectives and roles.

Key factors in group behaviour

Development

Group development is concerned with the processes it undergoes. In general, when a group forms it is concerned with establishing the tasks it needs to perform, the rules associated with their activities and so on. Unfortunately, very few groups concentrate on the processes they go through at this early stage, which means that much is left unsaid and unresolved until issues and/or personality difficulties emerge at a later date.

The next stage in the development cycle is where individuals explore the possibilities between them, generally known as 'storming' followed by establishing the norms relevant to the activities of the group; where individuals agree the way they will make and implement decisions. The group then begins to perform and get things done.

Size and cohesiveness

The size of the group influences its behaviour; a group with more than twelve individuals will lose cohesiveness and sub-groups will begin to form in order to develop closer working relationships. As implied, the cohesiveness of groups (or the attractiveness of the group to individual members) is inversely correlated to the size of the group.

Group norms

As norms are established for the overall behaviour of the group, any deviance, or the joining of a new member, will result in group pressures affecting their performance and behaviour, with the expectation that individuals will conform. Leaders are likely to bring relevant individuals to the group in order to optimize the group's effectiveness and limit unhealthy conflicts and competition.

However, if the leader is looking for changes or to break up any 'groupthink' (Janis, 1972) which may have developed (the denial of important or essential information or evidence which threatens the normal thinking and behaviour of the group and which is therefore manipulated or ignored), the leader may wish to bring in someone who is able to resist the pressures to conform. Such individuals will gradually gain credibility through whatever strengths they happen to possess and will eventually influence the original group away from its accepted norms.

To provide a practical example of this, it is appropriate at this stage to return to the interview with one of the two residential care managers at Enfield Social Services.

In this particular home there is the opportunity, after a long period of 'ringfencing', for the manager to recruit seven new people. The manager says that when the new people join, they will be encouraged to find out all relevant information including actions taken at the beginning of each shift (this has not been an accepted norm within the existing group) which, she is hoping, will influence the other care assistants to do the same.

The manager is looking for different types of people and while some of the existing people might resist the new influences and choose to leave, she is convinced that most will respond positively by eventually allowing the group norms to change in order to keep and develop their jobs.

Leadership

Leadership is discussed elsewhere in this chapter in some detail, but it must be remembered that without effective leadership which adopts the styles necessary to motivate and develop the group, the group is unlikely to ever become effective.

In looking once again at Enfield Social Services, the manager at Ian McLeod House is clear about her achievements so far; she has successfully turned around the longstanding culture demonstrated by previous assistant managers who have now moved on, to one where staff are developed and encouraged to find out what the residents think and want.

A young care assistant who has recently been promoted to care officer will be assisting the manager in the recruitment of the new staff. According to the manager, the care officer concerned is very young 'young enough to be daughter to some staff members' but who has the potential to become a good manager in time. The young woman has recently completed a supervisory skills course and is ready to put her learning into practice. The manager says she will only intervene when absolutely necessary; that she is a very assertive young woman who deals with the staff very well. According to the manager some members of staff have difficulty differentiating between anger and assertiveness and that they must learn when to say 'No' appropriately.

Individual role identity

Every member of a workgroup has something specific to offer; some will co-ordinate the activities and ideas of others; some prefer to come up with all the ideas, but have little patience for honing them to implementation; some will reflect on their own and others' actions and decisions and analyse their usefulness, etc. Others will analyse current situations and determine the logic of plans and ideas; others have contacts outside the immediate group and are good at finding out things and obtaining information and additional resources. Still others like to get jobs completed and move onto the next challenge and so on. (For a detailed analysis of ideal group membership, see Belbin, 1991.)

All membership has its purpose; each will exhibit mixtures of introversion and extroversion in varying degrees according to the occasion, circumstance and need. Each individual must be motivated, according to their various needs and expectations, through encouragement and recognition, without the fear of threat or recrimination and be dealt with sensitively by leaders who are aware.

Action planning

1 Analyse your own behaviour in terms of strengths (positive outcomes) and weaknesses (negative effects), in dealing with actual work-based occurrences with regards to the various relationship situations discussed in this chapter.

2 Decide how you might deal with them differently in the future and what are your immediate training requirements and future development needs.

3 Discuss them with your immediate boss and negotiate how you might address them.

9 Communicating effectively outside the organization

The overall competence focus of this chapter is:

● to maintain and improve service and product operations.

which will be developed by the ability to:

● maintain operations to meet quality standards;
● create and maintain the necessary conditions for productive work.

involving the following dimensions of personal competence:

- showing concern for excellence;
- setting and prioritizing objectives;
- monitoring and responding to actual against planned activities;
- showing sensitivity to the needs of others;
- relating to others;
- presenting oneself positively to others;
- obtaining the commitment of others;
- showing self-confidence and personal drive;
- managing personal emotions and stress;
- collecting and organizing information;
- identifying and applying concepts.

Objectives of this chapter

● recognize the role of communication in marketing;
● know and appreciate the value of various market research techniques;
● recognize the purpose, techniques and the range of activities in acquiring information about products, markets and customer needs and perceptions;
● understand the need to apply various environmental analysis techniques to strategic decision-making;
● recognize the function, benefits and processes involved in advertising activity;
● recognize the function, benefits and processes involved in public relations activities;
● practise the skills of active listening to identify needs;

- promote the benefits of a product/service to meet an identified need;
- recognize the function, benefits and processes involved in other means of marketing communications.

Introduction

Communication is a strategic activity. Not only is it a part of the process of developing goals and objectives but it is also an integral part of incorporating those goals and objectives in terms of profile and branding.

External communications are the processes by which we send the messages about our companies or organizations, and/or its products or services, to potential or actual customers.

For some organizations, communicating to the outside world is seen as merely advertising but it is, in fact, a much more complex and broad set of activities.

In the 1990s and beyond there will be many challenges facing organizations of all types and if they do not recognize the significance of these challenges to their own work practices, they are unlikely to survive into the twenty-first century.

Some of the challenges already having impact on the economy are:

- increased market competition;
- rapid technological change;
- the 'ageing' of people who work in these organizations, as demographic changes produce a reduction of available young people.

To meet these challenges, organizations are being prompted to invest in people and ensure that valuable human assets are given the best possible chance to maximize potential, just like any other appreciating valuable asset. This investment, it is contended, can only be truly realized through meaningful and relevant training (*Investors in People*, 1990).

The justification of this statement will become clear as this chapter unfolds; each section itself addressing the complexities involved in understanding, addressing and meeting customer needs in the coming decades.

Communicating with the customer

In the corporate context communication is essentially a sub-discipline of marketing. Marketing has to do with an exchange relationship in which all parties derive satisfaction. The exchange need not be for goods or money. Initially conceived in the commercial world, and still mainly associated with commerce – marketing principles are being adopted in the 'selling' of ideology (political parties), of personnel (employment applications), of a social consciousness ('Keep Britain Tidy'), of health (anti-smoking) and so on.

The concept is based on the exchange of value for mutual satisfaction, which depends for its success on the correct identification of the buyer's needs by the seller and supplying what the buyer actually needs so that satisfaction actually occurs. The supplier is also concerned to be satisfied; this may be in terms other than the commercial notion of profit. For example in the public sector; 'the effective, efficient and economic delivery of a service'.

Three elements must be present in order for an organization to claim it is truly marketing oriented:

1 It must be customer oriented – concerned primarily with the needs of customers and to co-ordinate activities which allow the organization to determine those needs.
2 Its efforts must be integrated to create consistency, avoid duplication, capitalize on individual skills and personal creativity, and by so doing, create 'synergy' (the value of effects which are more than the sum of the individual parts).
3 Clear objectives must be established with the identification of the performance 'indicators', (outcomes desired to determine relevant organizational activities needed to ensure the successful achievement of these outcomes) which will facilitate the development of appropriate control measurements to monitor performance and progress.

The marketing mix

The expression 'Marketing Mix' is a term first coined for the concept of marketing as an integrative function in 1952 by Neil Borden, a US advertising executive and has been used as part of the marketing vocabulary ever since. There are many elements to the marketing mix, but Jerome McCarthy (1960) popularized a four-fold classification of these variables, called the 'Four Ps': Product, Price, Place and Promotion.

Communications are vital to every element of the marketing mix and good communications techniques can be applied to each element of the mix in the following ways:

1 Price and positioning: messages about price competitiveness, value-added benefits, quality and style – positioning is not what you do with a product or service, but the effects your messages have on the minds of the customers.
2 Products: consumer information, analysis of benefits, etc.

3 Promotion: from advertising and sales promotion to packaging and point of sale displays.
4 Place: the physical distribution of the product or service where they will reach the targeted customer effectively and conveniently.

As with any other communication activity, we need to examine:

What :   the message is we are trying to communicate;
Whom: the message is for − the target market;
How :   to reach them − the media to carry the message;
Why :   choose the product mix we do? As the environment, the technology and the products change over time, so must the rationale.

Identifying the right 'messages'

Getting the message across

The variety of messages required to keep a company functioning efficiently in the market-place is vast. So too is the variety of target audiences and media to carry them.

In each case, the purpose is to ensure:

- recognition;
- quality;
- consistency.

of the message.

Media campaigns can be very efficient at promoting a single, often simple idea about a company or its products/services. They often concentrate on a USP (Unique Selling Point), with a memorable phrase, or strapline, e.g. 'When it positively, definitely, has to be there on time'; 'Probably the best lager in the world'. To what or whom do these lines refer? The recognition, quality and consistency factors apply in all aspects of a company's communications.

Corporate branding

It is often very important for a company to promote recognition of its own name, as well as its products or services. This is often done with the enhancement of visual recognition techniques such as colour, corporate logos, and so on.

London Underground is recognized, not just in London, or even nationally, but the world over, by its very distinctive corporate branding. This is based on the use of its distinct roundel, and the use of its own typeface (called New Johnstone, and a variation of the Gill typeface). Another very strong feature of this recognition comes from the distinctive London Underground map. It is unusual in that it is not a 'real' map, in the normal sense that the distances shown are to scale. It is a topological map, which shows the spatial relationships of the lines and stations. It was designed for London Underground in 1933, by Henry Beck, complete with the distinctive colours for the lines that existed then. In substance, it has changed very little since its invention.

The roundel, the insignia style and the Underground map are protected very carefully by London Underground, so as not to dilute the power of their distinctive symbols.

The telephone

The telephone is often the first line of response to customers, or the public at large, for many organizations. But what sort of impression do your customers get from your company/organization?

Try phoning your own organization from outside. What sort of response do you get? Is it prompt, helpful, informative, efficient?

It would be a pity to spend millions of pounds on a major media campaign to promote a product/service or company, and have it spoiled because customers are treated badly by your telephonists. Yet this does happen all too often. Malcolm Peel (1987) identifies five steps to help in his 'telephone checklist':

How to use the 'phone effectively –

  i) Get good equipment. Modern technology now enables real sophistication in call storage, diversion and transfer.
  ii) Give technical training. Obviously this applies to telephonists, but all staff should be able to use divert, 'follow me', and other facilities, if they are available.
  iii) Structure the job right. Good support and guidance for telephone operators are essential in helping them to give effective customer service.
  iv) Establish good discipline. How to deal with various types of enquiry, personal calls, peak time procedures. Are they allowed to take messages for individuals?
  v) Behavioural training. If telephonists are the voice of your organisation, make sure that it is a voice you would like your customers to hear when they 'phone. Is the greeting courteous? Does it identify the organisation in the proper way? These are all important.

Internal communications

While it may seem odd to consider internal communications in a chapter specifically concerned with external communications, there are occasions when it is impossible to separate the two. It should also be noted that the techniques and standards which should be applied are very similar in both cases. In much of the current literature about the effectiveness of management, and in the growing body of literature that examines successful organizations, a consensus is emerging. It suggests that successful organizations are those that communicate their mission to their own staff, motivate them to perform, and train and empower them to make decisions and to achieve success.

At each stage, communication plays a vital role. Obviously, an important aspect of this is the interpersonal communication that takes place throughout an organization and at every level. This is dealt with in more detail in previous chapters. Corporate communication to staff as a body is in itself like a marketing exercise to a specialized group of internal customers.

Such internal corporate communications can be used for many purposes:

- Information: ensuring everyone receives the information they need in order to fulfil their individual and departmental objectives, based upon the overall corporate mission.
- Corporate branding: to ensure all 'internal customers' have full understanding of the corporate image and reflect the agreed standards in all their activities.
- Training: to provide benefits to the organization which will be reflected in: increased profitability; increased turnover; higher quality; improved image/reputation; better ways of meeting client needs and so on.
- Teambuilding and integration: by defining and promoting cultural values and norms.
- Motivation: the organization's 'internal customers' will be more highly motivated if they understand what, and grow to identify with, the corporate image.
- Social bonding: internal messages about corporate image and identity will enhance interpersonal relationships and create a sense of belonging.

Establishing customer needs and simple market research techniques

Market research

If marketing is the process whereby we 'identify, anticipate and satisfy customer requirements profitably', then we need systematic means of undertaking each of these stages.

Market research is the process by which we research the nature of customer tastes and preferences, and by which we measure their satisfaction with products and services. It is one of the means of forecasting demand in the market-place which might be included among the following:

- buyer intentions;
- sales force assessment;
- trends analysis;
- market research;
- leading indicators;
- comparative studies;
- experimental research.

The scope of market research

Market research is generally agreed to give information about the following:

- buyers' habits;
- demography;
- consumer product/service knowledge;
- opinions/attitudes;
- intentions;
- motives;
- perceptions.

It operates in two key dimensions. The first is in acquiring information about current products/services, and their position in the market. The second is in identifying new market opportunities.

Some of the most important techniques

Panels

These are a selected sample of a target population who give interviews and express opinions on a regular basis. A problem with using panels is in assessing the reliability and validity of the information they give.

A more specific technique is the retail audit, which is used to establish brand share and volume sales.

Qualitative

This is the acquisition of opinions, reactions and behaviour. It can take many forms and it can be carried out by interview, questionnaire, or by informal means.

Media research

This involves identifying the size and nature of audiences for advertisements in various media. It can also be used to audit the effectiveness of specific advertisements. Researchers look for evidence of 'spontaneous recall', or 'prompted recall' of a product or service.

Test marketing

The various processes by which new products are tried out on customers to gauge reaction. It is used to reduce the chances of expensive failures.

Preference mapping

This is a specific technique for analysing the customer perceptions of the benefits of a product or product range.

Interviews and panels are used to identify significant attributes. These attributes are tested with sample groups to identify priority order, and eliminate unimportant ones. For instance, with training shoes, the key attributes might be price and style.

Then a selected sample of customers are asked to rate their ideal product/service in terms of the attributes identified. This rating is quantified so that the responses can be mapped onto a matrix like the one below (see Figure 9.1):

When more than two attributes are identified, the matrix becomes multidimensional. In the final phase, real products/services are rated and compared to the ideal product.

The advantage of this method is that a very clear picture of a product or service can be drawn in terms of customer response. So, if your product is identified as being too expensive, then countering strategies can be drawn up – either to reduce price, or to emphasize value added aspects.

This technique works better for well understood products or services, or ranges thereof, than it does for potential or innovative products or services.

Where customers or clients are also citizens with social needs

Some readers of this chapter may feel that marketing is of little relevance to them because they serve a 'market' of an entirely different sort. For instance, those working in parts of the public or

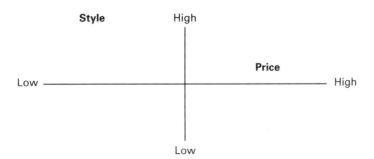

Figure 9.1 *Customer ratings matrix*

voluntary sectors may believe that some of the concepts discussed here are quite irrelevant when addressing, for example, the needs of the elderly in residential care homes.

For the purposes of relating some of these theories to such situations, consider the following information obtained from interviews with the two managers quoted earlier in this book:

1 Instead of enabling clients to develop their independence within one of the homes, a care assistant was actually leading others into 'disabling' the clients by telling them what to do, how to do it and what not to do, etc. The manager believes it is simply a matter of educating both staff and clients who may believe that providing attention in a continued 'fussing over others and doing things for them' manner is the correct behaviour. According to the manager 'it is difficult to convert to a customer care culture and to break down the "you do this and fit into our routine", approach, but an important challenge'.

Before the manager joined the care team, residents had no locks on their doors and the doors were also kept permanently wide open so that an 'eye could be kept on them'. When the manager discussed the idea of privacy and locks on residents' doors with the team, an uproar ensued. The general excuse made was that the 'corridor would be dark'. The locks were eventually fitted, but staff and residents alike found the idea very difficult to accept initially.

2 Clothing was another issue. Care assistants had habitually produced whatever clothes they thought the residents should wear. Now the clients are being asked what they would like to wear and proper discussions and questioning about such issues are replacing the well-intentioned, but inappropriate control of client interests.

3 The manager believes that staff must continue to identify residents' needs and wishes and work towards those, instead of always telling them what to do. If they continue to concentrate on residents' disabilities, the results will be negative. Therefore they must concentrate on individuals' strengths and abilities for positive outcomes. The negative results, and indeed the disabilities themselves, she says, will then recede into the background.

The organization and its environment

A major responsibility for organizations is to monitor and search the environment for new opportunities. Sometimes motivation of those concerned may be low in times of recession. In fact, difficult times require even more thorough searches, because it is at these times that opportunities are more easily missed. It can also be said that the lack of opportunity searching can be one of the causes of recessions in particular industries or even whole economies.

A company's marketing environment consists of the actors and forces external to the marketing management function of the firm that impinge on the marketing management's ability to develop and maintain successful transactions with its target customers.' Kotler, (1986).

The actors referred to by Kotler in his definition of an organization's marketing environment include those operating in the micro-environment and the macro-environment.

There are two basic tools used by managers to analyse and understand the environment in which their organizations operate:

1 Strengths, Weaknesses, Opportunities and Threats (or SWOT): analysis for the micro-environment and
2 Sociological, Technological, Economic and Political (STEP): analysis for the macro-environment.

SWOT analysis and the micro-environment

The Strengths and Weaknesses part of SWOT, stresses the internal environment and past and present experiences; while the Opportunities and Threats focus on the external environment and potential future experiences. Remember, every threat to an organization also poses an opportunity, or a challenge, although they are not entirely mutually exclusive!

1 The organization; requiring managers to constantly ask themselves questions like:
   • what are we in business for?
   • is the original mission still appropriate?
   • how often do we redefine our objectives?
   • should we be changing direction, e.g. markets, products/services?
   • what are the major strengths and weaknesses of the organization in the past and the present in providing appropriate goods or services.
2 The organization's suppliers; requiring a constant review of:
   • relevance of suppliers used;
   • whether the organization is 'supplier led'; what are the choices for alternatives?
   • whether they continue to supply effectively and efficiently;
   • whether their supplies are and will continue to be appropriate;
   • whether delivery continues to be reliable and timely;
   • would vertical integration (taking them over) be more beneficial to the organization?
3 marketing intermediaries, e.g.:
   • 'middlemen'; e.g. agents, brokers, wholesalers, etc.:
     – are they necessary?
     – are they cost effective and a value to the organization?

- are there alternative ways of reselling goods/services?
- physical distribution firms; requiring constant review of:
  - whether customers continue to be reached through their channels;
  - whether their selling pitch is appropriate and accurate;
  - their ability/inclination to promote the organization's products or services;
  - whether they need training/development in promoting the organization's products or services;
  - whether they continue to be needed at all;
  - would vertical integration be appropriate here?
- marketing service agencies: e.g. marketing research firms; consulting firms; advertising agencies, etc.:
  - how often are their services reviewed?
  - are they cost effective?
  - do they reach the relevant markets and so on?
- financial intermediaries: e.g. banks; credit companies; insurance companies, etc.:
  - does the organization continue to get good deals?
  - when were their services last reviewed?
  - what are the alternatives, etc.?
4 customers; how does the organization determine:
  - who they are?
  - where they are?
  - what their needs are?
  - does the organization address their needs?
  - does the organization fulfil their needs? and so on.
5 competitors; does the organization:
  - carry out regular competitor analyses to determine:
    - who they are?
    - where they are?
    - their strengths and weaknesses?
    - their major threats to the organization's goods and service?
    - whether they also analyse the market thoroughly to determine where the opportunities are?
  - determine what benefits the organization offers to customers which are specific and unique as compared to competitors?
6 public institutions: e.g. financial; media; government; education; citizen-action. Does the organization understand and address the influences these institutions have nationally in:
  - the ability of the organization to obtain funds;
  - the effects of publicity on the organization − good and bad;
  - what implications the impact of local government policies may have on organizational strategy;
  - the effects of any local initiatives in training and education policies;
  - public opinion towards the organization's products, services, recruitment and retention, environmental policies and so on.

While not very easy the first time you try it, SWOT analysis is an excellent tool to help managers reflect objectively. The criteria used is largely up to you; you may wish to analyse the management function areas appropriate to your organization or the desired outcomes/impacts which are expected as a result of strategic decision-making, whatever you consider most appropriate to your particular area of work. Once you have made the attempt, you will find future exercises will become more sophisticated as you repeat the procedure, and you will become more discerning in the criteria you use and the judgements you make.

STEP analysis and the macro-environment

Similarly a STEP analysis can become more useful to you as you become more practised in its application. This is a detailed analysis of the external environment looking nationally and internationally as necessary. STEP is an acronym for Sociological, Technological, Economic and Political environment. In detail managers might look at the following implications:

- demography: because people make up markets, organizations' need to constantly monitor the changes in:
  - birthrate: which is declining in the UK;
  - population: which is ageing and organizations' need to consider policies which address needs appropriately;
  - changes in the family: e.g. single parents; remarriage following divorce; increases in fostering and adoption, etc.;
  - rises in non-family households: more couples are choosing not to have families;
  - geographical shifts in population: these are likely to prove more important in the UK as multinationals move to rural districts;
  - better-educated population: increasing the need to address marketing in the service sectors;
  - changing ethnic and racial population: requiring different cultural needs to be addressed.
- economic environment: requiring the analysis of the total purchasing power which includes four main trends:
  - slowdown of the real-income growth;
  - continued inflationary pressure;
  - low savings and high debt − mortgages, bank loans, etc.;
  - changing consumer expenditure patterns.
- physical environment: which requires attention to causes of the erosion of the ozone layer; diminishing rain forests and the general diminution of the world's natural resources including:
  - impending shortages of certain raw materials;
  - increased cost of energy;
  - increased levels of pollution;
  - strong government intervention in natural-resource management.

- technological environment: as one of the most dramatic forces shaping people's destiny, requiring organizations to address:
  - the accelerating pace of technological change;
  - unlimited innovational opportunities;
  - improving research and development;
  - minor improvements rather than major discoveries;
  - increasing regulation of technological change.
- political/legal environment: comprising laws, government agencies and pressure groups, requiring organizations to consider the implications of:
  - substantial legislation regulating British business;
  - increases in government agencies and sub-contracting;
  - growth of public-interest groups.
- socio/cultural environment: which are the combined effects of experiences shaping people's beliefs, values, attitudes, norms and behaviour. Organizations need to consider:
  - how persistent are core cultural values in the changing environment?
  - that each culture consists of subcultures;
  - that secondary cultural values undergo shifts through time.

The issues within STEP which you use for analysis will vary between organizations and between the circumstances confronting them. Many major organizational changes are made as a result of analysing STEP regularly and thoroughly. The secret to successful application of SWOT and STEP analyses is a manager's ability to communicate the messages effectively to senior management teams.

The author sometimes superimposes the OT part of the SWOT analysis onto STEP; it can be very enlightening and insightful to an innovative manager.

Simple negotiation and selling techniques

Selling skills

If we consider selling to be 'convincing someone of the advantages of accepting your position', then we can interpret it in a wide way. Some of us will be involved in selling products or services to customers face to face. Many more will have a marketing role. Nearly everyone will be involved in persuading internal customers to 'buy' an idea we are 'selling', whether it be a new project, or a new system. The theory and practice of selling is a personal skill, and it is the communication skill par excellence. By putting the theory and practice to good use, everyone can benefit, not just those who have the responsibility for moving products or services to individual customers. It can inform much of our persuasive activity.

Features benefits and positioning

When we sell we are looking to satisfy customers' needs. Clearly the most important element of selling is to find out what those needs are. This is interesting because it contradicts many people's notions of what selling is. They seem to characterize it as talking and persuading. In fact listening is a much more important skill. Again, our active listening skills come to the fore. It is necessary to look more closely at products and services, and what they are in a customer's eyes.

The features of a product or service are the technical or user characteristics that make a product or service interesting. On a video recorder, a 7-day timer is a feature. For a shop, 7-day opening is a feature.

A benefit is the advantage gained by the customer by virtue of the features.

So, if we are selling furniture, we might sell the benefit of comfort. For certain types of car we might sell status or speed.

Positioning is about the way that we promote the image of a product/service, a range of products/services, or a brand name.

The most important aspect of this knowledge is that we sell benefits, not features. Most potential customers will not be interested in the finer working of the epicyclic overdrive capacitor. They will be seeking the answer to the question 'What can it do for me?' This can only be answered if we work to uncover what their needs really are.

Identifying needs

Most people have needs. They are not always expressed explicitly and strongly − particularly at the opening of a sales presentation. Initially, needs are expressed as a dissatisfaction with some aspect of the current situation. The need grows eventually to a stronger and more positive commitment to a particular solution. Research shows that selling is much more efficient when it is directed to a strong explicit need than to a weak and implicit one:

- A weak implicit need might be: 'Our order processing is not very efficient.'
- A strong, explicit need might be: 'I need a photocopier that will count copies used by our different departments.'

To return to some practical examples obtained from one of the residential care homes surveyed. As a result of interviewing and finding out their client needs, the management team improved the information and facilities available to residents as follows:

- brochures available from area doctors' surgeries;

- special transport arrangements in the area;
- a suggestion book;
- a simplified complaints procedure;
- computerized menus, with large print for the short-sighted;
- regular meetings for clients and relatives;
- various clubs were introduced;
- regular and special outings were arranged;
- pictures for walls were provided;
- public relations activities introduced;
- summer and Christmas bazaars introduced;
- open days were arranged;
- donations encouraged from residents, families, local services, etc. and proper mechanisms for thanking them.
  (Many things seem so obvious − after they have been discovered!)

If we know we are seeking to encourage customers to tell us their needs, we need to think about how to construct a sales presentation that enables us to do this.

The sales presentation

A one-to-one sales presentation should have structure and purpose, and should have the following phases:

- Courtesy/introduction: this involves introducing ourselves and establishing rapport. We have already talked about the importance of good first impressions and nowhere are they more important than here. Look back at the rules for creating a good impression.
- Exploration: this phase is really the one where we identify the needs of the customer. It is vital that we give the customer the opportunity to tell us what their needs are − not the other way around. Research shows that successful selling occurs when buyers do more talking than sellers. Where we do talk, we should be actively seeking − not telling at this stage. What we need to do is to talk about the most interesting thing in the world to our customer − themselves! Again, our active listening skills are crucial here.

Once we have explored and identified explicit needs, we move on to the next stage.

- Offering solutions: it is only now that we can offer solutions. The solution offered relates directly to the expressed need. The key idea is to match benefits to needs. This will be followed by discussion, objections, reinforcement.
  Many books on sales technique talk about buying signals. These are basically the customer 'trying out' the ideas in their minds. They may range from vague interest to a genuine objection. Your job is to pick up these signals, find out their significance and

respond accordingly. Once you see a level of commitment developing you should move on to the last phase.

- Closing the deal: there are really no rules about closing a deal, although there are many books that give advice, information, techniques and so on. The major objective is to seek a level of commitment. The level of that commitment will depend mainly on the customer and the circumstances.

'Would you like to pay cash or cheque', is a nice close, but it does not work like that every time. It may be that the maximum commitment a customer can or will give is to see the product/ service in action, to use it for a week on trial, or any other commitment up to on the spot purchase. The skill is finding the maximum level of commitment that the customer is comfortable with (and has the authority to provide!).

More formal presentations

These have more formal requirements:

Written and oral sales presentations

The written presentation should:

- summarize your understanding of the customer's situation and needs;
- describe key features and benefits of the proposed services and how they will meet customer needs;
- summarize costs;
- project your offer as different to and/or better than others';
- enable the client to evaluate your services, products and reputation;
- communicate your message in a way that is appealing and intelligible to the decision-makers.

Oral presentations should:

- get and keep the listeners' attention;
- keep them interested in what you have to say;
- spotlight four or five benefits or points of major interest to the customer;
- answer questions and clarify any points necessary.

What you should find out about the customer

1 Assemble and evaluate information about:
    - technical, financial and historical information, this may be abstracted from client documentation to ensure accuracy;
    - the personnel involved: their main interests; the level of their technical expertise, particularly in relation to your products and

services; the interpersonal relationships between them; (you will need to 'pitch' your presentation according to the culture of the organization and the apparent power bases);
- the state of the relevant industry: whether it is a new industry; if it is expanding or declining; who are the major competitors, etc.;
- major problems currently faced by the organization: a SWOT and STEP analysis is useful here, but at the very least you should discover whether the industry confronts the possibility of takeover; the implications of any major technological advances; important changes which are either pending or being avoided by the organization;
- the reasons the customer wishes to consider your proposal: it may be purely economic; for example a local authority may be more interested in in-company training provided by an academic institution than a leading consultancy, based purely on the costs involved; whether they are seeking to short circuit any improvements they should be considering; maybe your product or service is of higher quality standards than others, and so on;

2 Identify the prospective decision-makers and pitch your presentation according to expertise, degree of influence, the role they perform (their information needs will vary accordingly).
3 Gain information quickly and effectively. Make full use of published material, knowledge held by colleagues and associates and use questioning techniques appropriate to eliciting free speaking (open-ended questions), and specific information (closed questions).

Find out what the customer needs and how you can meet the need

1 Actively identify needs by responding fully to expressed (recognized) needs and seeking out unrecognized (but real) needs. Needs may be personal, task oriented, or organizational.
2 Decide which services could be helpful in meeting needs and assisting in the solution of problems, identify the benefits and link a feature (attributes of the service) to the benefit (what's in it for the customer) it brings.
3 Customers do not buy services; they are looking for a bundle of benefits.
4 Analyse the strengths and weaknesses of your organization's services; demonstrate the strengths and minimize the weaknesses.
5 Demonstrate clearly what your organization can do more effectively than any other.
6 Assess the personalities on your team as appropriate counterparts to the customer's team of decision-makers.

How to make the sale

1 Be effective: the content of your delivery should match the

customer's needs and your delivery should demonstrate that you are confident, perceptive, responsive and enthusiastic. You should use humour, listening skills and show ability to think on your feet; provide all information needed for the customer to make a decision; present information with different emphases according to the individuals in your audience.

2 Present the right image – personal and professional.

3 Communicate with skill (as discussed in other chapters of this book).

4 Deal with objections: anticipate them and formulate responses; seek to forestall them; if raised, respond to them by probing the nature of the problem raised – an apparent objection may be a device to seek further information.

5 Find out about your competitors: who they are; where they are; their strengths and weaknesses and which major strengths you will have to compete against in this instance.

6 If you are unsuccessful! Failure to obtain an organization's commitment is still a valuable learning experience. Capitalize on the investment put into it:

- review the whole process;
- identify precisely what you have learned;
- identify other opportunities for your services or products;
- build contacts.

The value and use of advertising and public relations

Advertising

Advertising has been called 'The means of making known in order to sell goods and services'.

It is easy to associate advertising with the high profile, expensive TV campaigns, but advertising can be carried in many different media:

- press,
- TV,
- posters and transport,
- cinema,
- radio,
- direct mail.

The choice depends on a number of factors, one of the most important of which is budget. There are, of course, other considerations. Examples would be the difference between trade and consumer advertising, and the amount of information needed to convey the message, or arouse interest. For instance, it would be difficult to describe the features of a high-tech item of equipment in a short TV ad, but it could be used to stimulate interest. Instructions can be provided for potential customers to seek further information.

Marketing tasks that can be performed well by advertising include:

- new product/service launches;
- complementing face-to-face or telephone advertising activities;
- entering new markets;
- inviting enquiries;
- direct selling;
- creating images;
- selling services.

Although many small and medium-sized enterprises will devise and execute advertising campaigns for themselves, larger companies will use specialist agencies to do this work for them. People who do this need to know how to get the best from such agencies, and their priorities and methods of working are instructive for the 'do it yourself' organizations.

Advertising agencies

Agencies have all the experience, expertise and resources necessary to manage the complex processes involved in any campaign. They are organized into specialist departments which undertake different functional activities. These usually include:

- Creative Department: these include the thinkers and visualizers, whose job it is to create concepts and ideas from a brief.
- Media Department: who recommend an appropriate media for a campaign, and who can also 'buy' the space for the individual advertisements.
- Production Department: their job is the writing, design, illustration, photography, film and print, to realize a concept.
- Account Management: whose job it is to manage the whole process to budget and schedule, and to act as liaison with the client.

Choosing an agency

Of course, there are many ways of choosing an agency. A common one for major accounts is called competitive pitching. In this, a number of agencies are invited to work up creative ideas in response to a written brief. This can work very well for the client, as they can judge the potential effectiveness of a campaign from the ideas proposed.

Not all agencies will expend the time and effort needed for this process. For instance, Bartle, Bogle and Hegarty are famous for declining to do just that. They will produce a credentials briefing, where they provide evidence of success based on completed projects. Only when they are contracted will they throw the full weight of their creative team into a campaign.

The brief

The needs of the client are specified in a document called a brief. Because it is the basis from which the creative team builds the campaign, it must contain all of the information they need, and it is vital to get it right. It is quite common for the agency to assist the client in drawing up the brief. Some are expert at turning the vague statements and ideas of the client into a powerful and workable brief. However, it is preferable for the client to control the whole process and better results will be obtained if they can communicate their needs clearly to the agency.

The brief should cover five main areas:

- objectives and tasks;
- background to company and products/services;
- target markets;
- constraints/issues/interests;
- media.

The more clues provided, the more accurate the response is likely to be.

Public relations

The function

Public Relations or PR is the range of activities that seeks to place messages and ideas about organizations and products or services into the media. Unlike advertising, it does not prepare and control specific adverts, but seeks to gain profile through news and features. However, it is not concerned solely with print media, and it can encompass a huge variety of activities. Among them are:

- press releases;
- research reports;
- events, such as conferences (including press conferences);
- personal appearances, e.g. on TV or radio talk shows;
- crisis management;
- information services;
- specific briefings, e.g. for financial journalists;
- sponsorship.

Quite often, some of the basic activities are covered by in-house press and publicity departments. Even where there is an internal service, one of its functions may be to brief and contract the outside specialist services of a PR consultancy. As well as having the whole range of expertise necessary to manage a campaign on a day-to-day basis, such agencies also have established contacts with people in the trade or consumer press, and can often place features, or gain exposure for press information beneficial to their clients.

As with advertising agencies, PR consultancies vary in their strengths, and in the services they offer. Some of this information can be obtained from trade directories such as Hollis, but a credentials pitch for a number of likely candidates is a better way to get a feel for the strengths of an agency. They differ in a number of ways:

- Size: from an individual consultant, up to the large consultancies like Biss Lancaster or the Rowland group;
- Style: from the traditional to the more youthful and upmarket agencies like Lynne Franks;
- Specialisms: most agencies are generic, but all have particular specialisms like finance, fashion or leisure.

Although it may seem like a soft spend, with little chance of auditing its own effectiveness, PR should be able to quantitatively justify its activities, like any other area of the business. If you wish to commission a PR consultancy you should expect them to project cost benefits from the work they do. One of the best measures of their effectiveness is the amount of column inches of advertising space that they have gained on your behalf. This can be costed quite easily.

The brief

As with advertising agencies, PR consultancies work best when they are properly briefed. The same criteria apply, and so the brief should contain:

- objectives and tasks;
- background to company and products;
- target markets (this could include customers, employees, share-holders, community and all other stakeholders);
- constraints/issues/interests;
- media.

In response to this brief, the consultancy should offer a complete service to manage outgoing information to reach target markets, whether they be trade or consumer, and it should specify the targeted media and the means of reaching them.

Campaigns usually involve a mixture of ongoing press activities, together with specific projects aimed at particular targets. In fact, it should be possible to list activities and target groups separately.

Alternatively, they can be shown in a matrix, giving specific details.

In order to draw up a PR programme for a local building project, for example it would be necessary to start by defining the target groups that need to be reached. These might include:

- banks/financial institutions;
- Department of Environment;
- local planning authorities;
- local politicians;
- national pressure groups;
- local residents;
- press;
- local pressure groups;
- professionals.

Events and activities might include:

- information pack;
- visits to site;
- press releases/articles;
- press conferences;
- photographs;
- competition/education;
- exhibitions.

These can then be plotted on a two by two matrix, and details added (see Figure 9.2):

Other marketing communications

There are a number of other means of promoting profile, products and services direct to potential customers. These can be broadly classified as marketing communications, and highlighted here are a few of the most important ones.

Direct mail

Direct mail is the sending of information to specified and identified target individuals or businesses. As end-user consumers, we often call it junk mail. Despite there being some negative connotations to the concept, its wide use testifies to its effectiveness, when it is well done and properly targeted. It usually contains product or service information, together with some sort of inducement to buy. Two of the most popular forms are leaflets and letters.

As a receiver of junk mail yourself, you will know that the one thing you do not want with unsolicited mail is to work hard to understand its meaning, or to respond to it. Therefore, simplicity,

	Banks	DoE	Local groups	Politicians	National groups	Residents etc.
Information packs						
Visits to site						
Press releases						
Press conferences						
Photographs						
Competitions						
Exhibitions						

Figure 9.2 *PR matrix for local building project*

directness and brevity are the key to its success. The most usual mistake is to try to send too many messages, and too much information. Ideally, there should be a single, simple message, whether contained in a letter or a leaflet.

In a letter, you should begin with a sentence that catches the interest and imagination. This should then be followed by the claim, and the justification for that claim. You must then make it clear how people should respond — and make it as easy as possible to do just that. (Complete the form, send it off.) It is not expensive to arrange a 'Freepost' reply facility, that attracts potential customers, not only because it is easy but also because they do not have to pay.

To summarize, an effective formula is:

- Did you know? — identify the problem;
- Look at this — here is the solution;
- Now do this — how to respond.

Technology can help enormously in making direct mail effective. There are three main aspects to this:

1 Consumer databases: it is possible to buy names and addresses that correspond to specified criteria such as income, status, demography, etc. The more constraints you specify, the more you pay for each name.

2 Word-processing/DTP: these systems can enable you to design and produce quite effective and inexpensive letters or leaflets within your organization.
3 Mailmerge: lists of names and addresses can be supplied or entered into a database, and this can be linked to the word processor package via a mailmerge package. This customizes each letter for the named individual and can also produce address labels.

Brochures

Brochures and other specialist publications can be a very effective means of influencing potential customers. Not only can they carry written information but also photographs or illustrations can show products in a very positive light and design can be branded which can promote very positive images. In order to achieve these effects, however, professionalism is required. Often, this expertise is available within an organization, but even large companies often subcontract agencies or freelancers to produce specific projects.

Whether the publication is to be produced internally or externally, it is the brief that is all important. The brief should reference similar elements to advertising or PR briefs. In addition, they should also be explicit about content, style, the nature and extent of illustration and the format (size, number of colours, etc.).

Video recordings

The potential of video recording is being realized increasingly. Its use can range from sales presentations or product briefings through footage for press and publicity purposes, to in-company newsletters.

In terms of execution, many of the comments about brochures also apply. That is, use specialists and brief them properly.

These are well used and popular forms of marketing communications. But all companies are individual in their needs, and often specific needs can be satisfied by a different or more imaginative approach, for example:

A major manufacturer of domestic electronic goods had a problem in that it was reliant on the sales staff of the major electrical retailers to promote its products. It needed to educate them to the benefits and features of its products and to encourage them to promote them to customers.

Their solution was to provide a sales training kit. It included:

- advice on sales technique;
- market information;
- five reasons for buying their equipment;
- information about how the equipment worked;

- features and benefits of their products;
- a script for a face-to-face sales presentation.

All this was supplied in filofax format, which was known to be useful and attractive to sales staff.

Action planning

1   What are your particular strengths when dealing/liaising with people or agencies outside your own organization?

2   Would you say you had any particular difficulties?

3   What are your development needs in relation to the concepts and practicalities discussed in this chapter?

4   How do you intend to address them?

10 Action planning

Introduction

A book of this nature can only get you started on the way to being more effective as a manager. If you have been using this book as part of a distance learning or taught course then you will have undertaken a range of assessed tasks. It is helpful to review your progress by considering what was involved in and learned through doing those tasks. This chapter will:

- identify aspects of ongoing learning;
- show how learning from non-success is particularly important;
- review the MCI competences and furnish you with specially developed questions to review your own situation;
- offer a model to plan for your development of increased effectiveness in areas of managerial and personal effectiveness;
- provides a checklist of the sort of Managerial Competence questions used by trained MCI assessors and advisors;
- give you a basis to plan personal development and change.

The importance of ongoing learning

The learning cycle identified in Chapter 1 is a critical concept for people who wish to continue to make progress in their managerial development. The learning cycle is an ongoing process. Experience forms the basis for reviewing and drawing conclusions and planning. Experience can arise just as easily from lack of success as from succeeding.

Failure is a word which has an unfortunate negative meaning associated with it. Who would wish to have the word applied to them. However, failure nearly always brings with it the opportunity to learn. It is only when failure is not used for learning that there is really true failure.

Roget's Thesaurus offers as an alternative to 'failure' the words 'cessation', 'discontinuance' or 'stall'. These words imply that some expected event or progress has not taken place. If a domestic appliance such as a vacuum cleaner stopped working then most intelligent people would consider some obvious reasons before calling in an expensive technician or throwing the appliance in the bin. By finding out why the cleaner did not work you would gain knowledge which you could apply to other electrical appliances in your house.

Similarly when, as a manager, you find that something you set out to accomplish does not work out as planned you have an opportunity to learn. The opportunity is to learn not only how you might have set about it differently but also how you might act in future situations. It is called learning from experience.

There is a perception of experience which is familiar to all who have to plough through piles of c.v.s or application forms. The phrase often appears: 'I have X years of experience'. The question which often goes through the reader's mind is: 'X years of experience or one year's experience repeated X times?' How much has the person learned from that experience?

Personal effectiveness is not simply acquired from reading a book or carrying out book based activities. It is something derived from the thoughtful and informed application of learning and experience.

Application of learning

The Managerial and Personal Competences identified by the Management Charter Initiative (MCI) may have considerable relevance for you as a manager. It is almost inconceivable that you would find that none had any application. Furthermore these competences have acquired wide acceptance as a basis for junior and intermediate management qualifications.

Therefore, we would suggest that you take the MCI competences as a basis and add or amend them as necessary. Clearly the standards may not precisely apply in your work situation. There may be other competences that are necessary. One local authority added a competence relating to equal opportunities in the workplace. When the MCI were researching the standards the competence of 'ability to lie convincingly' came up as a possibility. The MCI felt that it was inappropriate to include this as a standard and it is easy to see why.

There are few easy short cuts to becoming competent in any skill or occupational calling. Competence comes from knowledge and from practise based upon that knowledge. Possession of the knowledge is not a short cut. Rather it helps you avoid too much 'trial and error' learning.

Therefore, you need to plan how you can put into practice the knowledge base which this book offers in the area of personal effectiveness. The opportunities to do this are probably far greater than you might think.

- The obvious opportunities of your current job which you are currently making use of.
- The obvious opportunities of your current job which you are not currently using but which you could use if (for example) you managed your time better.

- Whatever aspects of your manager's job which he/she may be persuaded to let you undertake.
- The opportunities presented by jobs which colleagues undertake and which you may be able to negotiate.
- The opportunities offered by your work place to become involved in the organization and management of social, sports, trade union and welfare activities.
- The range of non-work involvements and activities which you are currently undertaking (sports, leisure, religious, etc.)
- The range of non-work involvements and activities which you are not currently undertaking (sports, leisure, religious, etc.) but which you could undertake if (for example) you managed your time better.
- The family-based activities which you are currently undertaking (problem-solving, planning, organizing, etc.)
- The family based activities which you are not currently undertaking (problem-solving, planning, organizing, etc.) but which you could undertake if (for example) you managed your time better.

A practical example

One of the MCI units of managerial competence is:

- Plan, allocate and evaluate work carried out by teams, individuals and self.

It includes various elements as follows:

- set and update work objectives for individuals;
- plan activities and determine work methods to achieve objectives;
- allocate work and evaluate teams, individuals and self against objectives;
- provide feedback to teams and individuals on their performance.

Now it is reasonable to assume that most managers will have to be able to do this effectively. However, it is quite likely that some readers of this book may either not have the opportunity to do all of the elements in their current job. Perhaps you do not manage a team of staff which you can set objectives, allocate and evaluate work and provide feedback to.

Figure 10.1 takes you through a flow chart which enables you to consider how you can develop (or further develop) a management skill or competence.

The first question(s) you should ask yourself is: 'Is it a part of my job' or more broadly: 'Is it conceivable that I should do it at some point in my job?'

Though you may not supervise staff as part of your normal activities perhaps the opportunity arises to take the responsibility from time

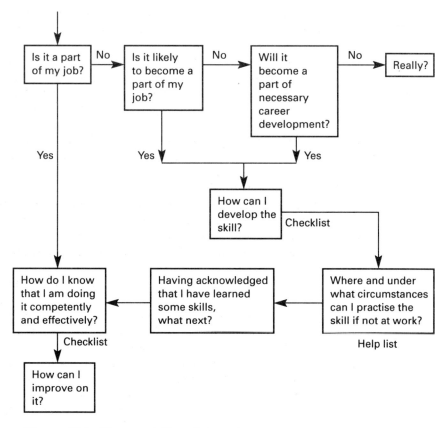

Figure 10.1 *The acquisition of competence*

to time. Most organizations involve staff in project teams or working parties. Co-ordination of such activities is not automatically associated with seniority. Sometimes it rests with the person who shows willingness to do it.

There is an attitude which paraphrased runs 'it's not in my job description and I'm not paid to do it'. This attitude is understandable when seen in terms of industrial relations or health and safety issues. After all you would not wish a hospital porter to be given the job of removing your appendix just because the porter was 'willing to do it'.

However, management skills are acquired through practice. Taking advantage of suitable opportunities is crucial. A person who does not reach beyond proficiency in their current job is, in effect, making a statement that they do not seek to progress further.

The checklist we provide further in this chapter offers questions which, as a Crediting Competence Centre, we use in assessing the extent to which managers possess the competences covered in this book.

Let us suppose that the particular competence is not one which currently is not part of your job taking a fairly broad definition. The next question you might put to yourself is: 'Is it likely to become a part of my job (in the future)?'

This might involve a bit of crystal ball gazing. At the time of writing many organizations are 'downsizing' which is management speak for reducing staff and layers of management. This exercise almost inevitably brings new responsibilities to bear on those staff who remain. There is an awareness that the environment is constantly changing for many organizations. Their staff need to be focused on innovation and develop new skills. So it is quite possible that the skills your job does not require now may be essential for your job next year − if your job is to remain yours!

Let us assume that the particular managerial or personal competence is one which you cannot see as applicable for your job now or in the foreseeable future. The next question to ask yourself is: 'Does it represent a skill that I might need for my own future career development?'

Now before answering that question it may be worth pausing and considering the views of Charles Handy (1985), a respected management writer who spends a lot of his time analysing what the future might hold for the world of work and organizations. He believes that in the future it is not employment which will be important but rather 'employability'. The possession of a job will not count for much unless the person has saleable skills since security of employment is becoming a thing of the past. Indeed we would argue that security of employment is already a thing of the past.

So the question revolves around whether possessing the competence is something which improves your attraction to employers. Possibly you may feel it does not. The Management Charter Initiative certainly should not defend their particular competences against the march of time. However, if the competence is no longer relevant then it is likely that some other competences are emerging as important for future managers. What are they and how might you acquire them?

The question thus becomes: 'How can I develop the skill or competence?'

The 'help list' (see Figure 10.2) is a simple checklist which you can use and add to. It sets out a number of possible sources for the development of a desired skill or competence.

Some of these are related to work activities (Section A). These are ongoing things which you may be doing which enable you to practise the particular skill within the work setting itself. The list is, of course, not exhaustive and we have deliberately left spaces for you to add additional items.

Often their is a need to acquire more information either to establish what the desired skill is and where it might be found within the organization. We have listed some information sources available within most organizations.

Management competence help list

A Work related	C Leisure activities

1 Subordinate feedback	1 Team memberships
2 Colleague feedback	2 Committee involvements
3 Line manager feedback	3 Obtaining resources
4 Customer feedback	4 Using resources
5 Team meetings	5 Decision-making
6 Liaison work	6 Problem-solving
7 Staff supervision	7 Evaluation
8 Report writing	8
9 Verbal reports	9
10 Interviewing	**D Home/family**
11 Progress chasing	1 Decision-making
12 Planning	2 Problem-solving
13 Negotiating	3 Negotiating
14 Quality checking	4 Obtaining resources
15 Standard setting	5 Using resources
16 Advice provision	6
17 Using resources	7
18 Decision-making	8
19 Problem-solving	
20 Evaluation	
21	
22	

B Work info. sources	E Self help and learning
1 Staff manual	1 Coach/mentor
2 Annual reports	2 Management course material
3 Business plans	3 Fellow course participants
4 Job descriptions/specs	4 Short courses
5 Finance procedures	5 Management tutors
6 Personnel procedures	6 Library resources
7 Review documents	7
8 Meeting minutes	8
9 Computer database	9
10 Information leaflets	
11 Working party reports	
12 Company newsletters etc.	

Figure 10.2 *Help list. Based on model provided by Richard Hooper of the London Borough of Enfield*

In some cases you may desire to develop a competence but you cannot locate any possibility to do it within your current work situation. Perhaps you have no responsibility and your own manager is unable or unwilling to delegate to you. How do you get the opportunity to experience using the competence?

There are essentially three areas of possibility.

1 You may find the opportunity within your actual or potential leisure pursuits. Many students have found that the experience of organizing and managing a sports or social club at school or college has made a major positive impression on employers – sometimes enabling them to get ahead of their academically better qualified colleagues.

2 In your home life you may find that you can develop and practise competence. Sound management of the economy, as Margaret (now Baroness) Thatcher used to say, is all about good housekeeping. Time management, priority-setting, problem-setting and decision-making are all activities that most people have to handle in everyday life.

3 Finally, there is the possibility of self-help and learning through study. Some skills can be acquired through 'simulation'. That is how people learn First Aid. Handling disciplinary situations is best practised in the classroom before trying it out in the 'real world'. However, well-planned training courses can often provide a realistic experience for students.

Checklist of managerial competence questions (MCI-based)

Units of management competence 1, 5, 6, 7, 8 and 9

Unit 1: Maintain and improve service and product operations

Aspects of this unit are covered in Chapters 1, 4, 5, 6 and 9 of this book.

 Customers

1   What/where are your largest client bases?

2   How do you find out about client needs?

3   How do you make customers aware that services are available?

4   How effective are these processes/media?

5   What would you do if there was a low takeup?

✎ Quality

1 How are service units currently co-ordinated in order to develop service provision?

2 Is there a particular system of Total Quality Management or Quality Assurance at your place of work?

3 How are performance standards determined and by whom?

4 How do you ensure that quality performance standards are being met?

5 How do you measure these standards?

6 What have been your experiences of your company's customer complaints procedure?

7 How are Health and Safety requirements currently addressed at your workplace?

✎ Liaison/communication

1 How appropriate is your location for the service you provide?

2 Which outside agencies do you currently liaise with?

3 Are there any areas of Joint Working in your service?

4 Within which agencies do you 'joint-work'? For what purpose?

5 How do you liaise with off-site staff or staff in boundary locations?

6 How is information fed back into the decision-making process?

7 What, if any, interdepartmental group activities do you participate in?

8 What are the main purposes of these groups?

Unit 5: develop teams, individuals and self to enhance performance

Aspects of this unit are covered in Chapters 1 and 6 of this book.

✎ Employee induction and training

1 Who are the parties involved in starting and inducting those for whom you will be responsible?

2 What is the induction programme and what does it cover?

3 Is there a method of determining individual training and development needs of your new staff members?

4 How might these be addressed?

5 Are there any specific job, safety and quality-related courses or programmes necessary for new members of staff?

6 Is there a probationary period applied to new members of your staff?

7 What procedures/criteria are used in determining whether probationary periods have been successfully completed?

8 How is induction and training evaluated for effectiveness?

9 What happens if a candidate proves unsuccessful at this juncture?

✎ Employee development

1 Are there any formal mechanisms to determine career progression once a member of staff is considered to be 'permanent'.

2 Is there a system to ensure staff remain up to date with such programmes?

3 How are these programmes evaluated for their effectiveness?

✎ Developing team

1 How do you develop your team?

2 What activities do you use for team development?

3 What planning goes into putting these into practice?

4 Have you taken any steps to improve equality of opportunity in the development of your team?

5 What were the outcomes?

✎ Developing individuals

1 What development activities have you used for individuals?

2 How did they evolve?

3 How did you review and subsequently improve them?

4 What other ways do you use to review development activities for individuals?

5 What specific incidences have caused you concern for the equal opportunities of development for all individuals?

✎ Developing self

1 How would you identify your own development needs within the job role?

2 How would you meet the needs you had identified?

3 How do you evaluate your progress?

Unit 6: Plan, allocate and evaluate work carried out by teams, individuals and self

Aspects of this unit are covered in Chapters 1 and 6 of this book.

✎ Objective setting

1 Do you set work objectives for individuals and/or teams?

2 Can you explain how you would arrive at these objectives both for an individual and for a team?

3 Can you also explain how you would update them?

4 Can you identify an objective you have had to meet and specify how you planned the work activities to meet the objective?

5 How did you decide which method would work best?

Motivation and delegation

1 How do you decide how to allocate work to people in your team?

2 What would you say is your leadership style?

3 What are the effects of your style on the individuals in your team? E.g. are you making the most of the skills available to you?

4 How does this tie in with the overall work objectives set?

Monitoring, review and appraisal

1 Do you have a means of evaluating your own performance against your work objectives?

2 How do you evaluate the performance of other individuals against their objectives?

3 How do you evaluate the performance of teams against their objectives?

4 What methods do you use to give feedback to individuals about their performance?

5 What methods do you use to give feedback to teams about their performance?

6 Can you pin-point anything which you consider particularly important when giving feedback?

7 Do you incorporate equal opportunities issues into this aspect of your work? If so, how?

Unit 7: Create, maintain and enhance effective working relationships

Aspects of this unit are covered in Chapters 1, 2 and 8 of this book.

 Trust and support of subordinates and colleagues

1 Describe the main working relationships you maintain?

2 How do you/would you maximize productive relationships and networks?

3 How do you/would you promote equal opportunities within your relationships and those of your colleagues and staff?

4 What are the key elements, in your opinion, in promoting effective working relationships?

5 What do you see as your strengths in establishing good working relationships and which aspects would you want to develop further?

6 How would you/do you go about establishing and developing working relationships with the following groups:

- staff?
- colleagues (internal and external)?
- managers/bosses?
- clients?
- associates?
- other?

What actions would you/have you taken with staff at times of particular difficulty or change?

✎ Trust and support of boss

1 How easy/difficult do you find asking support of or taking problems to your manager?

_____

2 How could it be improved?

_____

3 How easy/difficult do you think your staff find asking you for support or bringing problems to you?

_____

4 How could it be improved?

_____

✎ Trust and support beyond the team

1 What support would you/do you give to staff/team members in their relations with others outside the team?

_____

2 How could these relationships be improved?

_____

✎ Handling conflict

1 What formal and informal actions would you/have you taken to actively promote effective working relationships and prevent breakdown?

_____

2 How do you/would you deal with conflict in your relationships or in the relationships of your staff or colleagues arising from:

- differences of opinion on courses of action?
- personal animosity?
- racism?
- sexism?
- other discriminatory behaviour?
- non-compliance with organizational rules, norms or values?

_____

3 What are the systems and procedures, both statutory and organizational, for handling grievance and discipline?

4 How do you apply them in practice?

✎ **Counselling**

1 What do you see as counselling in the workplace?

2 What is its purpose and limitations?

3 What is your role as counsellor − both formally and informally?

4 What are the key elements of effective workplace counselling?

Unit 8: Seek, evaluate and organize information for action

Aspects of this unit are covered in Chapters 1, 3 and 5 of this book.

✎ **Obtaining information**

1 What information do you need to do your job and for what purposes?

2 Do you have any problems obtaining this information?

3 To whom do you supply information?

4 How much time do you spend in:

− gathering information?
− analysing information?
− giving information?

5   Do you have any pre-formatted documents for any of these purposes?

_____

6   How is information currently stored and retrieved?

_____

Unit 9: Exchange information to solve problems and make decisions

Aspects of this unit are covered in Chapters 1, 2, 4 and 5 of this book.

 Holding meetings

1   How often do you hold meetings (formal and informal), briefings and group discussions?

_____

2   For what purposes do you hold meetings, etc.?

_____

3   How often do meetings:

- start on time?
- finish on time?
- achieve their objectives?

_____

4   Do you have the necessary information in advance of the meetings?

_____

5   Do you supply the necessary information in advance of the meetings?

_____

6   Are you confident about:

- chairing meetings?
- contributing to the purpose of meetings?
- taking minutes?

_____

✎ Effectiveness of meetings

1   Would you say your meetings are:

- well prepared?
- well administered?
- well controlled?

2   Are the people at your meetings there because they:

- have a part to play?
- have an interest?
- have been sent?

3   What are the meetings' follow-up processes?

4   Do your meetings result in positive action?

5   Have you attended committees in your current role and prepared reports for these committees?

Acknowledgement

Questions devised by the Crediting Competence Team at South Bank University and reproduced with permission.

Bibliography

ACAS Code of Practice No. 2 – Disclosure of Information to Trade Unions for Collective Bargaining Purposes.

Adair, John (1975), *Management Decision Making*, Gower Press.

Adair, John (1979), *The Action Centred Leader*.

Adair, John (1985), *Effective Decision Making*, London: Pan. For his functional management diagram.

Adair, John (1988), *How to Manage Your Time*, Talbot Adair.

Back, Ken and Back, Kate (1991), *Assertiveness at Work*, McGraw-Hill.

Belbin, R. M. (1991), *Management Teams*, London: Heinemann, 2nd edn.

British Institute of Management (1990), *BIM Certificate in Management*, London: BIM. For whom this book was commissioned in support of their course. Chapters 1, 2, 3, 8 and 9 incorporate the course material as a framework for the expanded texts.

Carter, Steve (1990), *BIM Certificate in Management Course*, London: BIM. For his building project matrix, p. 85.

Cooke, Steve and Slack, Nigel (1991), *Making Management Decisions*, Prentice-Hall.

Cooper, Gary L., Cooper, Rachel D. and Eaker, Lynn H. (1988), *Living with Stress*, NJ: Penguin Books.

Eberle, R., Scamper, Cooper and Cummings (1972), *Games for Imagination Development*, Buffalo, NY: D.O.K. Press.

Fisher, R. and Ury, W. (1984), *Getting to Yes*, Hutchinson Business Books. For his four principles of successful negotiating.

Fletcher, Winston (1988), *Creative People*, Hutchinson Business Books.

Handy, Charles B. (1985), *Understanding Organizations*, London: Penguin Books, Ch. 5, 3rd ed. For his power and influence concepts which were abbreviated for the purposes of this book.

Hardy, W. G. (1990), *Effective Business Writing*, London: BIM. For an extended version of his 'purposes for writing' in BIM Certificate in Management Course, p. 65.

Harvey Jones, Sir John (1988), *Making It Happen*, Fontana.

Hind, David (1989), *Transferable Personal Skills: A Student Guide*, Tyne & Wear: Business Education Publishers. For his criteria for assertiveness; the art of clear and direct communication – as the basis for discussion.

Honey, Peter and Mumford, Alan (1990), *The Manual of Learning Opportunities*, Maidenhead: Honey. For a condensed version of Sections 1 and 2 as an introduction to competence development for certificate level managers.

Iacocca, Lee with Novak, William (1984), *Iacocca; An Autobiography*, Bantam Books.

Janis, I. L. (1972), *Victims of Groupthink*.

Kepner, Charles H. and Tregoe, Benjamin B. (1981), *The New Rational Manager*, Princeton, NJ: Kepner Tregoe Inc.

Kotler, Philip (ed.) (1984), 5th ed. *Marketing Management: Analysis, Planning & Control*, NJ: Prentice-Hall. For his definition of the marketing environment and simplified/adapted version of his micro- and macro-environmental analyses.

Lloyd, Sam R. (1988), *How to Develop Assertiveness*, Kogan Page.

Looker, Terry and Gregson, Olga (1989), *Stresswise*, Hodder and Stoughton Educational.

McCarthy, Jerome (1960), *Basic Marketing: A Managerial Approach*, Homewood: Illinois, USA, 1st ed.

Mager, Robert (1991), *Goal Analysis*, Kogan Page.

Margerison, Charles J. (1974), *Managerial Problem-Solving*, McGraw-Hill.

Mali, Paul (1986), *MBO Updated*, John Wiley & Sons.

Melrose Films (1991), *Certificate in Management* Course, London: Melrose. For their influencing problems, dealing with excuses and coping with aggression, which were 'loosely' used as a basis for exploring these ideas.

Mintzberg, Henry (1973), *The Nature of Managerial Work*, Harper & Row.

Open University, The (1990), *The Effective Manager*; Open Business School Certificate B784. For their eight barriers to effective communication.

Pease, Allan (1988), *Body Language: How to Read Others' Thoughts by Their Gestures*, London: Sheldon Press.

Peel, Malcolm (1987), *Customer Service*, Kogan Page. For his 'telephone checklist'.

Peel, Malcolm (1988), *How to Make Meetings Work*, Kogan Page. For his 'Six Deadly Sins of Meetings'.

Rawlinson, John Geoffrey (1981), *Creative Thinking and Brainstorming*, Gower.

Rickards, Tudor (1990), *Creativity and Problem-Solving at Work*, Gower.

Tannenbaum, R. and Schmidt, W. H. (1958), *How to choose a leadership pattern*, *Harvard Business Review*, Mar.–Apr. pp. 55–101. For the continuum of leadership behaviour and the background theory.

Training Agency, The and Training Research Advisory Consultancy Enterprises Ltd (1990), *Marketing Training*, London: HMSO.

Treacy, Declan (1991), *Clear Your Desk*, Business Books Ltd.

Vroom, V. H. and Yetton, P. W. (1973), *Leadership and Decision-Making*, Pittsburgh Press.

Training Agency, The (1990), *Investors in People*, London: HMSO.

Index